STAR-LORD GAMORA ROCKET RACCOON GROOT DRAX VENOM CAPTAIN MARVEL

GUARDIANS OF THE GALAXY

ORIGINAL SIN

WRITER: **BRIAN MICHAEL BENDIS**

ISSUES #18-20

PENCILERS: **ED McGUINNESS** WITH **VALERIO SCHITI** (#20)

INKERS: **MARK FARMER** (#18-19), **MARK MORALES** (#19),
JOHN LIVESAY (#19), **ED McGUINNESS** (#19) & **VALERIO SCHITI** (#20)

COLORISTS: **JUSTIN PONSOR** (#18) & **JASON KEITH** (#19-20)

COVER ART: **ED McGUINNESS, MARK FARMER** & **JUSTIN PONSOR**

ISSUES #21-23

ARTIST: **VALERIO SCHITI** WITH **DAVID LOPEZ** (#22)   COLORIST: **JASON KEITH**

COVER ART: **VALERIO SCHITI** WITH **JUSTIN PONSOR** (#21) & **JASON KEITH** (#22)
AND **CHRISTIAN WARD** (#23)

LETTERER: **VC'S CORY PETIT**   ASSISTANT EDITOR: **XANDER JAROWEY**   EDITOR: **MIKE MARTS**

COLLECTION EDITOR: **JENNIFER GRÜNWALD**   ASSISTANT EDITOR: **SARAH BRUNSTAD**
ASSOCIATE MANAGING EDITOR: **ALEX STARBUCK**   EDITOR, SPECIAL PROJECTS: **MARK D. BEAZLEY**
SENIOR EDITOR, SPECIAL PROJECTS: **JEFF YOUNGQUIST** SVP PRINT, SALES & MARKETING: **DAVID GABRIEL**

EDITOR IN CHIEF: **AXEL ALONSO**   CHIEF CREATIVE OFFICER: **JOE QUESADA**
PUBLISHER: **DAN BUCKLEY**   EXECUTIVE PRODUCER: **ALAN FINE**

GUARDIANS OF THE GALAXY VOL. 4: ORIGINAL SIN. Contains material originally published in magazine form as GUARDIANS OF THE GALAXY #18-23. First printing 2015. ISBN# 978-0-7851-9245-9. Published by MARVEL WORLDWIDE, INC., a subsidiary of MARVEL ENTERTAINMENT, LLC. OFFICE OF PUBLICATION: 135 West 50th Street, New York, NY 10020. Copyright © 2015 Marvel Characters, Inc. All rights reserved. All characters featured in this issue and the distinctive names and likenesses thereof, and all related indicia are trademarks of Marvel Characters, Inc. No similarity between any of the names, characters, persons, and/or institutions in this magazine with those of any living or dead person or institution is intended, and any such similarity which may exist is purely coincidental. **Printed in the U.S.A.** ALAN FINE, EVP - Office of the President, Marvel Worldwide, Inc. and EVP & CMO Marvel Characters B.V.; DAN BUCKLEY, Publisher & President - Print, Animation & Digital Divisions; JOE QUESADA, Chief Creative Officer; TOM BREVOORT, SVP of Publishing; DAVID BOGART, SVP of Operations & Procurement, Publishing; C.B. CEBULSKI, SVP of Creator & Content Development; DAVID GABRIEL, SVP Print, Sales & Marketing; JIM O'KEEFE, VP of Operations & Logistics; DAN CARR, Executive Director of Publishing Technology; SUSAN CRESPI, Editorial Operations Manager; ALEX MORALES, Publishing Operations Manager; STAN LEE, Chairman Emeritus. For information regarding advertising in Marvel Comics or on Marvel.com, please contact Niza Disla, Director of Marvel Partnerships, at ndisla@marvel.com. For Marvel subscription inquiries, please call 800-217-9158. Manufactured between 1/23/2015 and 3/2/2015 by R.R. DONNELLEY, INC., SALEM, VA, USA.
10 9 8 7 6 5 4 3 2 1

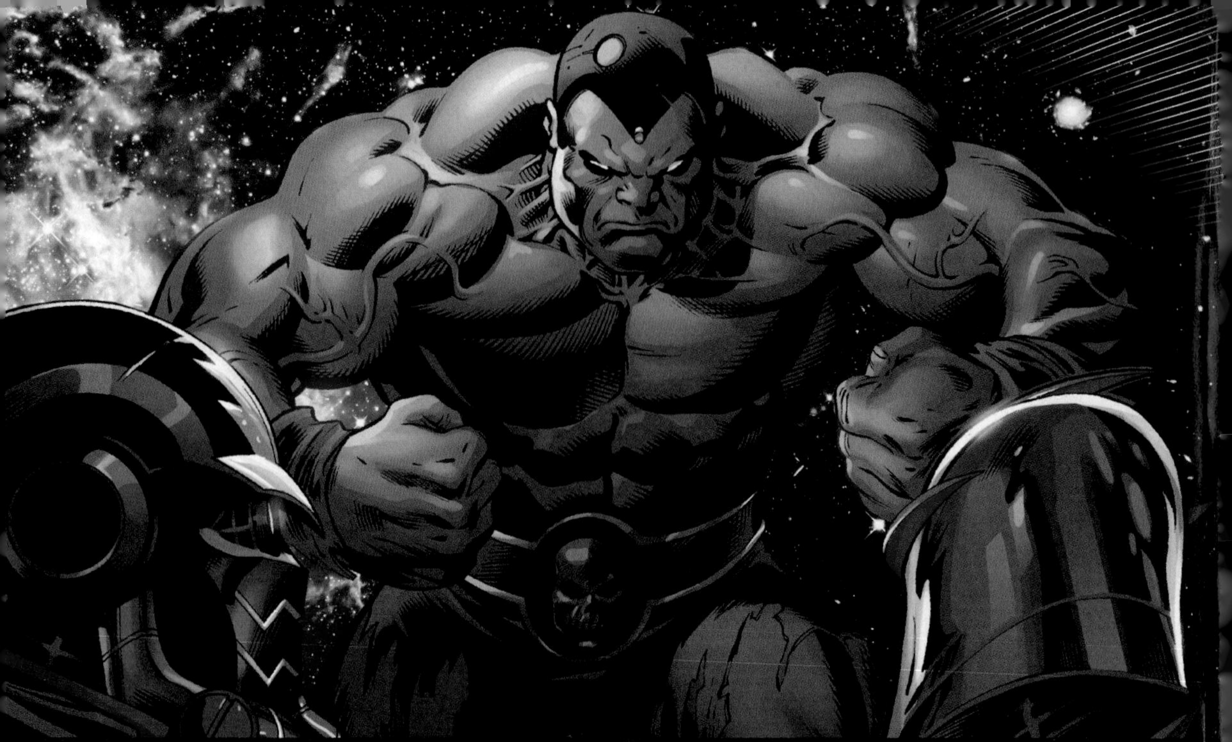

PREVIOUSLY...

DURING A CONFLICT WITH THANOS, PETER QUILL AND RICHARD RIDER, A.K.A. NOVA, AIMED TO STOP THE MAD TITAN ONCE AND FOR ALL BY TRAPPING HIM, ALONG WITH THEMSELVES, IN A PARASITIC PARALLEL DIMENSION KNOWN AS THE CANCERVERSE. A SUICIDE MISSION BY ALL ACCOUNTS, BUT WORTH IT TO SAVE THE GALAXY FROM THANOS. WITH THE COLLAPSE OF THE FAULT THAT CONNECTED THE CANCERVERSE, PETER AND NOVA WERE BELIEVED TRAPPED FOREVER.

AFTER MOURNING THEIR DEATHS, THE REMAINING GUARDIANS WERE RELIEVED TO DISCOVER THAT PETER — ALONG WITH THE FORMERLY DECEASED DRAX — WAS SOMEHOW ALIVE, BUT RELIEF TURNED TO HORROR WHEN THEY REALIZED THANOS HAD SURVIVED THE CANCERVERSE AS WELL. HOW THEY SURVIVED REMAINED A MYSTERY...UNTIL NOW.

MEANWHILE, PETER QUILL MAY HAVE FINALLY SETTLED DOWN FOR A RELATIONSHIP WITH THE X-MEN'S KITTY PRYDE — IF YOU CAN CALL HOLOGRAM CALLS FROM STAR SYSTEMS AWAY "DATING." AND FLASH THOMPSON, A.K.A. VENOM, HAS BEEN PLACED WITH THE GUARDIANS OF THE GALAXY AS THE AVENGERS' EARTH REPRESENTATIVE. HOWEVER, AFTER BEING KIDNAPPED AND SEPARATED FROM THE GROUP, VENOM MAY NOT BE KEEN ON INTERSTELLAR ADVENTURES. SPACE HAS DONE STRANGE THINGS TO HIS SYMBIOTE, AND AS EACH DAY PASSES IT GROWS STRONGER AND MORE DIFFICULT TO CONTROL.

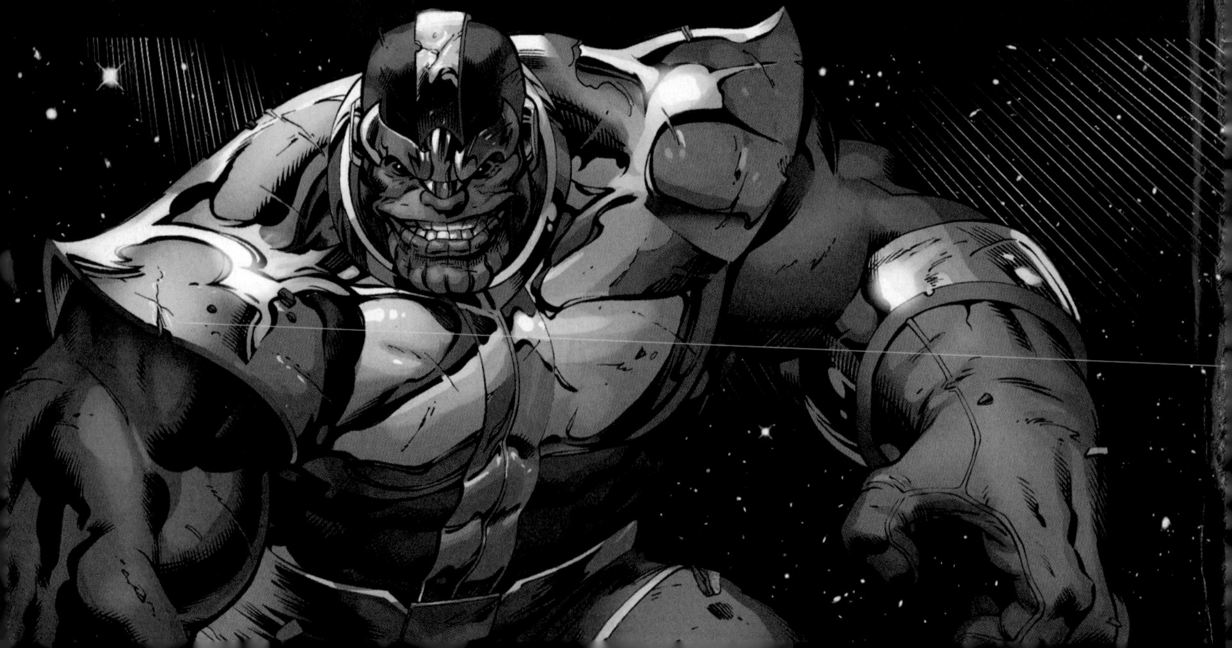

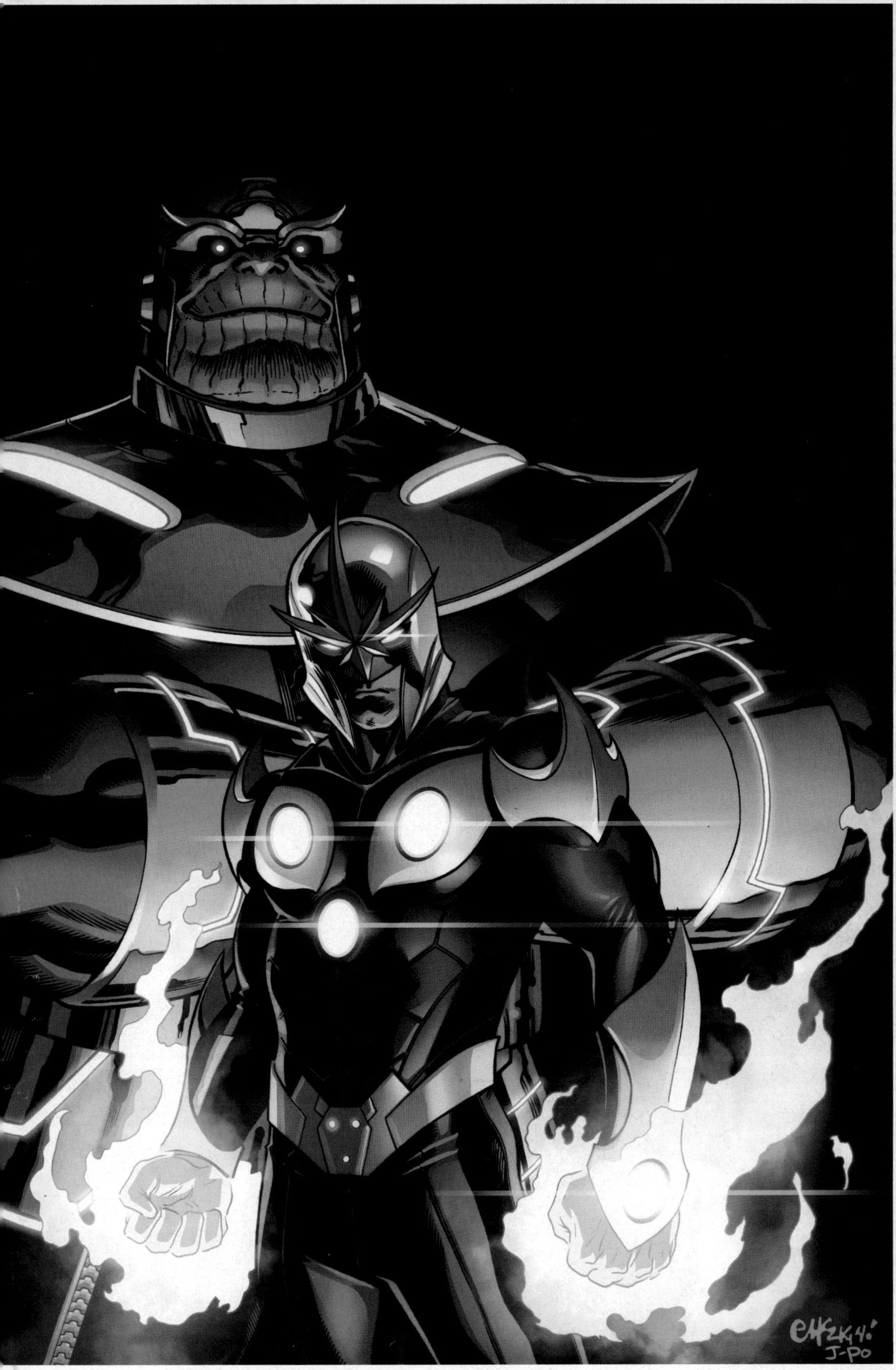

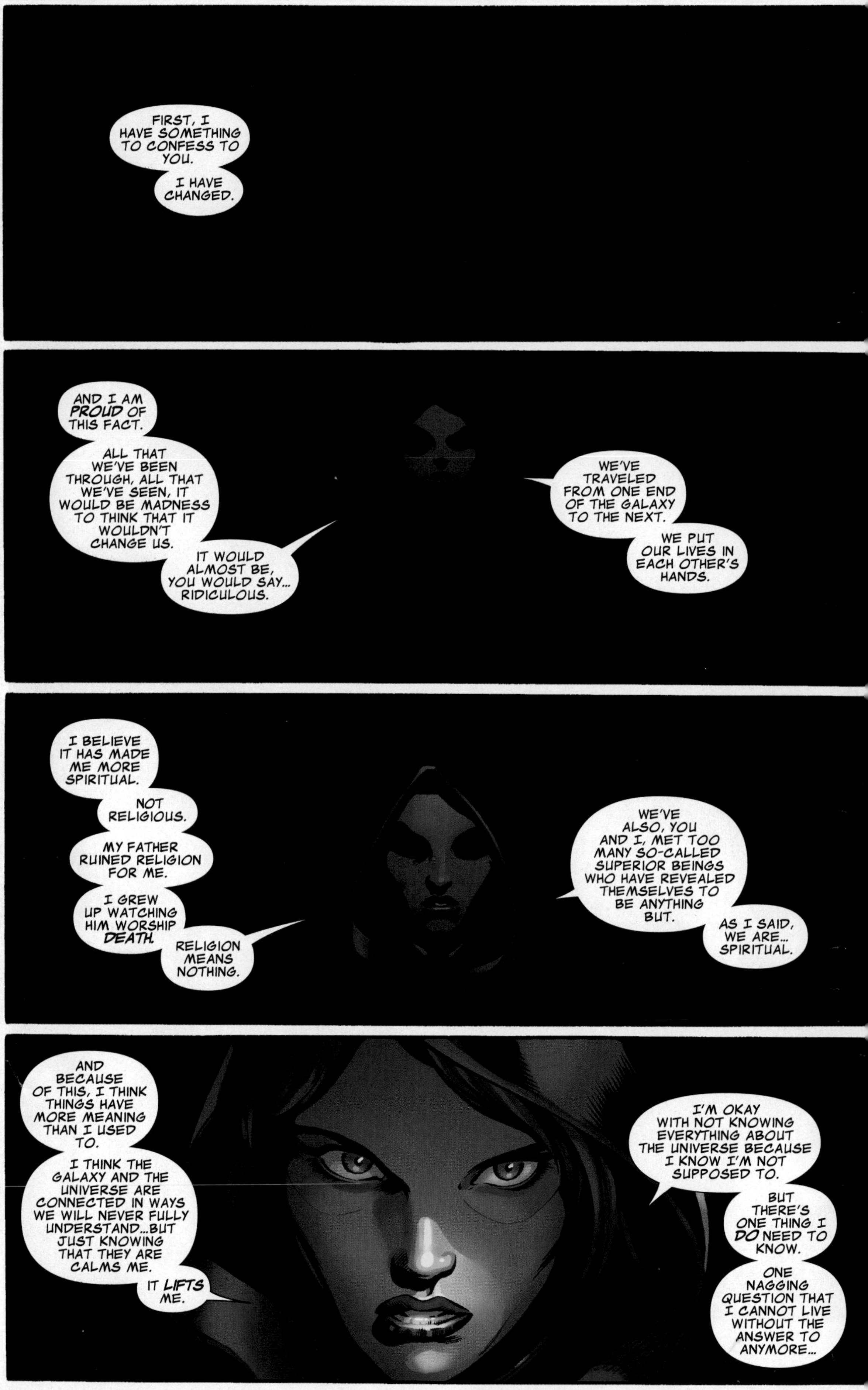

FIRST, I HAVE SOMETHING TO CONFESS TO YOU.
I HAVE CHANGED.
AND I AM PROUD OF THIS FACT.
ALL THAT WE'VE BEEN THROUGH, ALL THAT WE'VE SEEN, IT WOULD BE MADNESS TO THINK THAT IT WOULDN'T CHANGE US.
IT WOULD ALMOST BE, YOU WOULD SAY... RIDICULOUS.
WE'VE TRAVELED FROM ONE END OF THE GALAXY TO THE NEXT.
WE PUT OUR LIVES IN EACH OTHER'S HANDS.
I BELIEVE IT HAS MADE ME MORE SPIRITUAL.
NOT RELIGIOUS.
MY FATHER RUINED RELIGION FOR ME.
I GREW UP WATCHING HIM WORSHIP DEATH.
RELIGION MEANS NOTHING.
WE'VE ALSO, YOU AND I, MET TOO MANY SO-CALLED SUPERIOR BEINGS WHO HAVE REVEALED THEMSELVES TO BE ANYTHING BUT.
AS I SAID, WE ARE... SPIRITUAL.
AND BECAUSE OF THIS, I THINK THINGS HAVE MORE MEANING THAN I USED TO.
I THINK THE GALAXY AND THE UNIVERSE ARE CONNECTED IN WAYS WE WILL NEVER FULLY UNDERSTAND...BUT JUST KNOWING THAT THEY ARE CALMS ME.
IT LIFTS ME.
I'M OKAY WITH NOT KNOWING EVERYTHING ABOUT THE UNIVERSE BECAUSE I KNOW I'M NOT SUPPOSED TO.
BUT THERE'S ONE THING I DO NEED TO KNOW.
ONE NAGGING QUESTION THAT I CANNOT LIVE WITHOUT THE ANSWER TO ANYMORE...

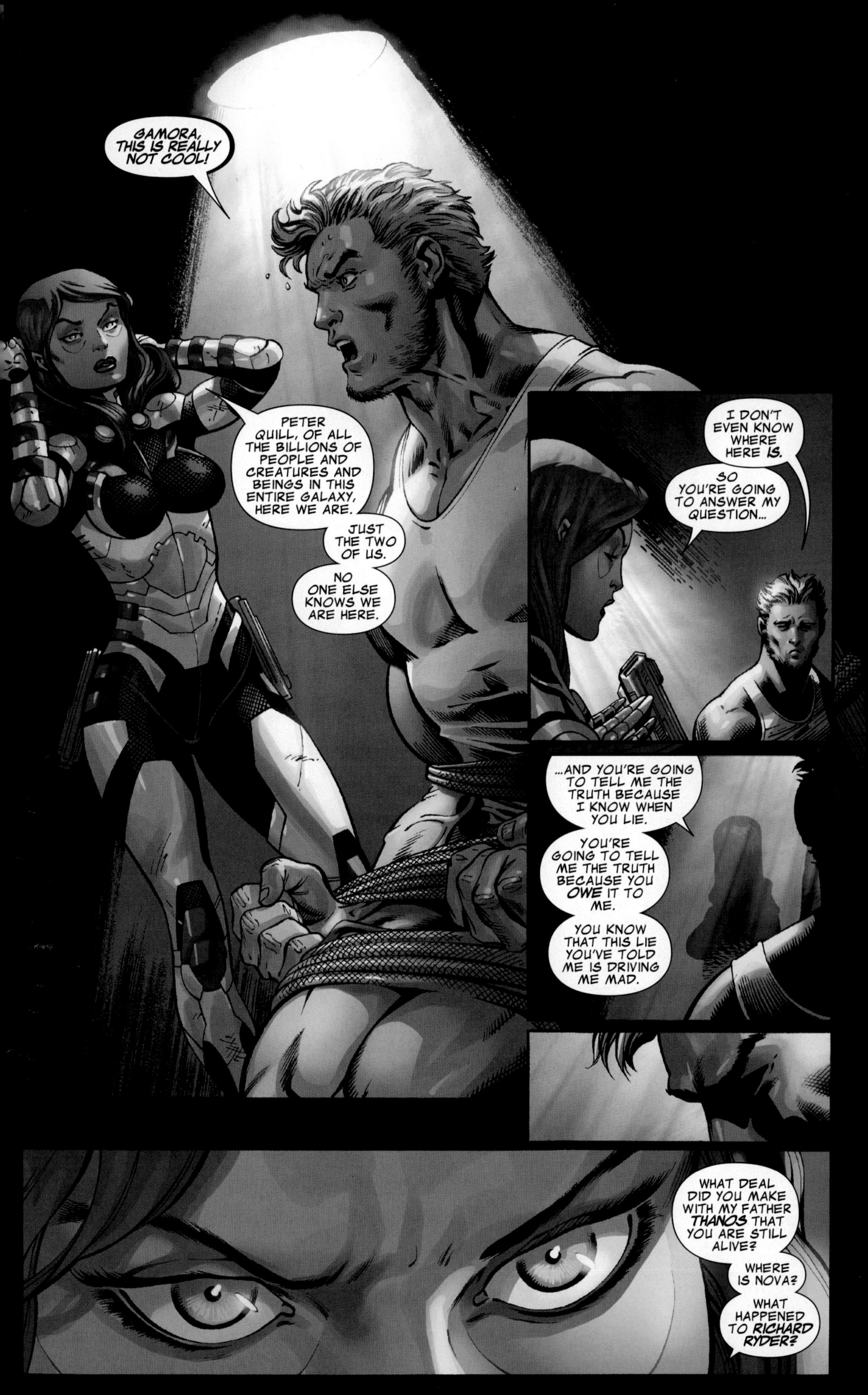
GAMORA, THIS IS REALLY NOT COOL!
PETER QUILL, OF ALL THE BILLIONS OF PEOPLE AND CREATURES AND BEINGS IN THIS ENTIRE GALAXY, HERE WE ARE.
JUST THE TWO OF US.
NO ONE ELSE KNOWS WE ARE HERE.
I DON'T EVEN KNOW WHERE HERE *IS*.
SO YOU'RE GOING TO ANSWER MY QUESTION...
...AND YOU'RE GOING TO TELL ME THE TRUTH BECAUSE I KNOW WHEN YOU LIE.
YOU'RE GOING TO TELL ME THE TRUTH BECAUSE YOU *OWE* IT TO ME.
YOU KNOW THAT THIS LIE YOU'VE TOLD ME IS DRIVING ME MAD.
WHAT DEAL DID YOU MAKE WITH MY FATHER *THANOS* THAT YOU ARE STILL ALIVE?
WHERE IS NOVA?
WHAT HAPPENED TO *RICHARD RYDER?*

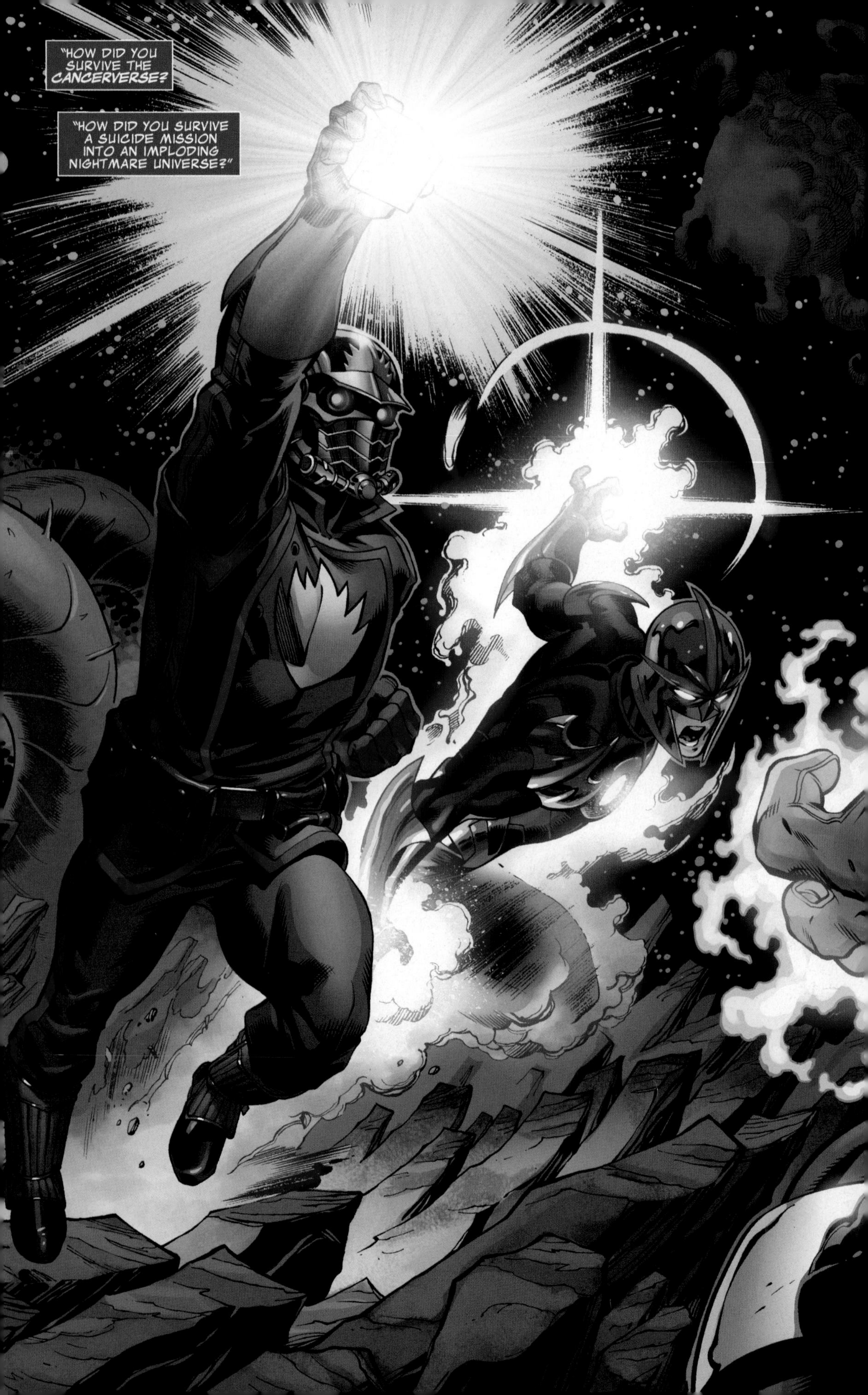
"HOW DID YOU SURVIVE THE CANCERVERSE?
"HOW DID YOU SURVIVE A SUICIDE MISSION INTO AN IMPLODING NIGHTMARE UNIVERSE?"

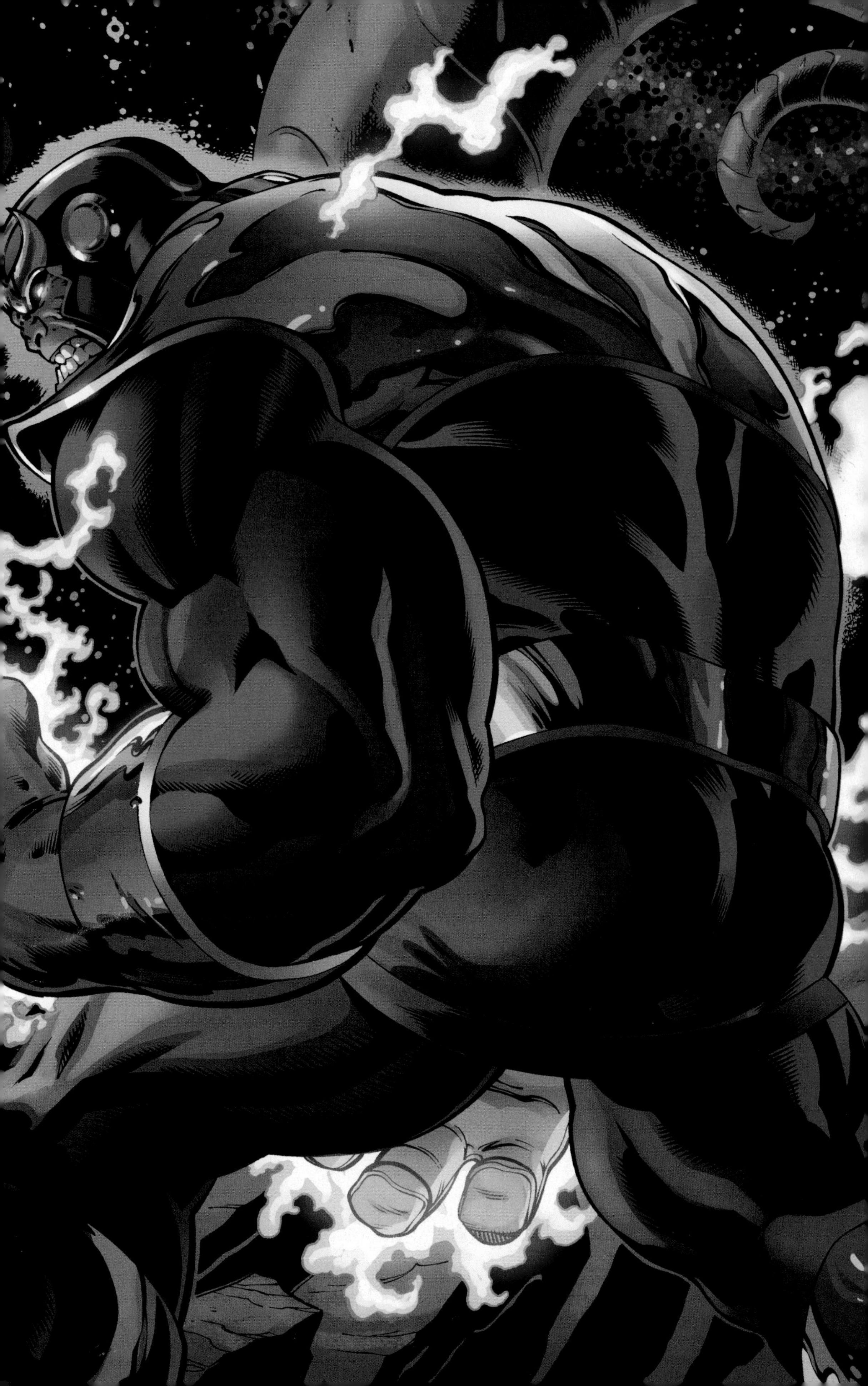

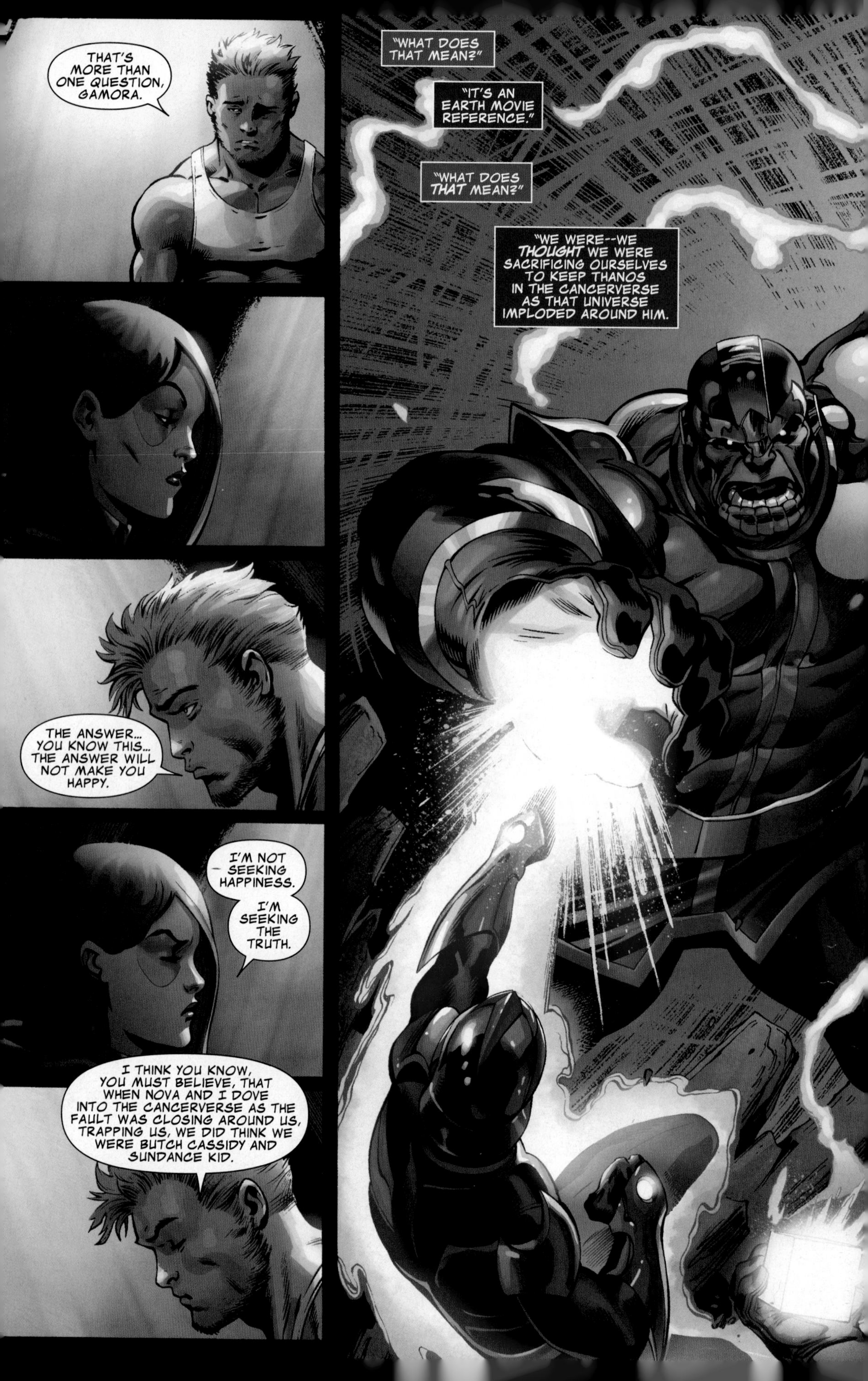
THAT'S MORE THAN ONE QUESTION, GAMORA.
THE ANSWER... YOU KNOW THIS... THE ANSWER WILL NOT MAKE YOU HAPPY.
I'M NOT SEEKING HAPPINESS.
I'M SEEKING THE TRUTH.
I THINK YOU KNOW, YOU MUST BELIEVE, THAT WHEN NOVA AND I DOVE INTO THE CANCERVERSE AS THE FAULT WAS CLOSING AROUND US, TRAPPING US, WE DID THINK WE WERE BUTCH CASSIDY AND SUNDANCE KID.
"WHAT DOES THAT MEAN?"
"IT'S AN EARTH MOVIE REFERENCE."
"WHAT DOES *THAT* MEAN?"
"WE WERE--WE *THOUGHT* WE WERE SACRIFICING OURSELVES TO KEEP THANOS IN THE CANCERVERSE AS THAT UNIVERSE IMPLODED AROUND HIM.

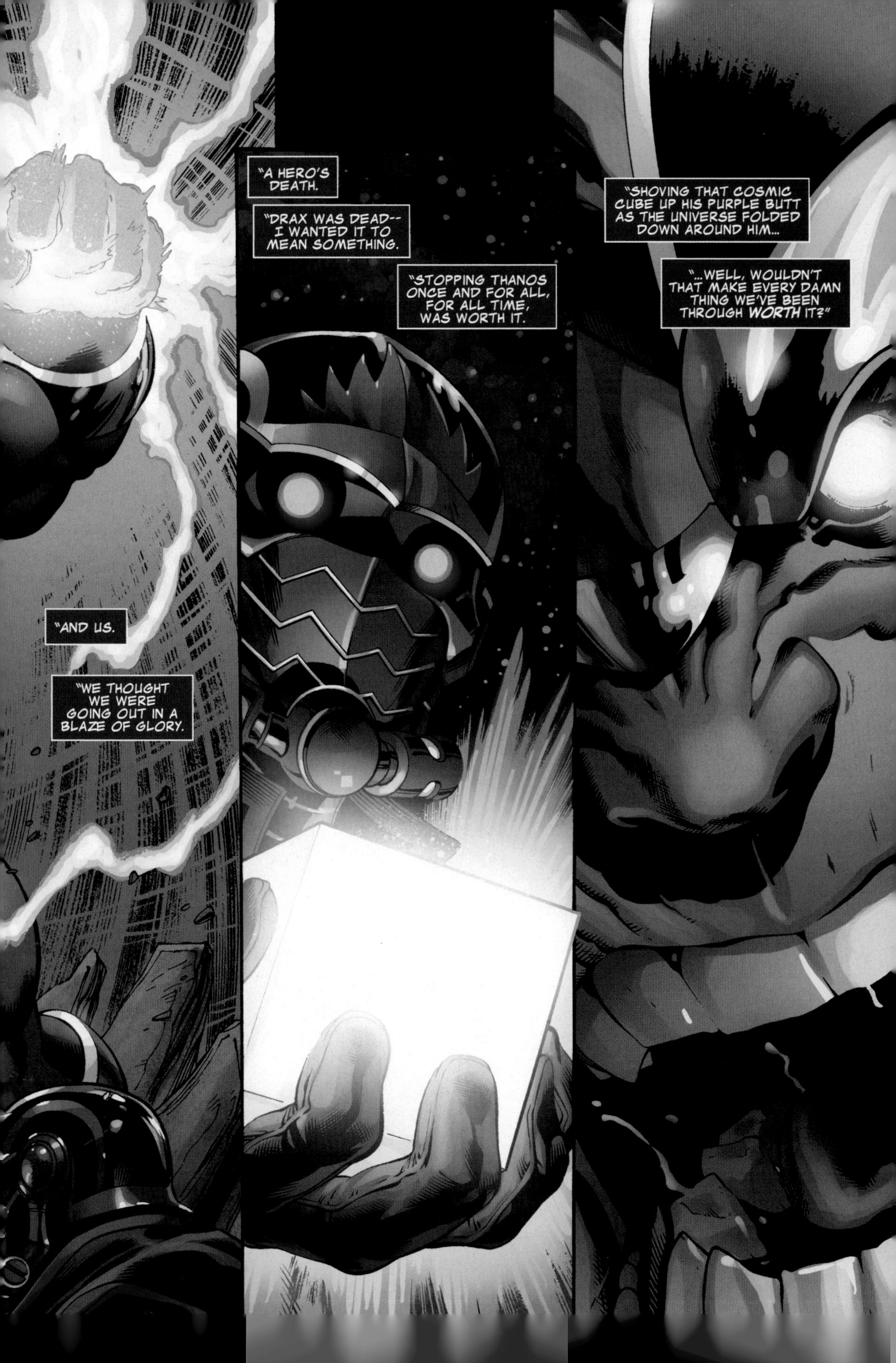
"AND US.
"WE THOUGHT WE WERE GOING OUT IN A BLAZE OF GLORY.
"A HERO'S DEATH.
"DRAX WAS DEAD-- I WANTED IT TO MEAN SOMETHING.
"STOPPING THANOS ONCE AND FOR ALL, FOR ALL TIME, WAS WORTH IT.
"SHOVING THAT COSMIC CUBE UP HIS PURPLE BUTT AS THE UNIVERSE FOLDED DOWN AROUND HIM...
"...WELL, WOULDN'T THAT MAKE EVERY DAMN THING WE'VE BEEN THROUGH WORTH IT?"

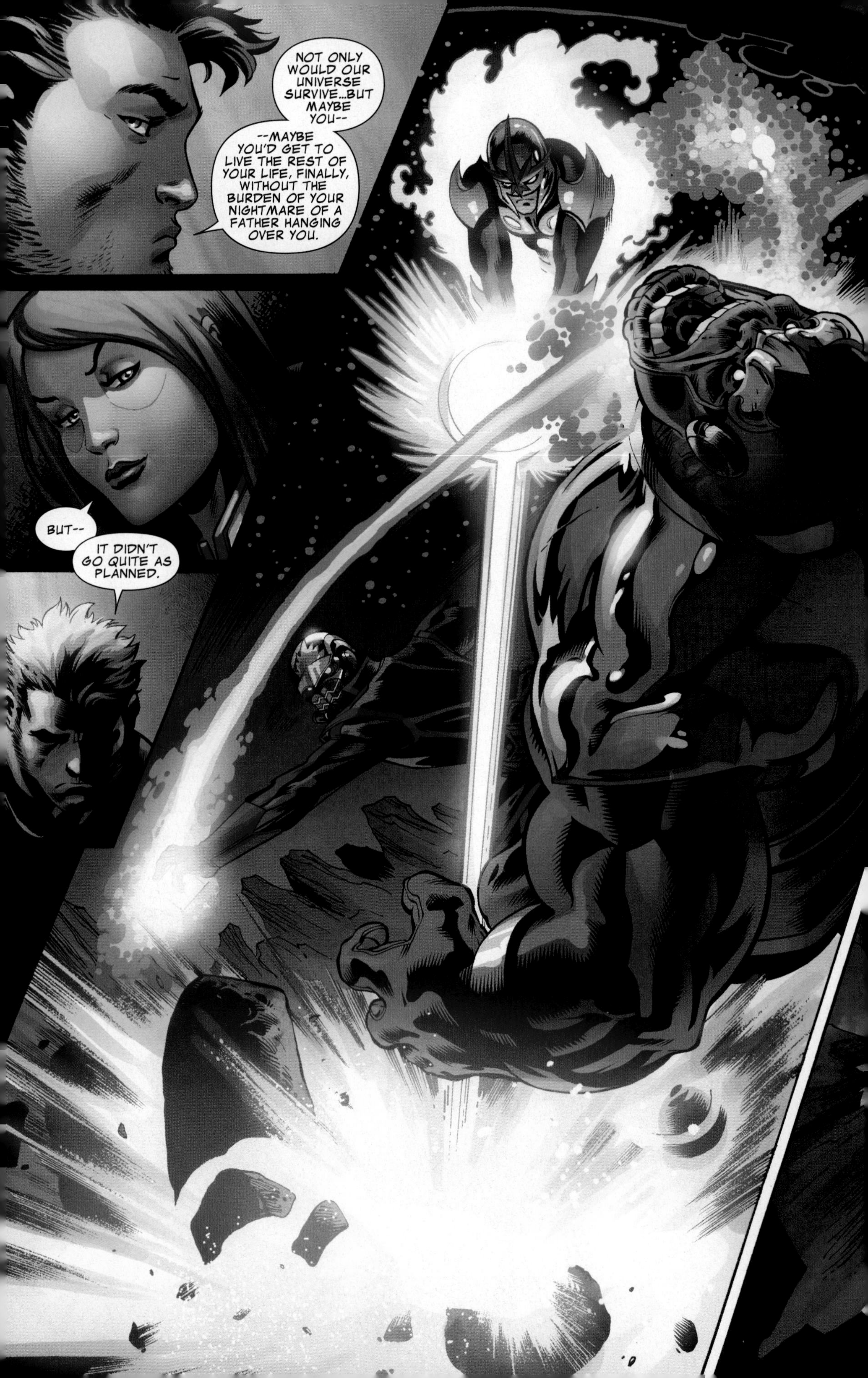
NOT ONLY WOULD OUR UNIVERSE SURVIVE...BUT MAYBE YOU--
--MAYBE YOU'D GET TO LIVE THE REST OF YOUR LIFE, FINALLY, WITHOUT THE BURDEN OF YOUR NIGHTMARE OF A FATHER HANGING OVER YOU.
BUT--
IT DIDN'T GO QUITE AS PLANNED.

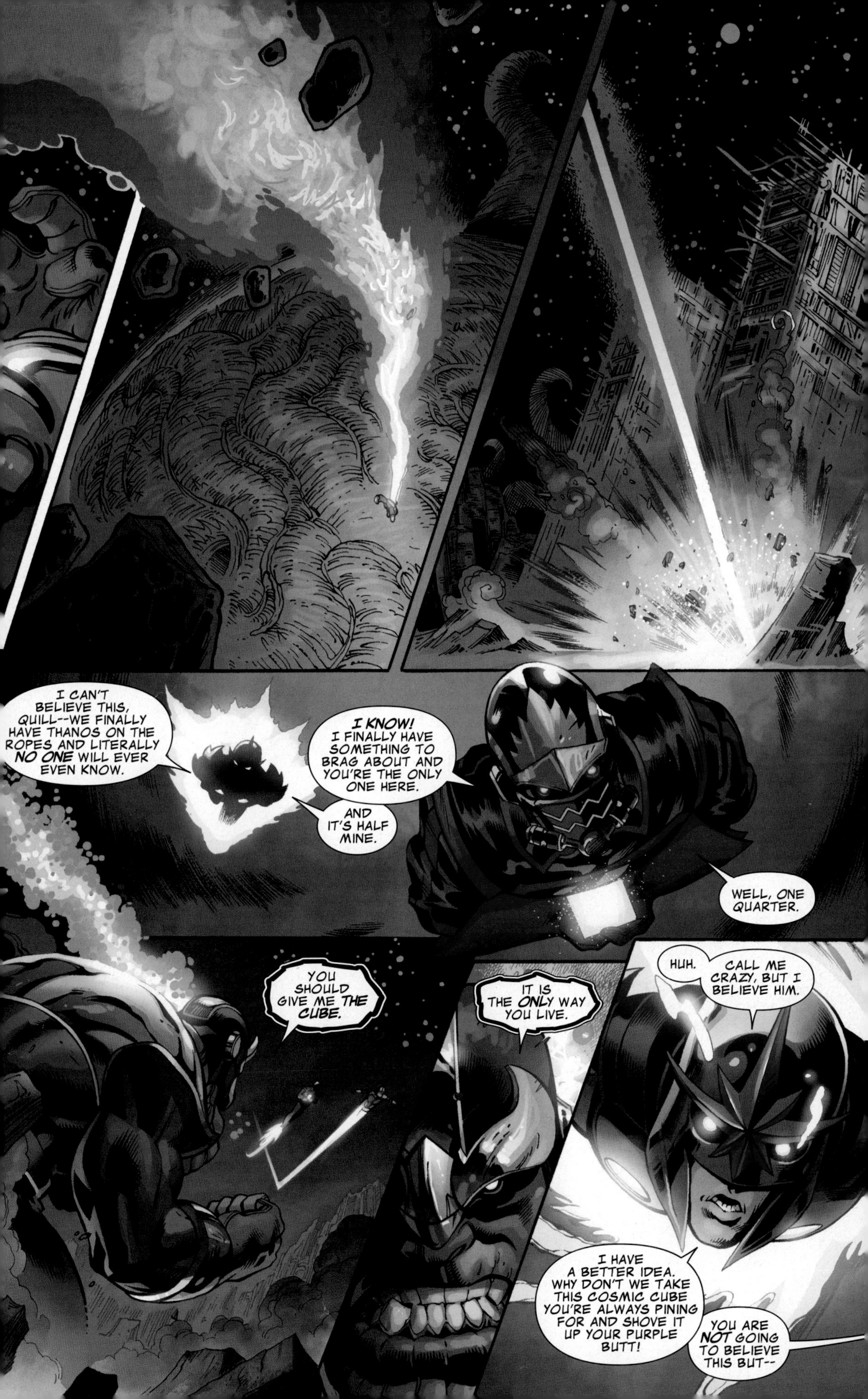
I CAN'T BELIEVE THIS, QUILL--WE FINALLY HAVE THANOS ON THE ROPES AND LITERALLY NO ONE WILL EVER EVEN KNOW.
I KNOW! I FINALLY HAVE SOMETHING TO BRAG ABOUT AND YOU'RE THE ONLY ONE HERE.
AND IT'S HALF MINE.
WELL, ONE QUARTER.
YOU SHOULD GIVE ME THE CUBE.
IT IS THE ONLY WAY YOU LIVE.
HUH.
CALL ME CRAZY, BUT I BELIEVE HIM.
I HAVE A BETTER IDEA. WHY DON'T WE TAKE THIS COSMIC CUBE YOU'RE ALWAYS PINING FOR AND SHOVE IT UP YOUR PURPLE BUTT!
YOU ARE NOT GOING TO BELIEVE THIS BUT--

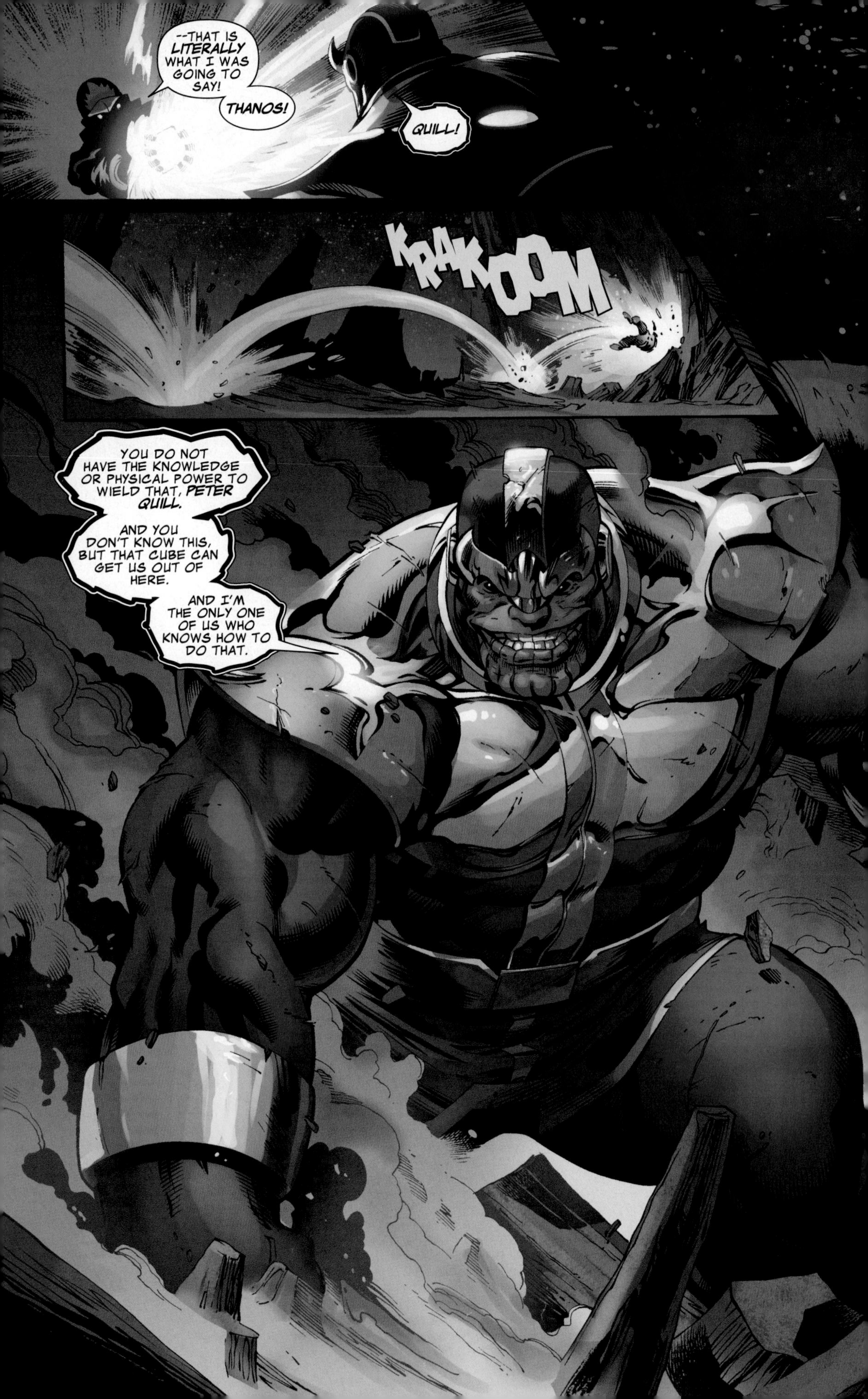

--THAT IS LITERALLY WHAT I WAS GOING TO SAY!
THANOS!
QUILL!
KRAKOOM
YOU DO NOT HAVE THE KNOWLEDGE OR PHYSICAL POWER TO WIELD THAT, PETER QUILL.
AND YOU DON'T KNOW THIS, BUT THAT CUBE CAN GET US OUT OF HERE.
AND I'M THE ONLY ONE OF US WHO KNOWS HOW TO DO THAT.

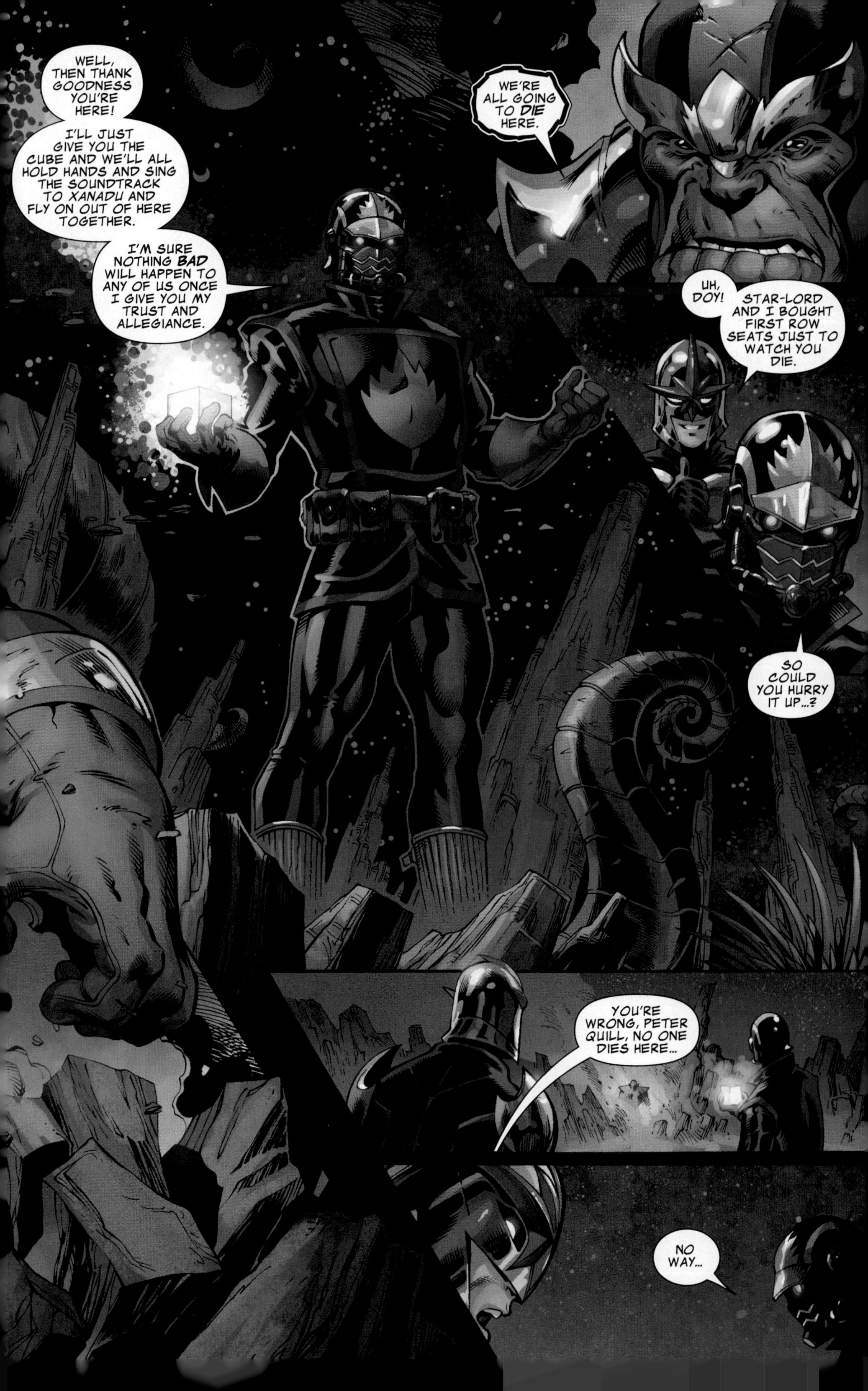
WELL, THEN THANK GOODNESS YOU'RE HERE!
I'LL JUST GIVE YOU THE CUBE AND WE'LL ALL HOLD HANDS AND SING THE SOUNDTRACK TO XANADU AND FLY ON OUT OF HERE TOGETHER.
I'M SURE NOTHING BAD WILL HAPPEN TO ANY OF US ONCE I GIVE YOU MY TRUST AND ALLEGIANCE.
WE'RE ALL GOING TO DIE HERE.
UH, DOY!
STAR-LORD AND I BOUGHT FIRST ROW SEATS JUST TO WATCH YOU DIE.
SO COULD YOU HURRY IT UP...?
YOU'RE WRONG, PETER QUILL, NO ONE DIES HERE...
NO WAY...

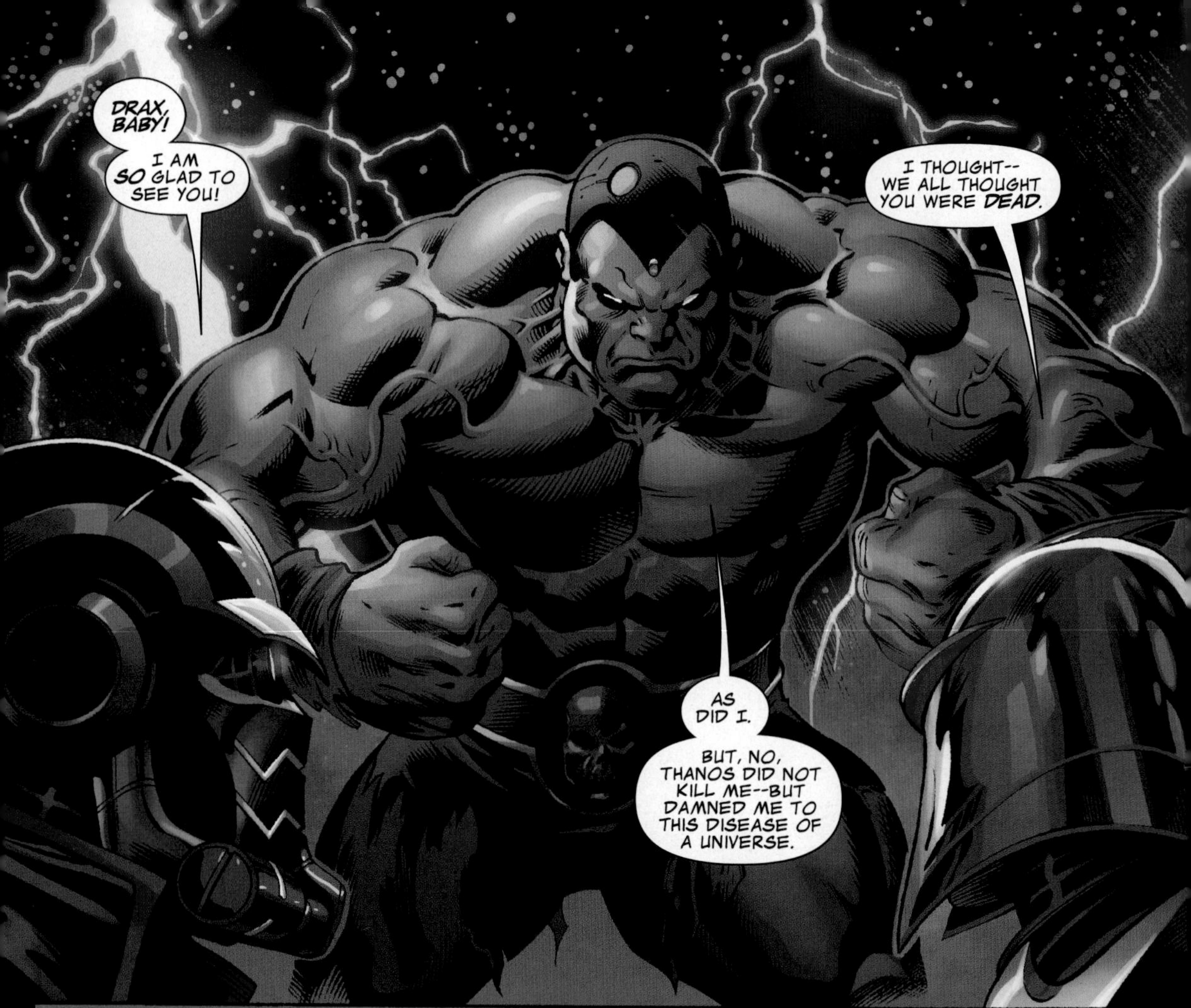
DRAX, BABY!
I AM SO GLAD TO SEE YOU!
I THOUGHT-- WE ALL THOUGHT YOU WERE DEAD.
AS DID I.
BUT, NO, THANOS DID NOT KILL ME--BUT DAMNED ME TO THIS DISEASE OF A UNIVERSE.

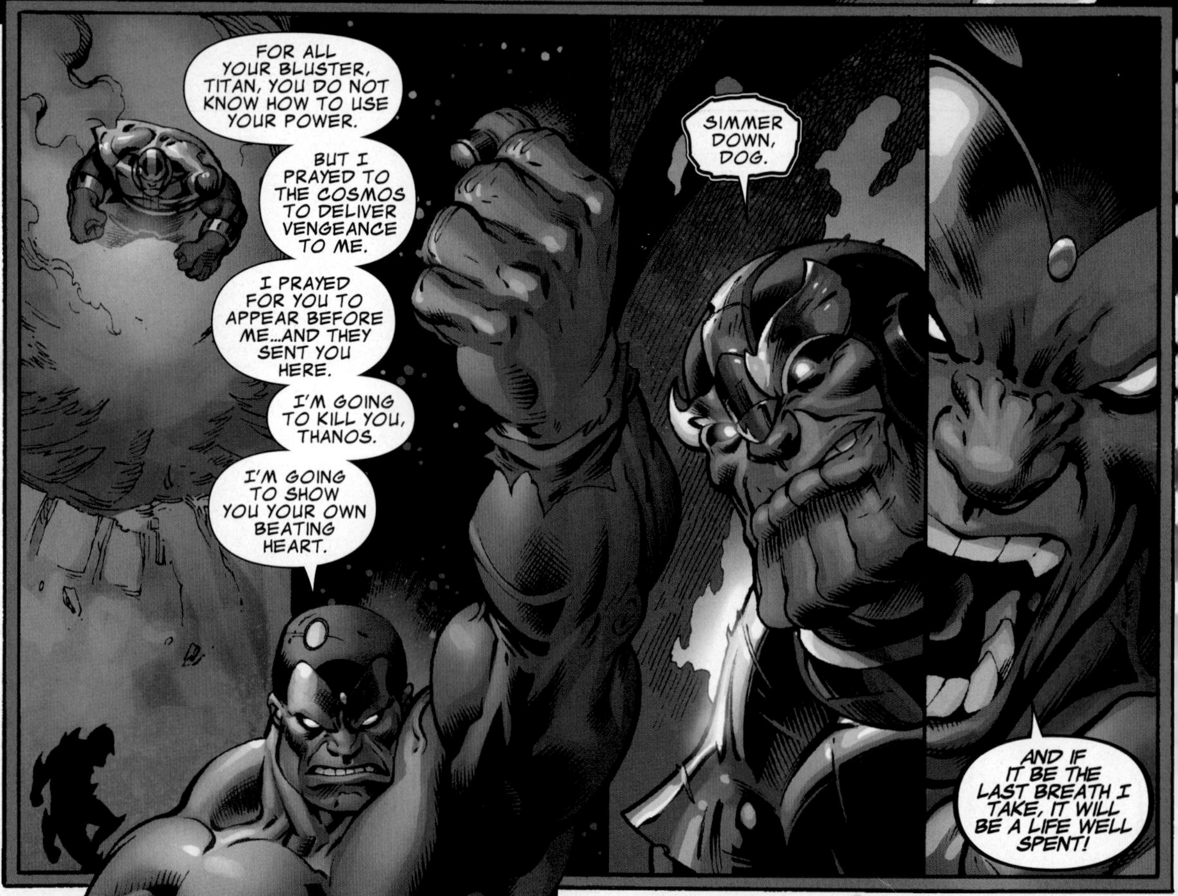
FOR ALL YOUR BLUSTER, TITAN, YOU DO NOT KNOW HOW TO USE YOUR POWER.
BUT I PRAYED TO THE COSMOS TO DELIVER VENGEANCE TO ME.
I PRAYED FOR YOU TO APPEAR BEFORE ME...AND THEY SENT YOU HERE.
I'M GOING TO KILL YOU, THANOS.
I'M GOING TO SHOW YOU YOUR OWN BEATING HEART.
SIMMER DOWN, DOG.
AND IF IT BE THE LAST BREATH I TAKE, IT WILL BE A LIFE WELL SPENT!

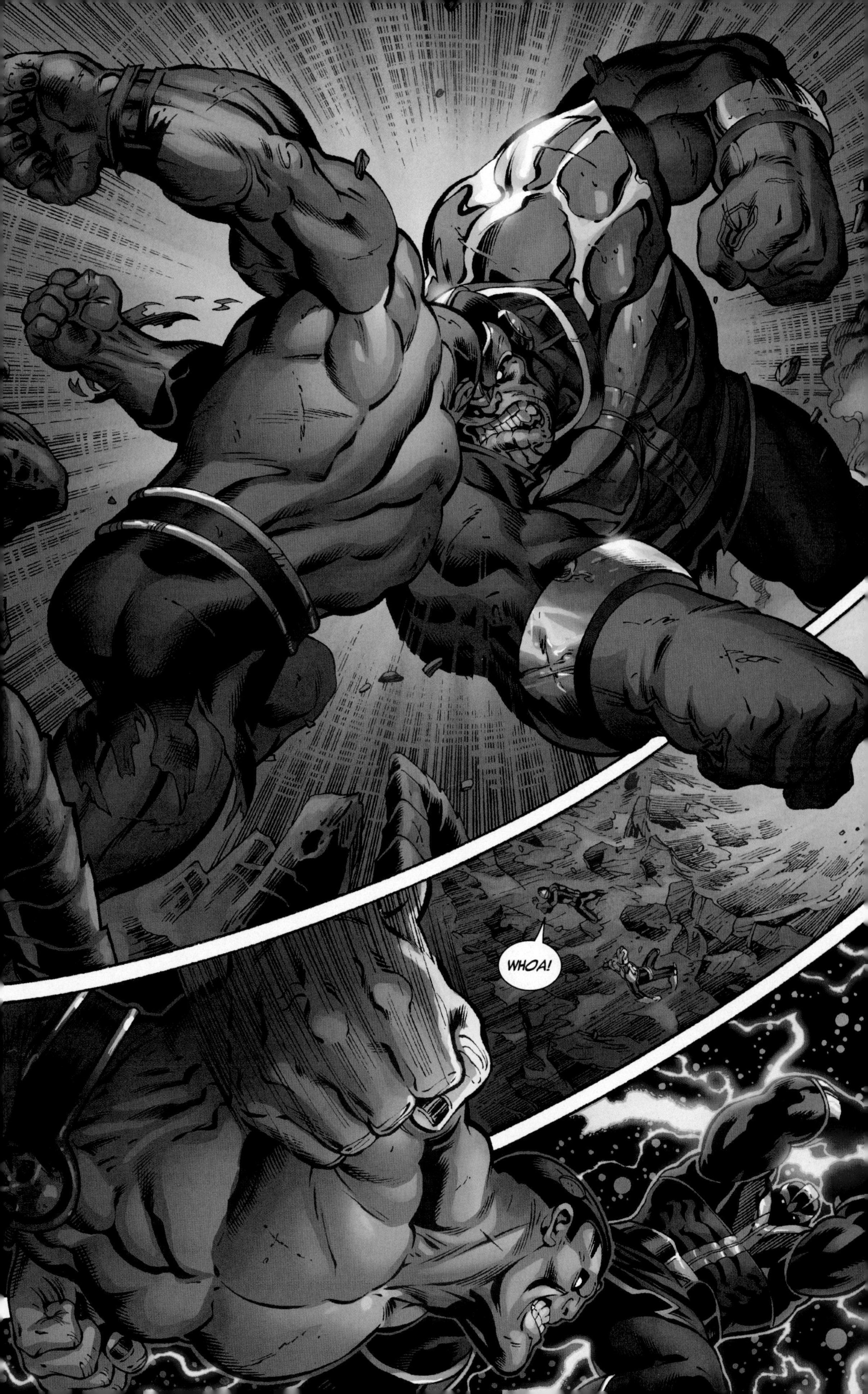
WHOA!

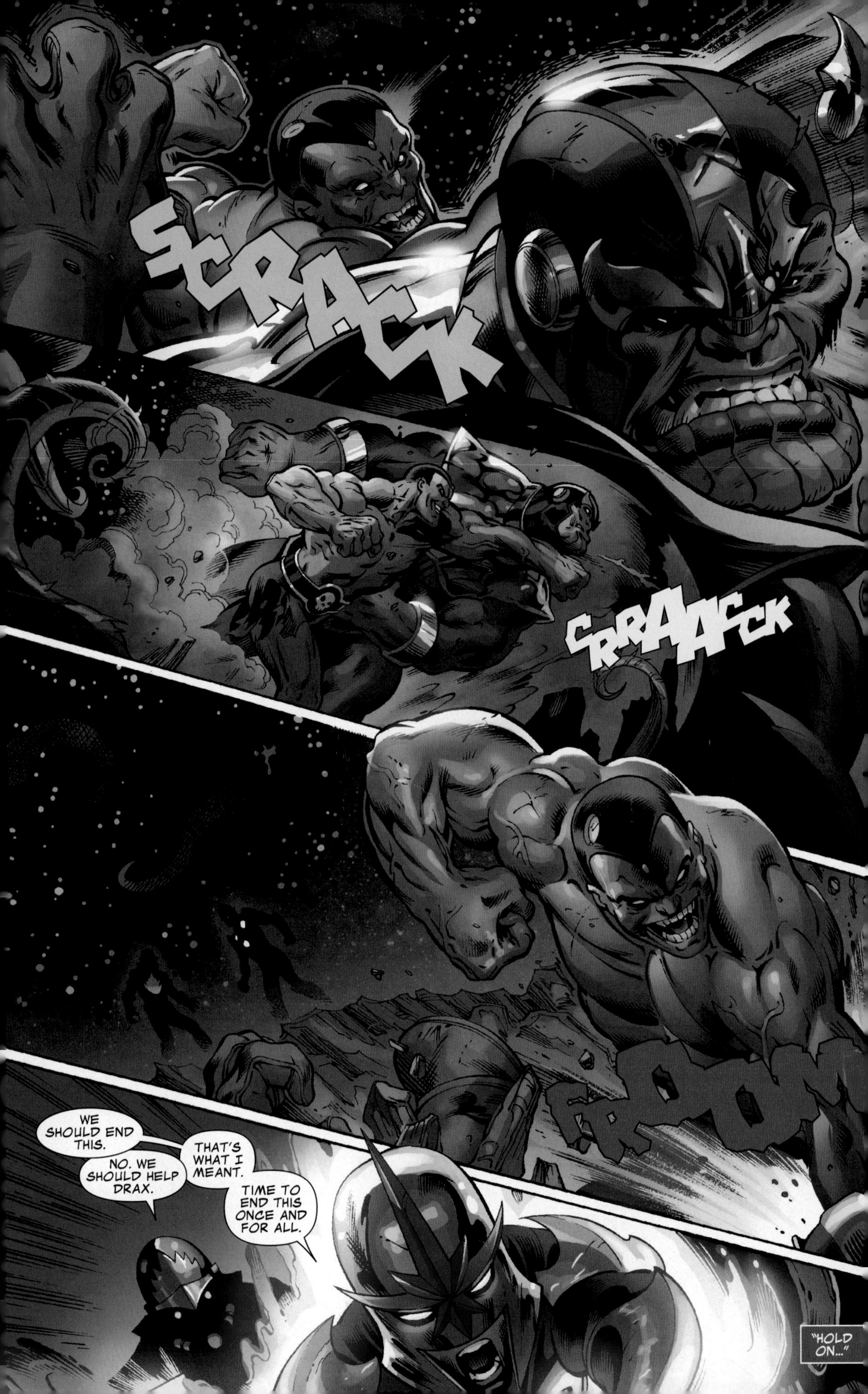
SCRACK
CRRAACK
WE SHOULD END THIS.
THAT'S WHAT I MEANT.
NO. WE SHOULD HELP DRAX.
TIME TO END THIS ONCE AND FOR ALL.
"HOLD ON..."

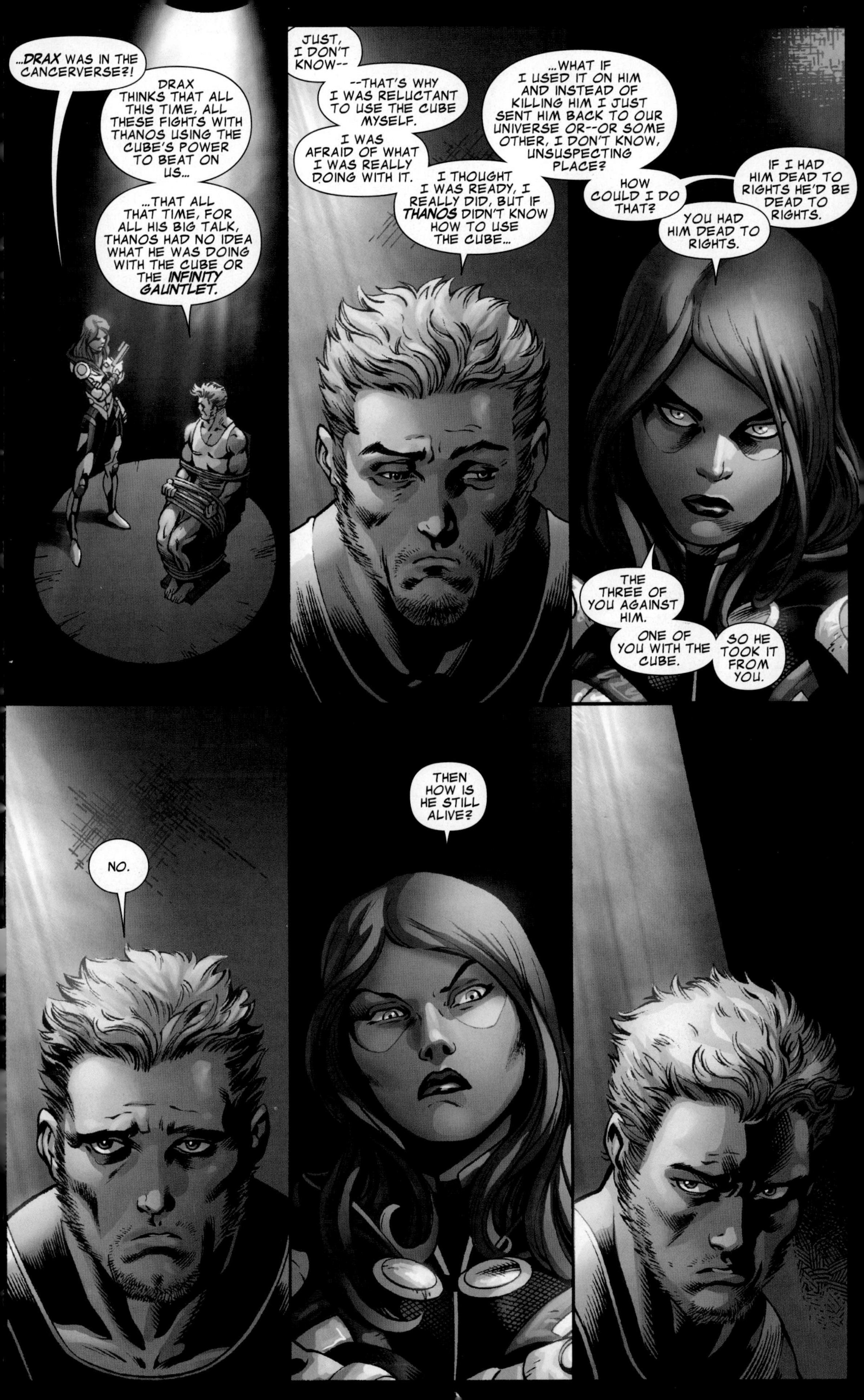
...DRAX WAS IN THE CANCERVERSE?!
DRAX THINKS THAT ALL THIS TIME, ALL THESE FIGHTS WITH THANOS USING THE CUBE'S POWER TO BEAT ON US...
...THAT ALL THAT TIME, FOR ALL HIS BIG TALK, THANOS HAD NO IDEA WHAT HE WAS DOING WITH THE CUBE OR THE INFINITY GAUNTLET.
JUST, I DON'T KNOW--
--THAT'S WHY I WAS RELUCTANT TO USE THE CUBE MYSELF.
I WAS AFRAID OF WHAT I WAS REALLY DOING WITH IT.
I THOUGHT I WAS READY, I REALLY DID, BUT IF THANOS DIDN'T KNOW HOW TO USE THE CUBE...
...WHAT IF I USED IT ON HIM AND INSTEAD OF KILLING HIM I JUST SENT HIM BACK TO OUR UNIVERSE OR--OR SOME OTHER, I DON'T KNOW, UNSUSPECTING PLACE?
HOW COULD I DO THAT?
IF I HAD HIM DEAD TO RIGHTS HE'D BE DEAD TO RIGHTS.
YOU HAD HIM DEAD TO RIGHTS.
THE THREE OF YOU AGAINST HIM.
ONE OF YOU WITH THE CUBE.
SO HE TOOK IT FROM YOU.
NO.
THEN HOW IS HE STILL ALIVE?

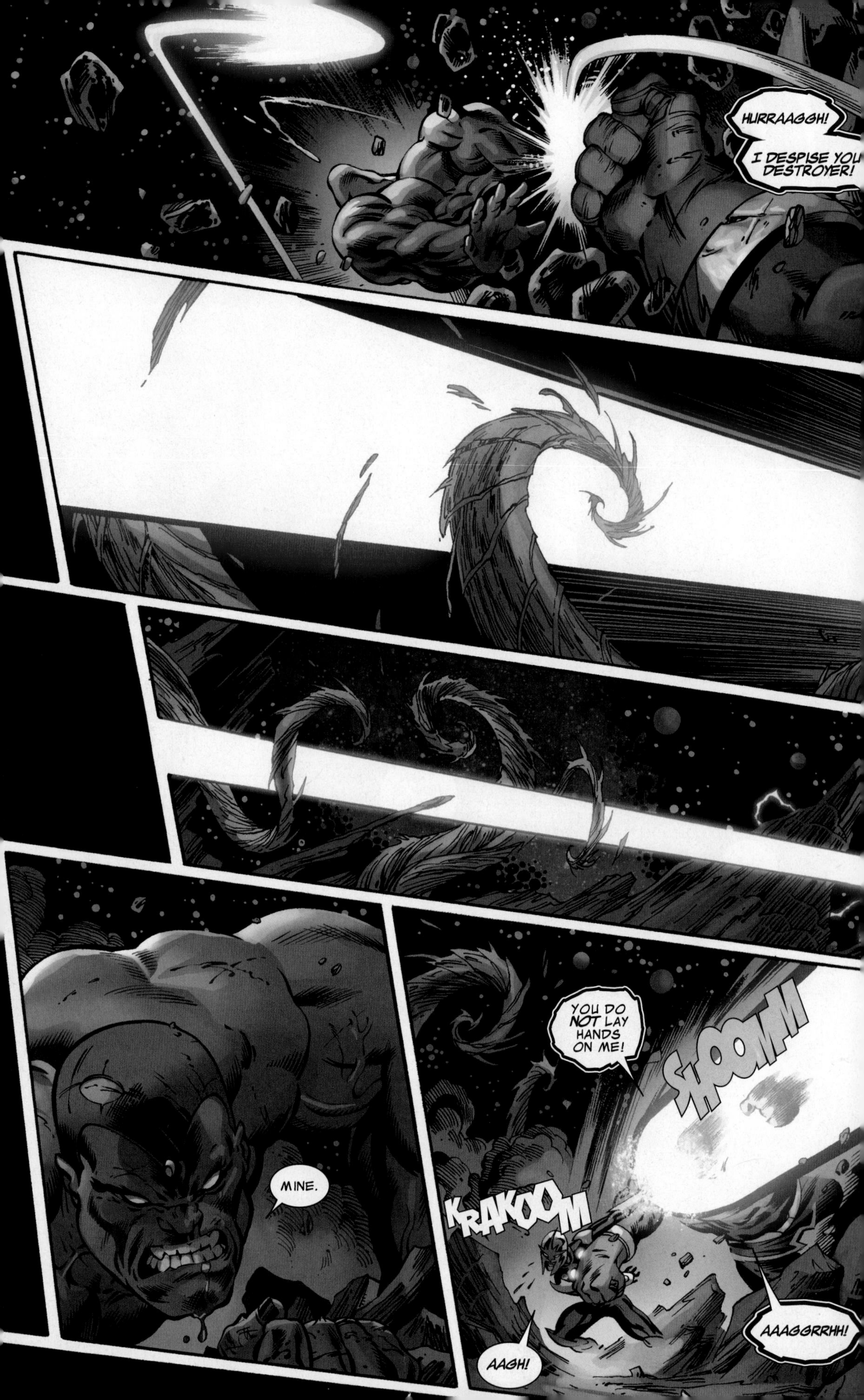
HURRAAGGH!
I DESPISE YOU DESTROYER!
MINE.
YOU DO NOT LAY HANDS ON ME!
SHOOMM
KRAKOOM
AAGH!
AAAGGRRHH!

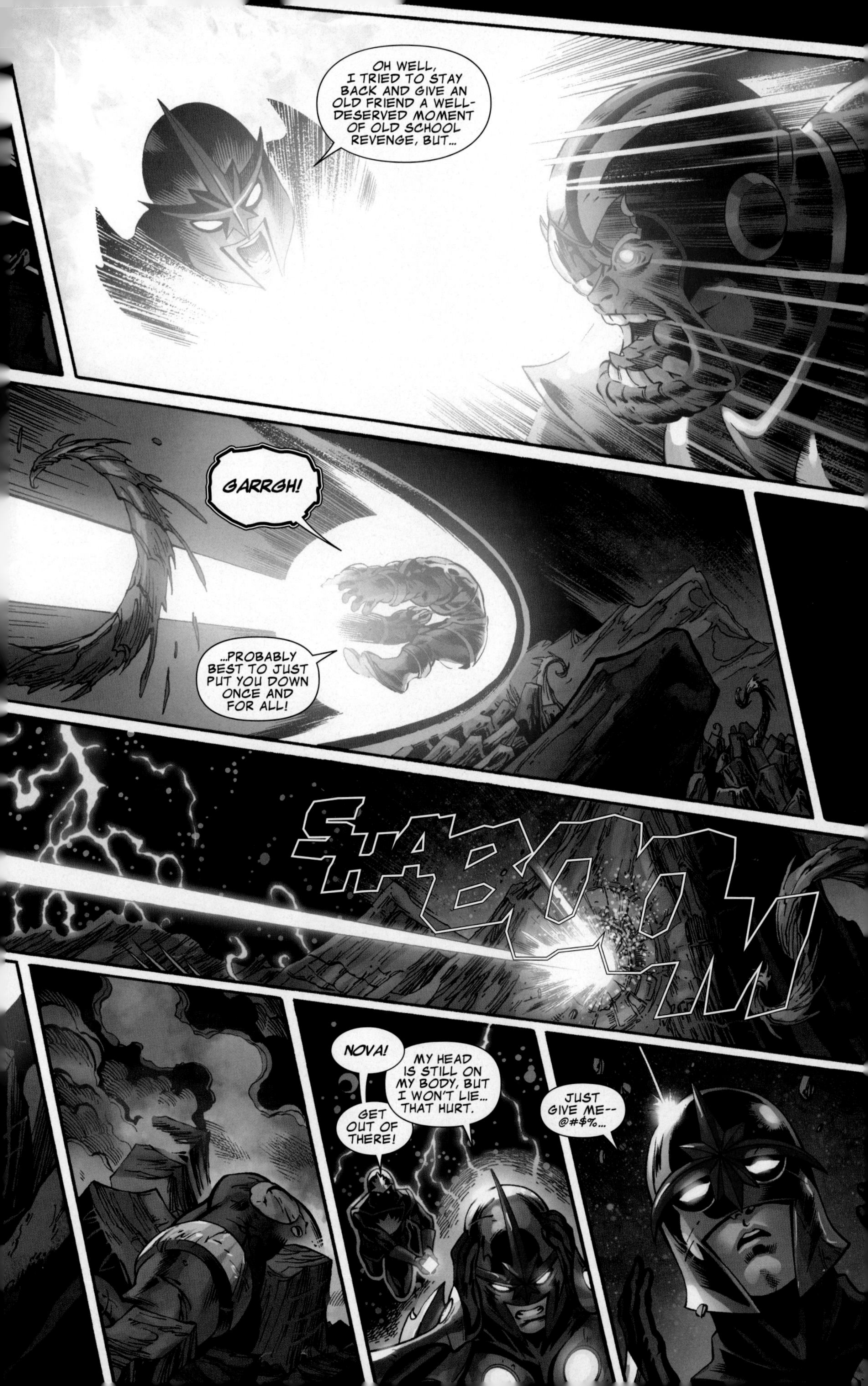
OH WELL, I TRIED TO STAY BACK AND GIVE AN OLD FRIEND A WELL-DESERVED MOMENT OF OLD SCHOOL REVENGE, BUT...
GARRGH!
...PROBABLY BEST TO JUST PUT YOU DOWN ONCE AND FOR ALL!
SHABOOM
NOVA!
GET OUT OF THERE!
MY HEAD IS STILL ON MY BODY, BUT I WON'T LIE... THAT HURT.
JUST GIVE ME-- @#$%...

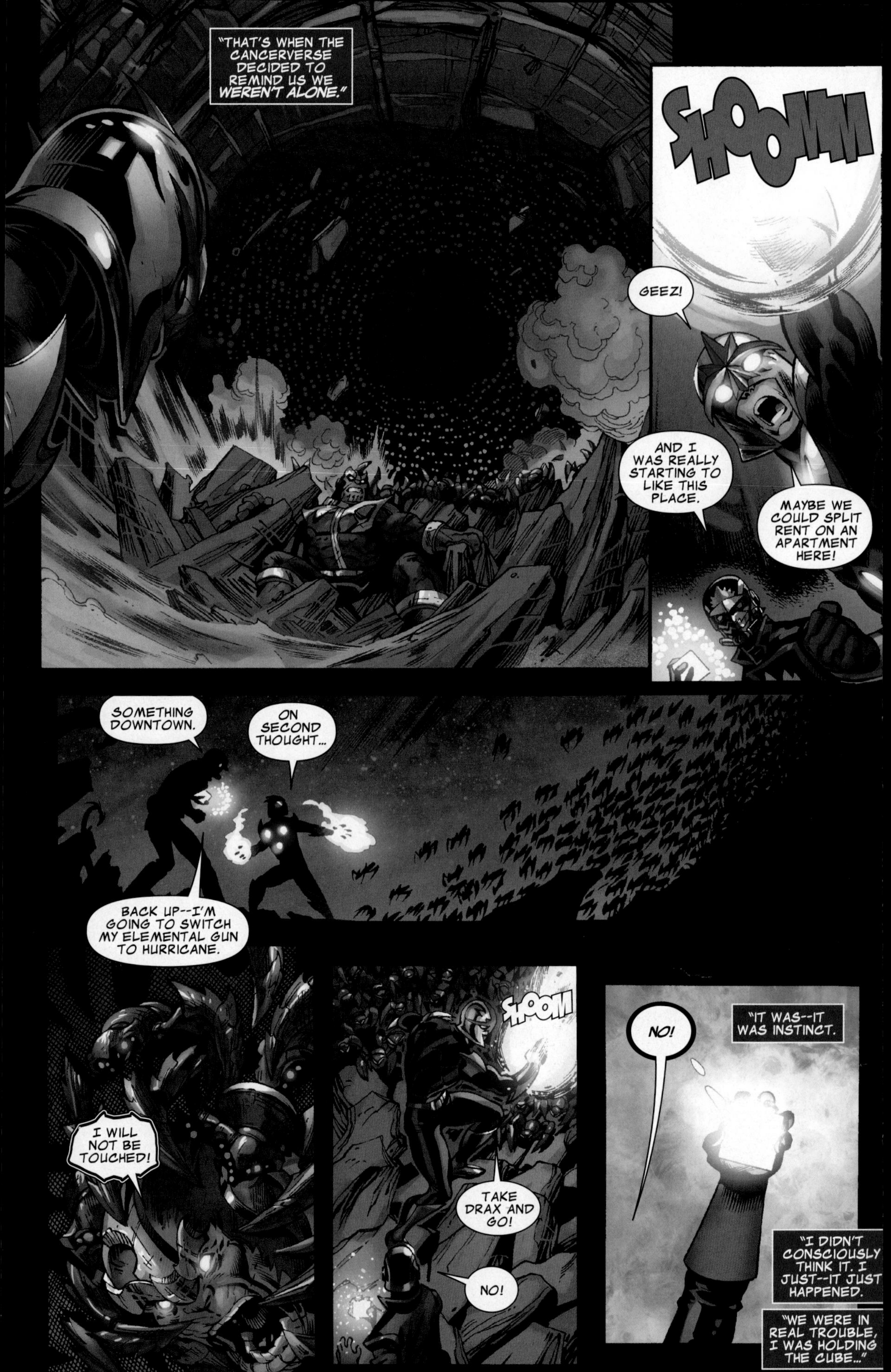
"THAT'S WHEN THE CANCERVERSE DECIDED TO REMIND US WE *WEREN'T ALONE.*"
SHOOMM
GEEZ!
AND I WAS REALLY STARTING TO LIKE THIS PLACE.
MAYBE WE COULD SPLIT RENT ON AN APARTMENT HERE!
SOMETHING DOWNTOWN.
ON SECOND THOUGHT...
BACK UP--I'M GOING TO SWITCH MY ELEMENTAL GUN TO HURRICANE.
I WILL NOT BE TOUCHED!
SHOOM
TAKE DRAX AND GO!
NO!
NO!
"IT WAS--IT WAS INSTINCT.
"I DIDN'T CONSCIOUSLY THINK IT. I JUST--IT JUST HAPPENED.
"WE WERE IN REAL TROUBLE, I WAS HOLDING THE CUBE..."

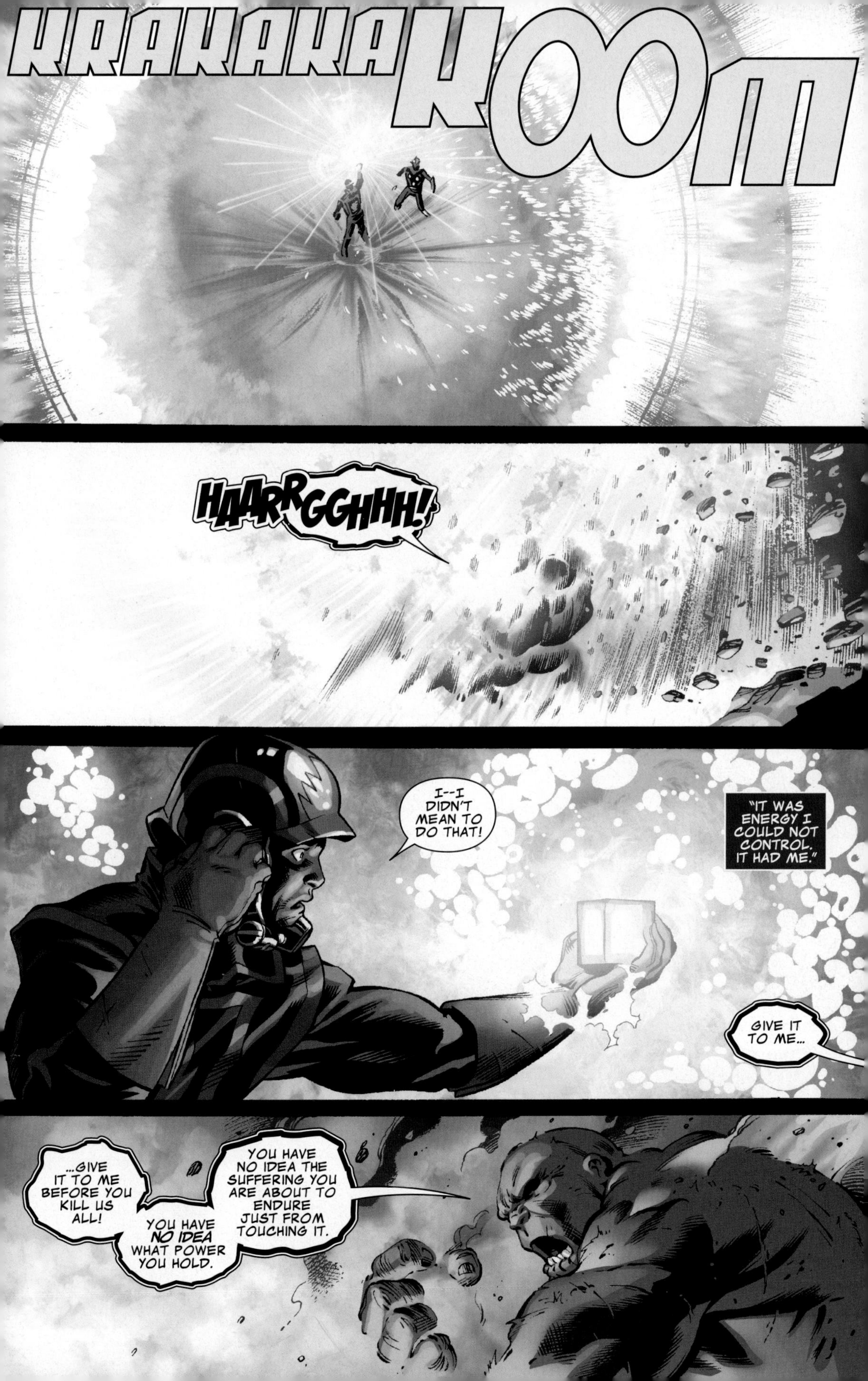
KRAKAKAKOOM
HAARRGGHHH!
I--I DIDN'T MEAN TO DO THAT!
"IT WAS ENERGY I COULD NOT CONTROL. IT HAD ME."
GIVE IT TO ME...
...GIVE IT TO ME BEFORE YOU KILL US ALL!
YOU HAVE NO IDEA WHAT POWER YOU HOLD.
YOU HAVE NO IDEA THE SUFFERING YOU ARE ABOUT TO ENDURE JUST FROM TOUCHING IT.

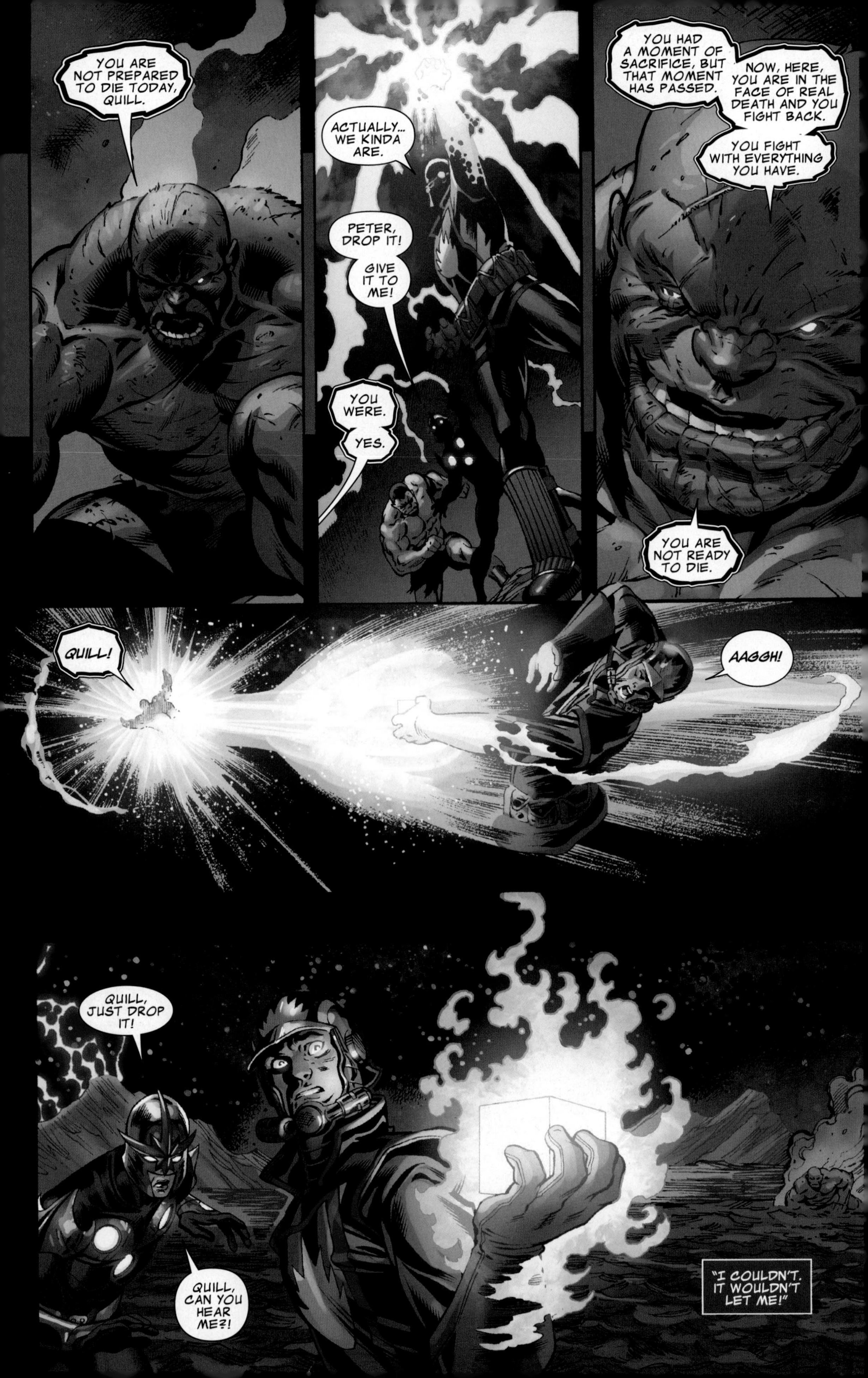
YOU ARE NOT PREPARED TO DIE TODAY, QUILL.
ACTUALLY... WE KINDA ARE.
PETER, DROP IT!
GIVE IT TO ME!
YOU WERE.
YES.
YOU HAD A MOMENT OF SACRIFICE, BUT THAT MOMENT HAS PASSED.
NOW, HERE, YOU ARE IN THE FACE OF REAL DEATH AND YOU FIGHT BACK.
YOU FIGHT WITH EVERYTHING YOU HAVE.
YOU ARE NOT READY TO DIE.
QUILL!
AAGGH!
QUILL, JUST DROP IT!
QUILL, CAN YOU HEAR ME?!
"I COULDN'T. IT WOULDN'T LET ME!"

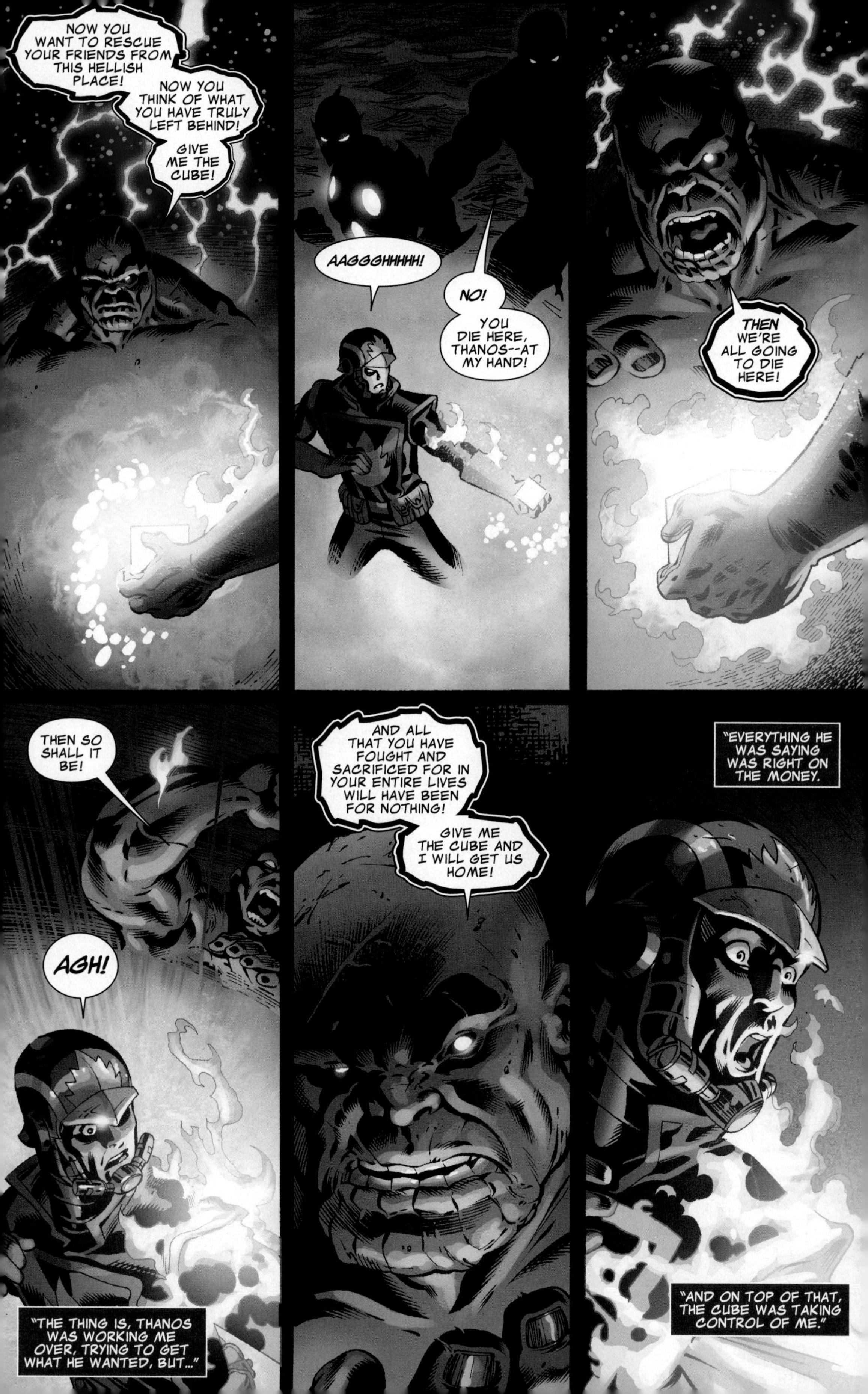
NOW YOU WANT TO RESCUE YOUR FRIENDS FROM THIS HELLISH PLACE!
NOW YOU THINK OF WHAT YOU HAVE TRULY LEFT BEHIND!
GIVE ME THE CUBE!
AAGGGHHHHH!
NO!
YOU DIE HERE, THANOS--AT MY HAND!
THEN WE'RE ALL GOING TO DIE HERE!
THEN SO SHALL IT BE!
AGH!
"THE THING IS, THANOS WAS WORKING ME OVER, TRYING TO GET WHAT HE WANTED, BUT..."
AND ALL THAT YOU HAVE FOUGHT AND SACRIFICED FOR IN YOUR ENTIRE LIVES WILL HAVE BEEN FOR NOTHING!
GIVE ME THE CUBE AND I WILL GET US HOME!
"EVERYTHING HE WAS SAYING WAS RIGHT ON THE MONEY.
"AND ON TOP OF THAT, THE CUBE WAS TAKING CONTROL OF ME."

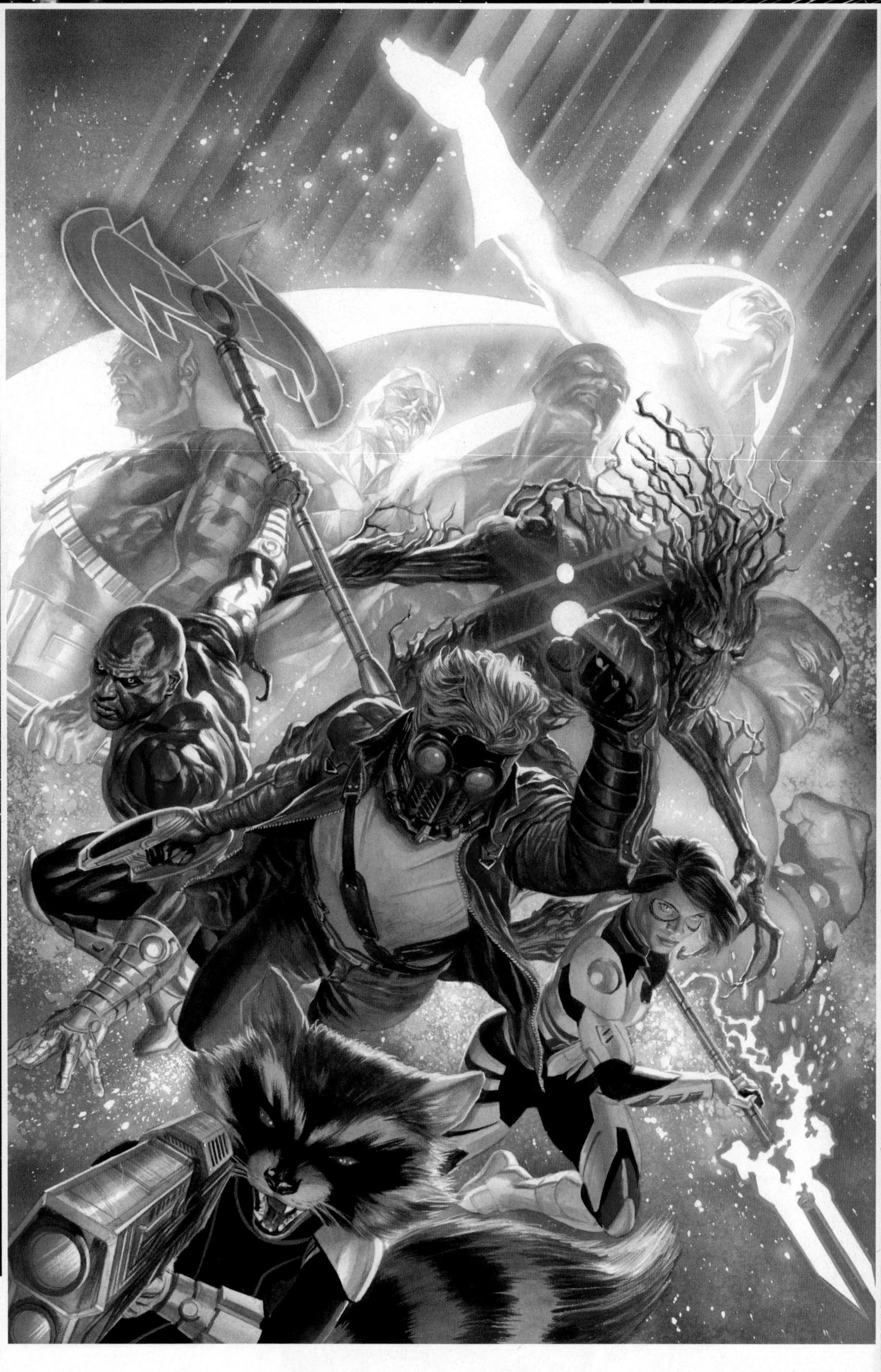

#*18* 75TH ANNIVERSARY VARIANT BY ALEX ROSS

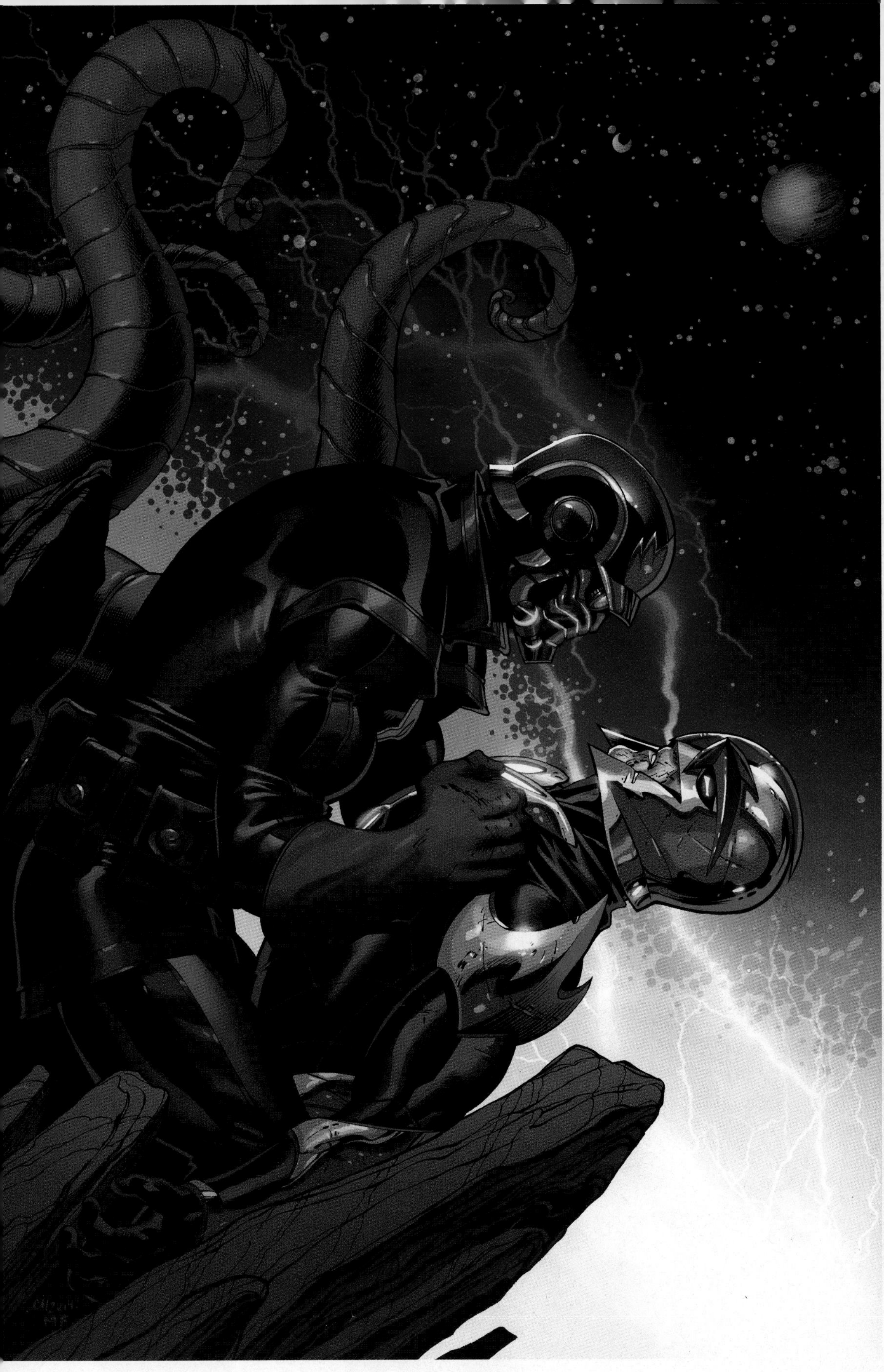

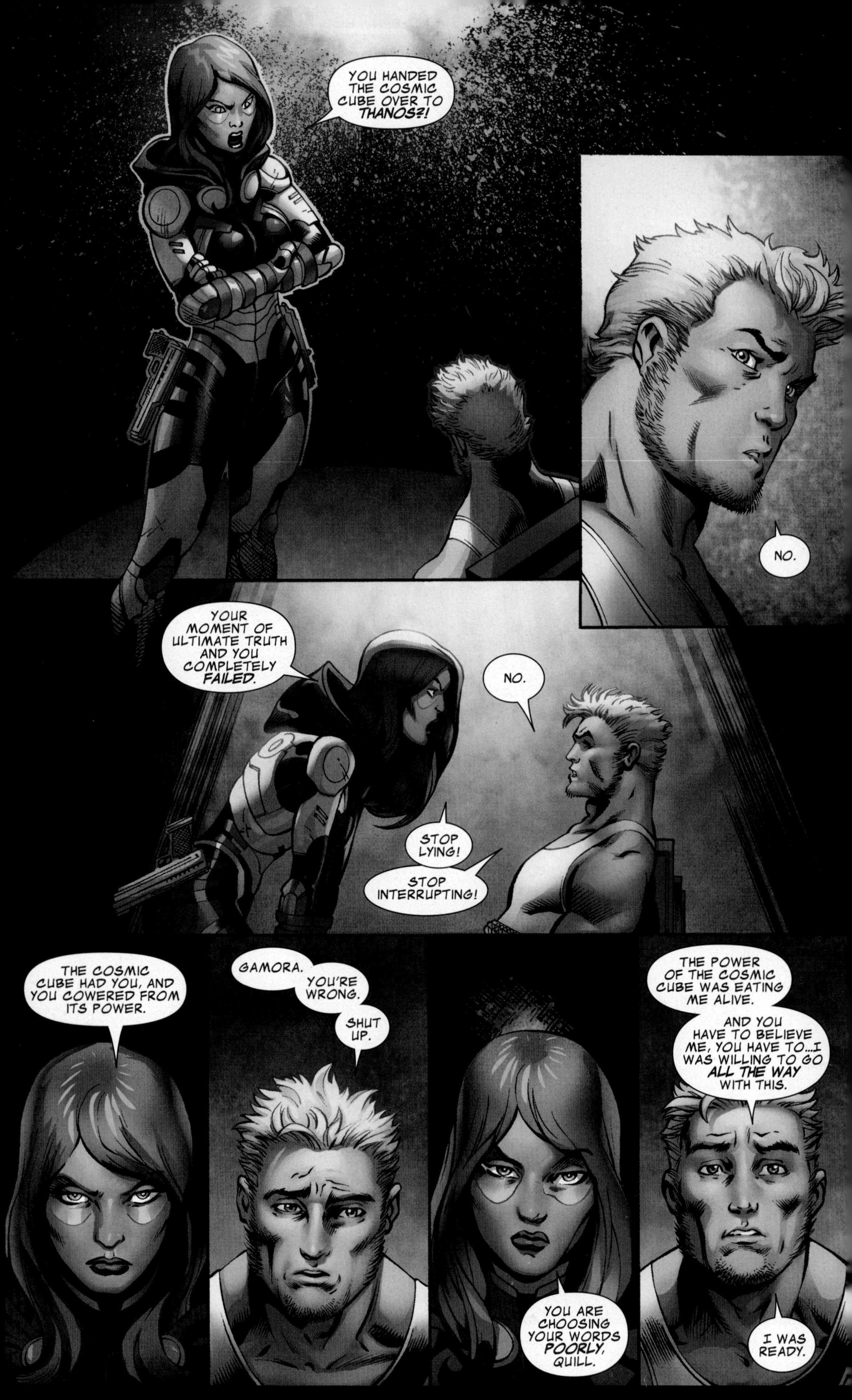
YOU HANDED THE COSMIC CUBE OVER TO *THANOS?!*
NO.
YOUR MOMENT OF ULTIMATE TRUTH AND YOU COMPLETELY *FAILED*.
NO.
STOP LYING!
STOP INTERRUPTING!
THE COSMIC CUBE HAD YOU, AND YOU COWERED FROM ITS POWER.
GAMORA.
YOU'RE WRONG.
SHUT UP.
YOU ARE CHOOSING YOUR WORDS *POORLY*, QUILL.
THE POWER OF THE COSMIC CUBE WAS EATING ME ALIVE.
AND YOU HAVE TO BELIEVE ME, YOU HAVE TO...I WAS WILLING TO GO *ALL THE WAY* WITH THIS.
I WAS READY.

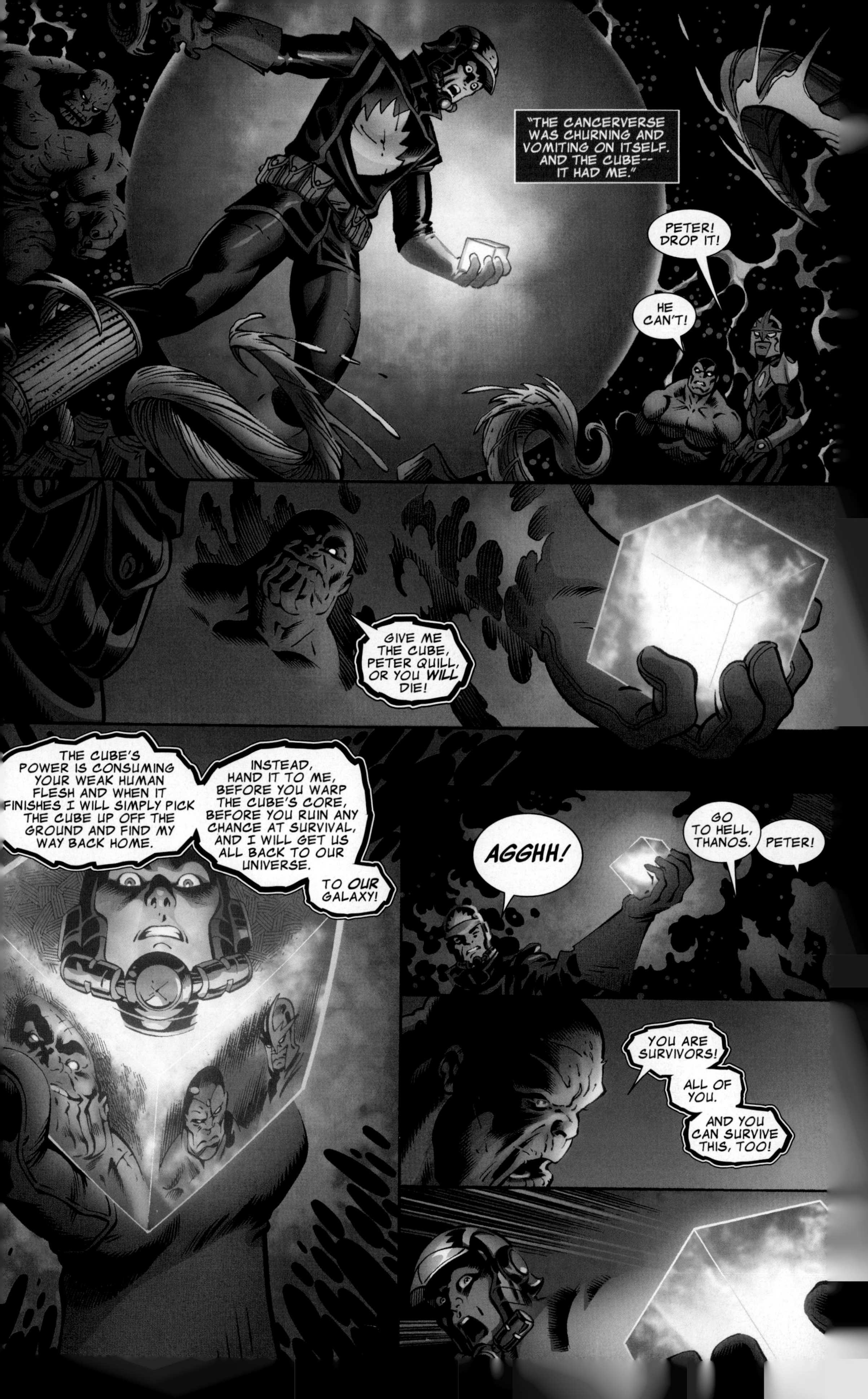
"THE CANCERVERSE WAS CHURNING AND VOMITING ON ITSELF. AND THE CUBE-- IT HAD ME."
PETER! DROP IT!
HE CAN'T!
GIVE ME THE CUBE, PETER QUILL, OR YOU WILL DIE!
THE CUBE'S POWER IS CONSUMING YOUR WEAK HUMAN FLESH AND WHEN IT FINISHES I WILL SIMPLY PICK THE CUBE UP OFF THE GROUND AND FIND MY WAY BACK HOME.
INSTEAD, HAND IT TO ME, BEFORE YOU WARP THE CUBE'S CORE, BEFORE YOU RUIN ANY CHANCE AT SURVIVAL, AND I WILL GET US ALL BACK TO OUR UNIVERSE.
TO OUR GALAXY!
AGGHH!
GO TO HELL, THANOS.
PETER!
YOU ARE SURVIVORS!
ALL OF YOU.
AND YOU CAN SURVIVE THIS, TOO!

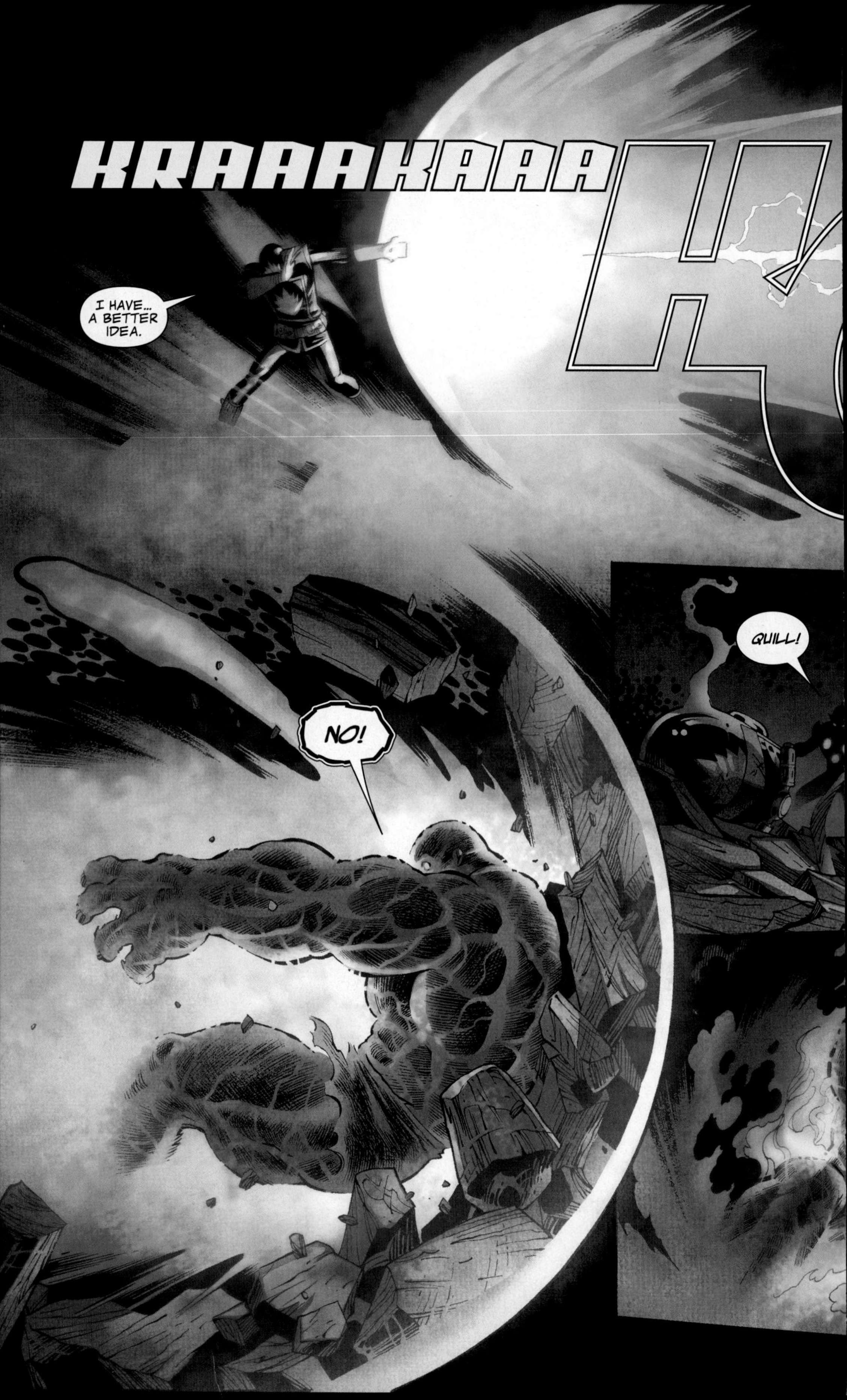
KRAAAAKAAAA
I HAVE... A BETTER IDEA.
NO!
QUILL!

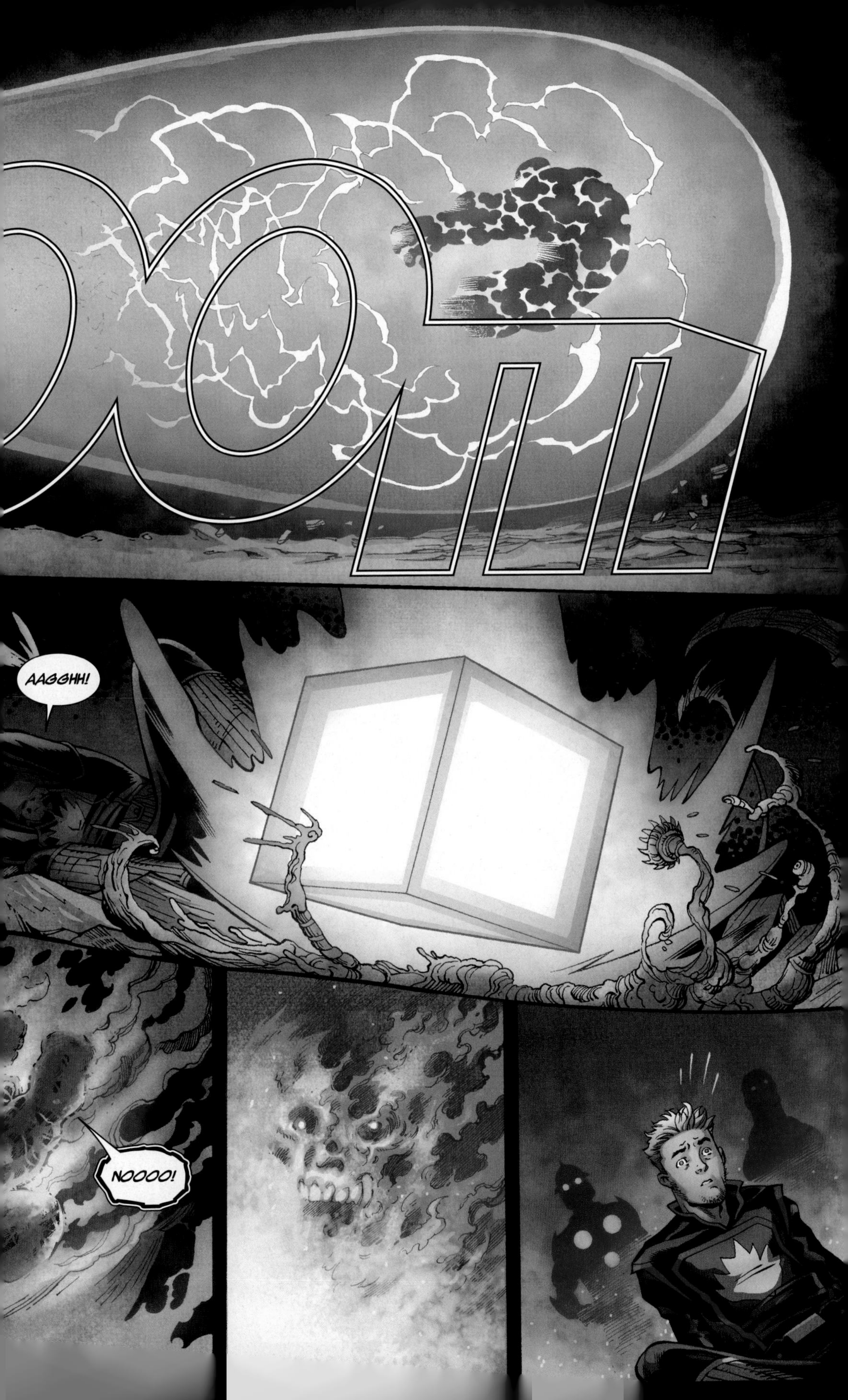
DOOM
AAGGHH!
NOOOO!

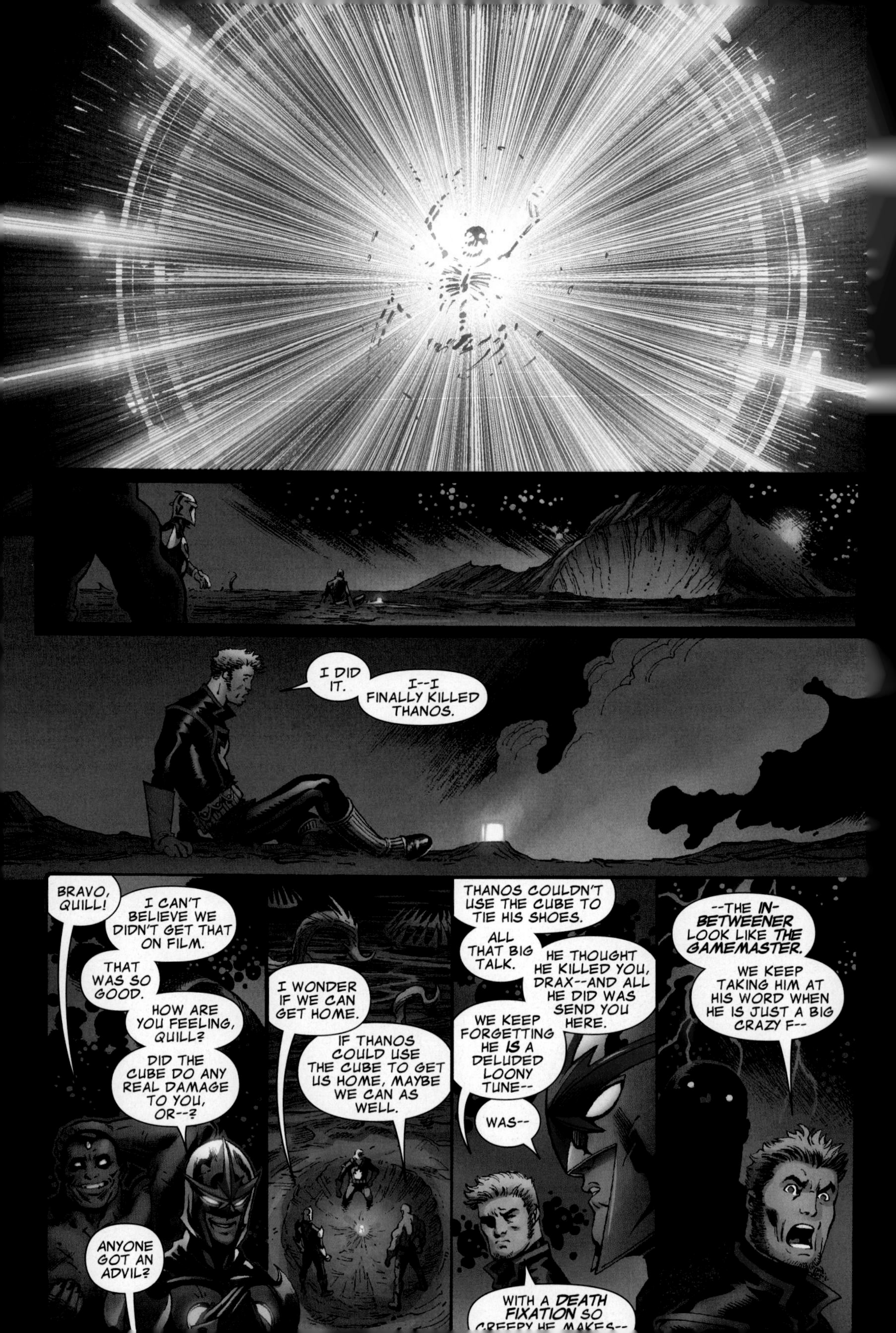

I DID IT.
I--I FINALLY KILLED THANOS.
BRAVO, QUILL!
I CAN'T BELIEVE WE DIDN'T GET THAT ON FILM.
THAT WAS SO GOOD.
HOW ARE YOU FEELING, QUILL?
DID THE CUBE DO ANY REAL DAMAGE TO YOU, OR--?
ANYONE GOT AN ADVIL?
I WONDER IF WE CAN GET HOME.
IF THANOS COULD USE THE CUBE TO GET US HOME, MAYBE WE CAN AS WELL.
THANOS COULDN'T USE THE CUBE TO TIE HIS SHOES.
ALL THAT BIG TALK.
HE THOUGHT HE KILLED YOU, DRAX--AND ALL HE DID WAS SEND YOU HERE.
WE KEEP FORGETTING HE IS A DELUDED LOONY TUNE--
WAS--
WITH A DEATH FIXATION SO CREEPY HE MAKES--
--THE IN-BETWEENER LOOK LIKE THE GAMEMASTER.
WE KEEP TAKING HIM AT HIS WORD WHEN HE IS JUST A BIG CRAZY F--

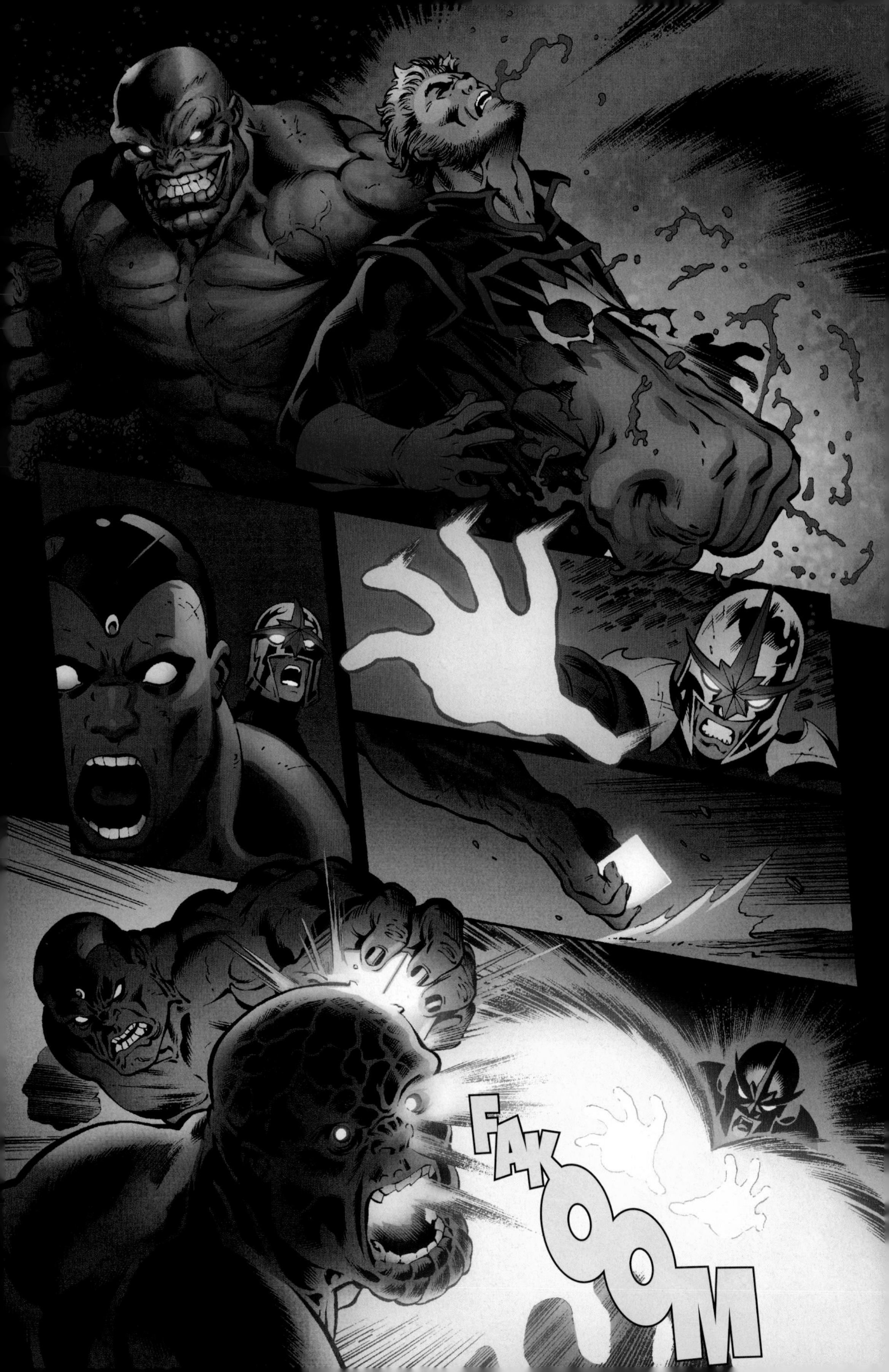
FAKOOOM

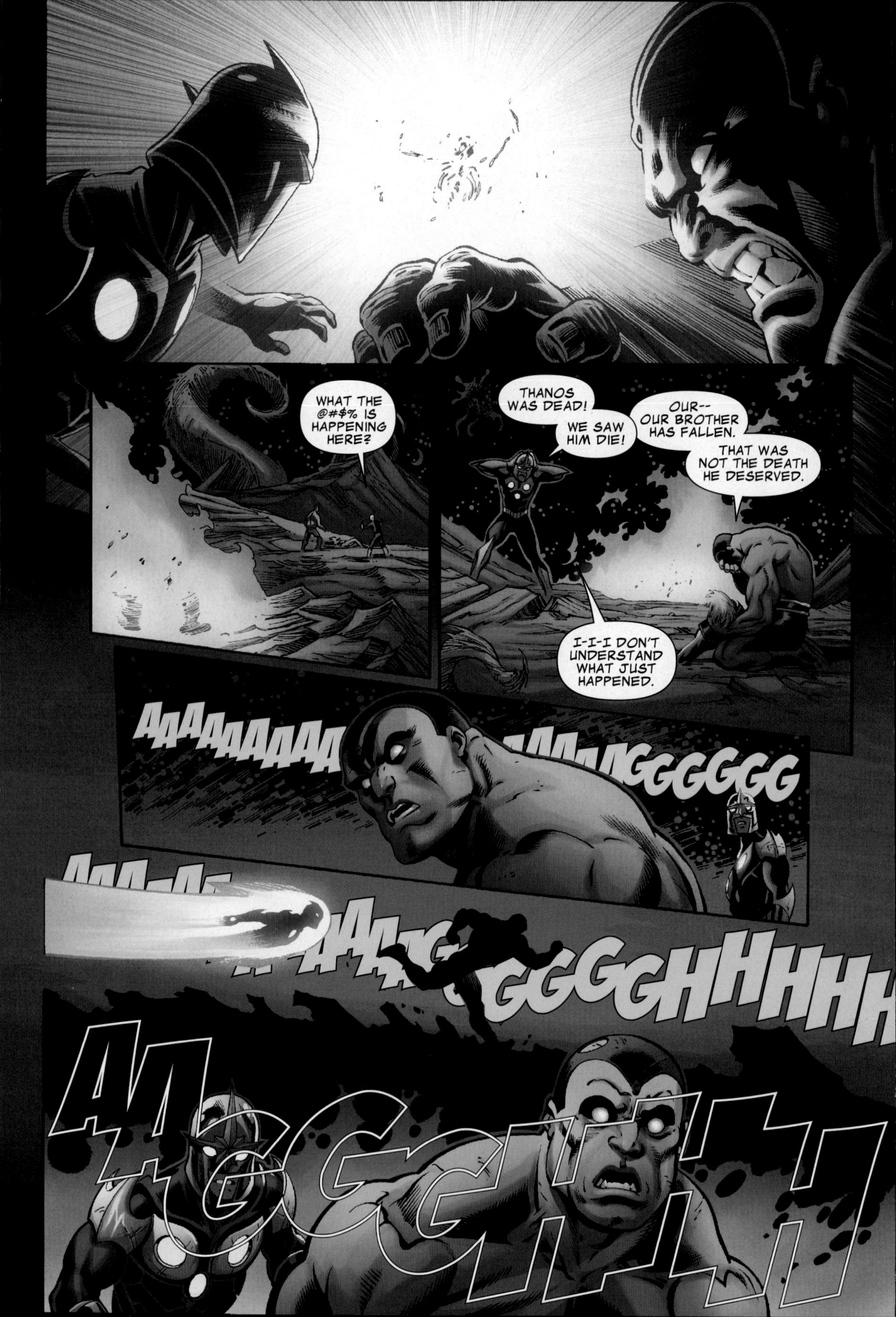
WHAT THE @#$% IS HAPPENING HERE?
THANOS WAS DEAD!
WE SAW HIM DIE!
OUR--OUR BROTHER HAS FALLEN.
THAT WAS NOT THE DEATH HE DESERVED.
I-I-I DON'T UNDERSTAND WHAT JUST HAPPENED.
AAAAAAAAAAAAAAAAGGGGGG
GGGGHHHHH
AAGGHHH

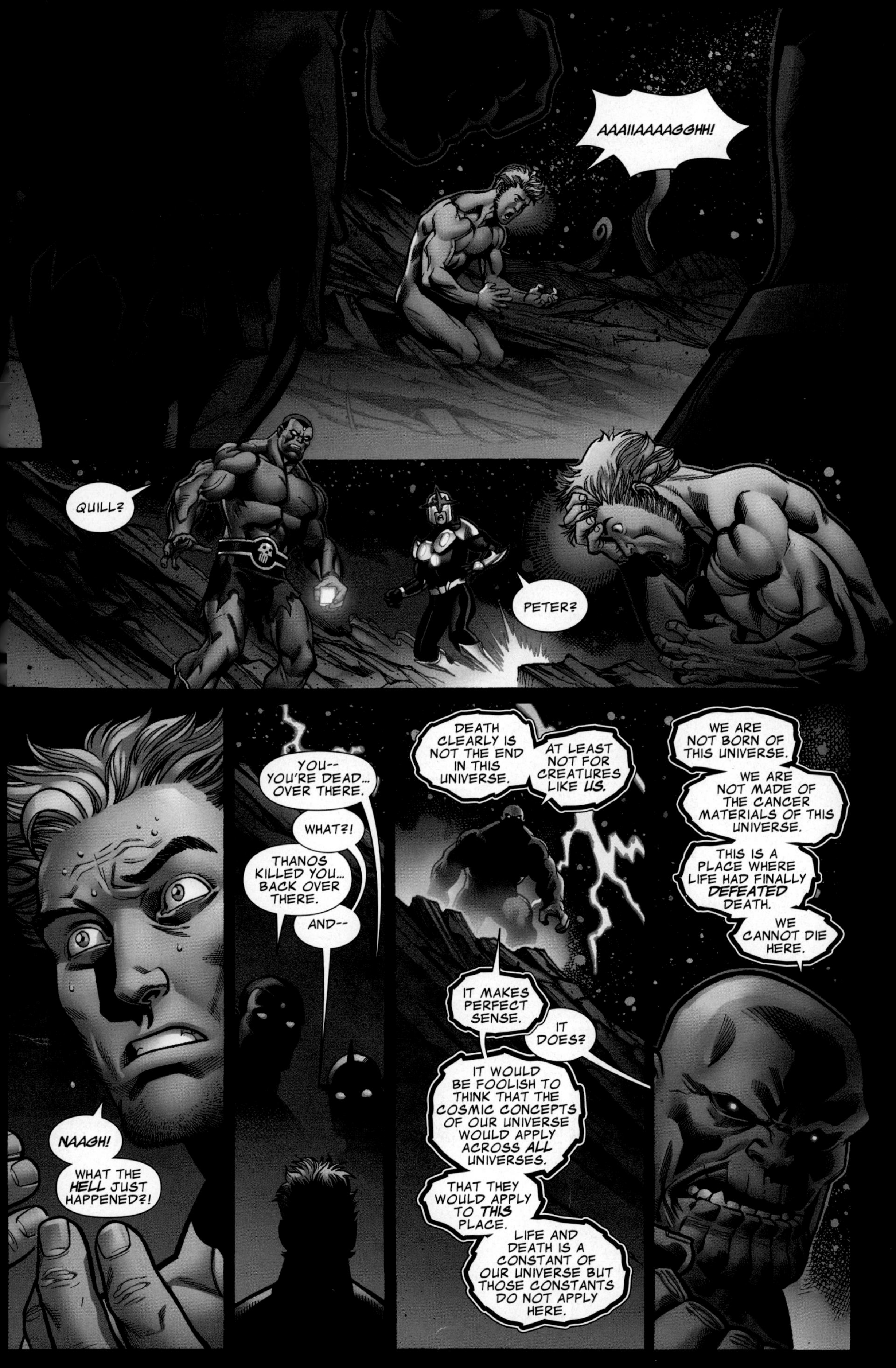
AAAIIAAAAGGHH!
QUILL?
PETER?
NAAGH!
WHAT THE HELL JUST HAPPENED?!
YOU-- YOU'RE DEAD... OVER THERE.
WHAT?!
THANOS KILLED YOU... BACK OVER THERE.
AND--
DEATH CLEARLY IS NOT THE END IN THIS UNIVERSE.
AT LEAST NOT FOR CREATURES LIKE US.
IT MAKES PERFECT SENSE.
IT DOES?
IT WOULD BE FOOLISH TO THINK THAT THE COSMIC CONCEPTS OF OUR UNIVERSE WOULD APPLY ACROSS ALL UNIVERSES.
THAT THEY WOULD APPLY TO THIS PLACE.
LIFE AND DEATH IS A CONSTANT OF OUR UNIVERSE BUT THOSE CONSTANTS DO NOT APPLY HERE.
WE ARE NOT BORN OF THIS UNIVERSE.
WE ARE NOT MADE OF THE CANCER MATERIALS OF THIS UNIVERSE.
THIS IS A PLACE WHERE LIFE HAD FINALLY DEFEATED DEATH.
WE CANNOT DIE HERE.

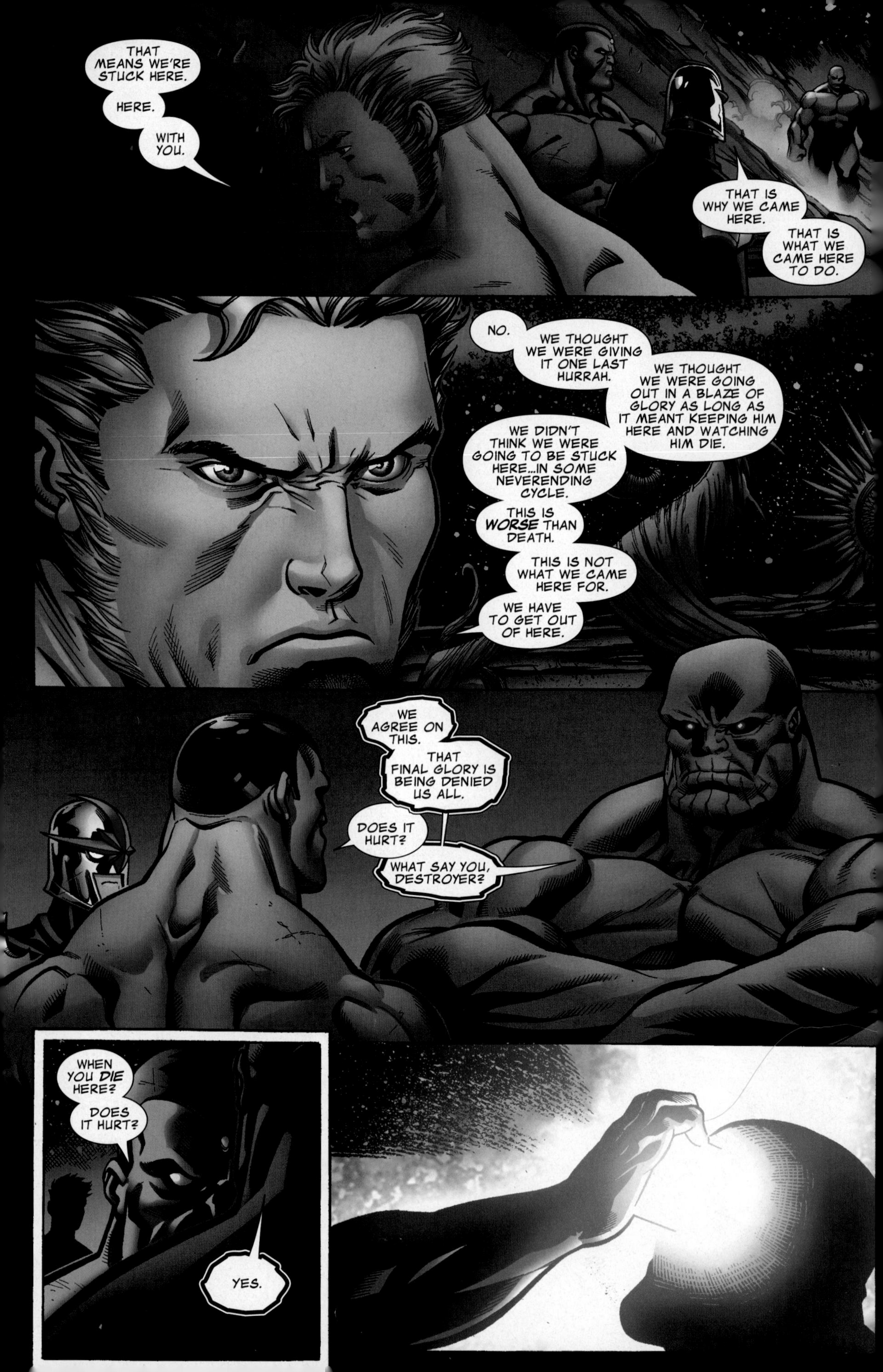
THAT MEANS WE'RE STUCK HERE.
HERE.
WITH YOU.
THAT IS WHY WE CAME HERE.
THAT IS WHAT WE CAME HERE TO DO.
NO.
WE THOUGHT WE WERE GIVING IT ONE LAST HURRAH.
WE THOUGHT WE WERE GOING OUT IN A BLAZE OF GLORY AS LONG AS IT MEANT KEEPING HIM HERE AND WATCHING HIM DIE.
WE DIDN'T THINK WE WERE GOING TO BE STUCK HERE...IN SOME NEVERENDING CYCLE.
THIS IS WORSE THAN DEATH.
THIS IS NOT WHAT WE CAME HERE FOR.
WE HAVE TO GET OUT OF HERE.
WE AGREE ON THIS.
THAT FINAL GLORY IS BEING DENIED US ALL.
WHAT SAY YOU, DESTROYER?
DOES IT HURT?
WHEN YOU DIE HERE?
DOES IT HURT?
YES.

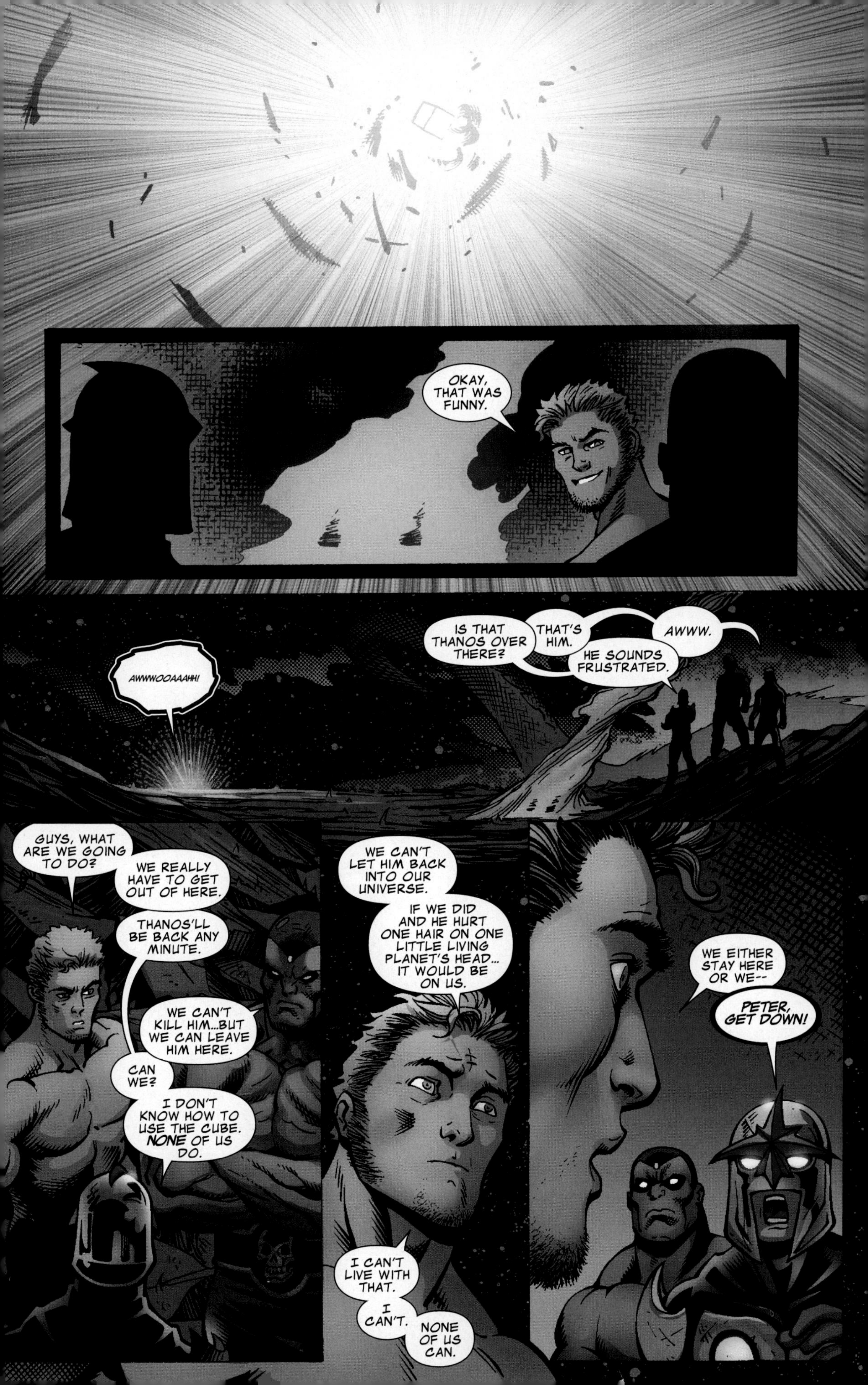

OKAY, THAT WAS FUNNY.
AWWWOOAAAHH!
IS THAT THANOS OVER THERE?
THAT'S HIM.
AWWW.
HE SOUNDS FRUSTRATED.
GUYS, WHAT ARE WE GOING TO DO?
WE REALLY HAVE TO GET OUT OF HERE.
THANOS'LL BE BACK ANY MINUTE.
WE CAN'T KILL HIM...BUT WE CAN LEAVE HIM HERE.
CAN WE?
I DON'T KNOW HOW TO USE THE CUBE. NONE OF US DO.
WE CAN'T LET HIM BACK INTO OUR UNIVERSE.
IF WE DID AND HE HURT ONE HAIR ON ONE LITTLE LIVING PLANET'S HEAD... IT WOULD BE ON US.
I CAN'T LIVE WITH THAT.
I CAN'T.
NONE OF US CAN.
WE EITHER STAY HERE OR WE--
PETER, GET DOWN!

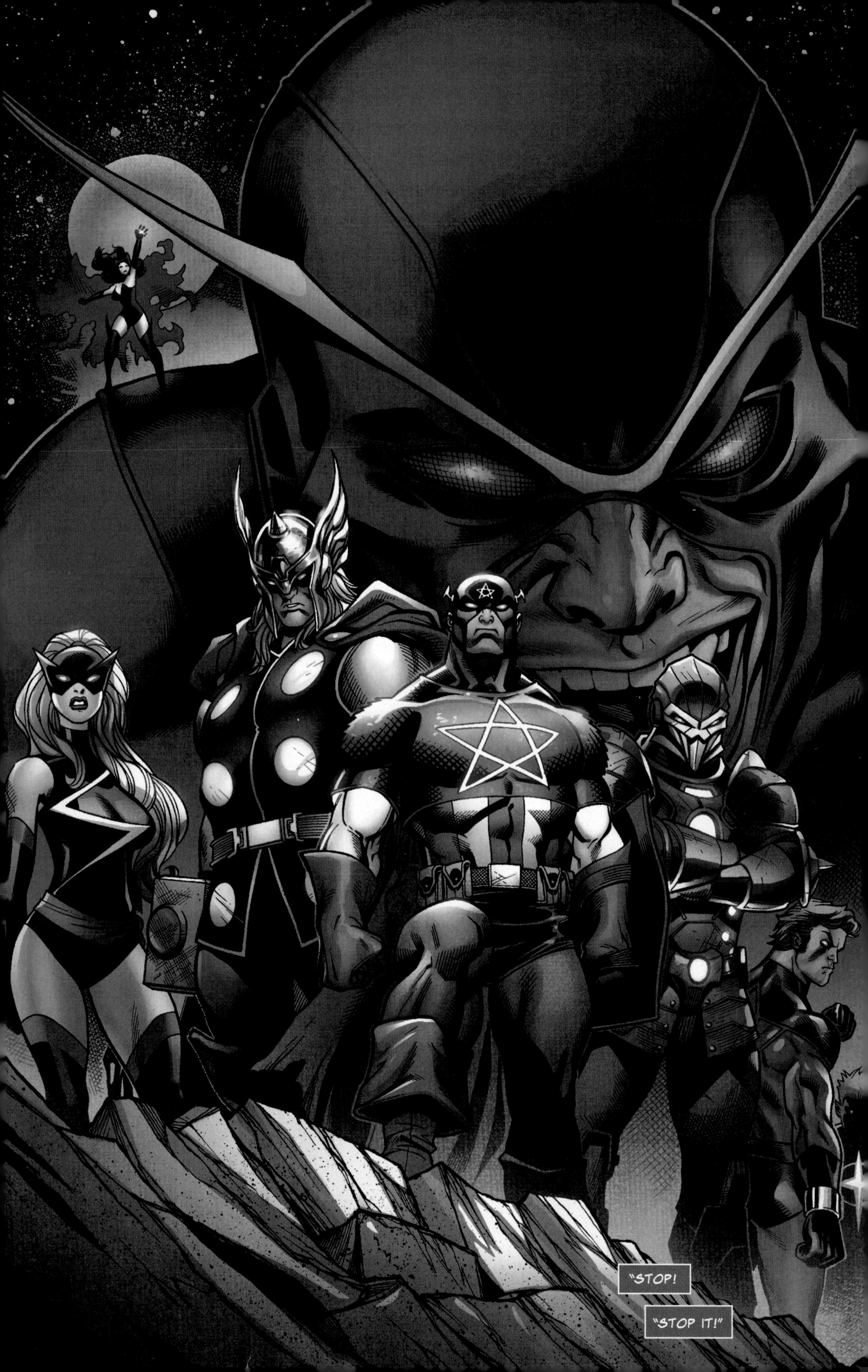
"STOP!
"STOP IT!"

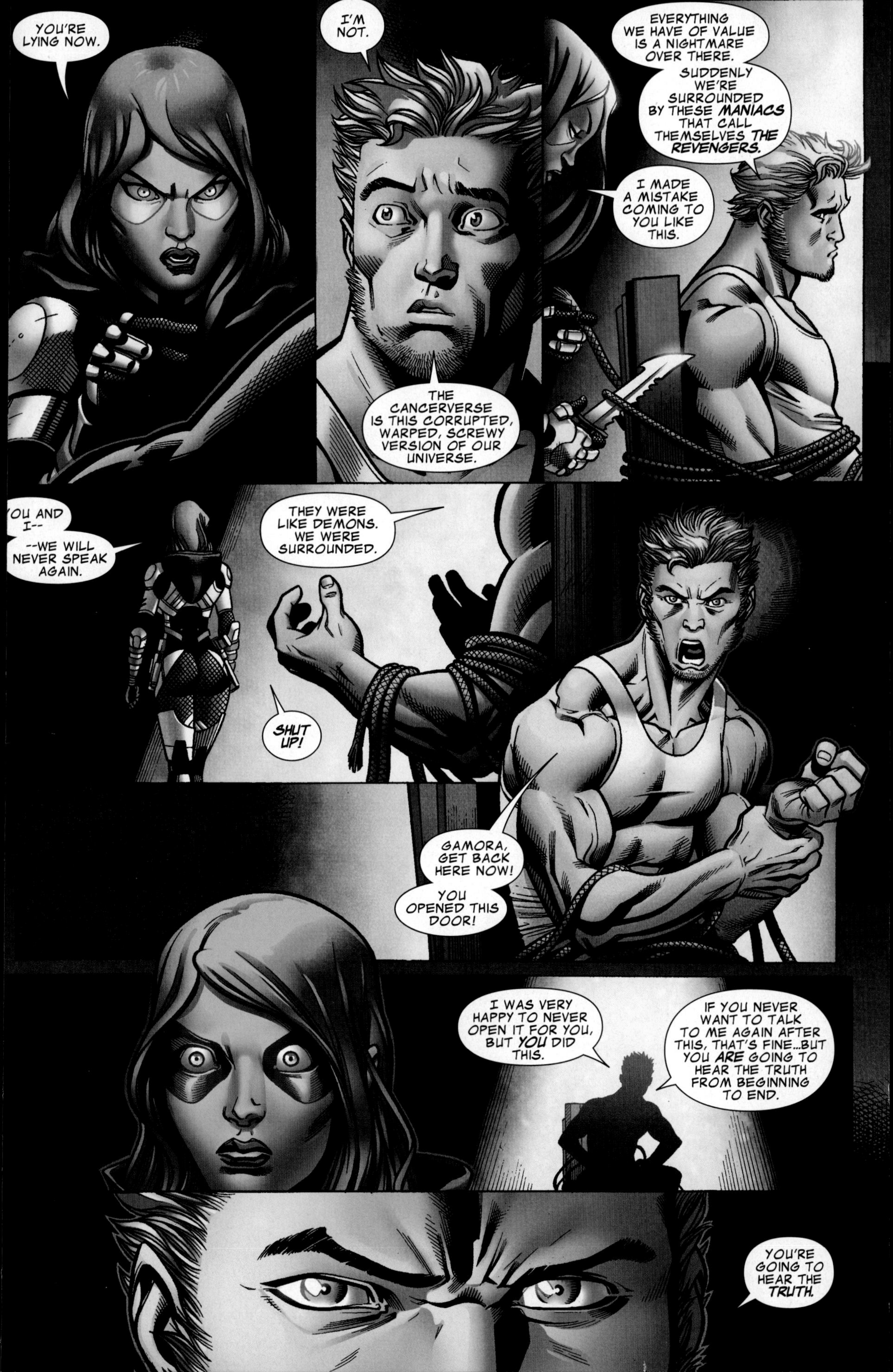

YOU'RE LYING NOW.
I'M NOT.
THE CANCERVERSE IS THIS CORRUPTED, WARPED, SCREWY VERSION OF OUR UNIVERSE.
EVERYTHING WE HAVE OF VALUE IS A NIGHTMARE OVER THERE.
SUDDENLY WE'RE SURROUNDED BY THESE MANIACS THAT CALL THEMSELVES THE REVENGERS.
I MADE A MISTAKE COMING TO YOU LIKE THIS.
OU AND I--
--WE WILL NEVER SPEAK AGAIN.
THEY WERE LIKE DEMONS. WE WERE SURROUNDED.
SHUT UP!
GAMORA, GET BACK HERE NOW!
YOU OPENED THIS DOOR!
I WAS VERY HAPPY TO NEVER OPEN IT FOR YOU, BUT YOU DID THIS.
IF YOU NEVER WANT TO TALK TO ME AGAIN AFTER THIS, THAT'S FINE...BUT YOU ARE GOING TO HEAR THE TRUTH FROM BEGINNING TO END.
YOU'RE GOING TO HEAR THE TRUTH.

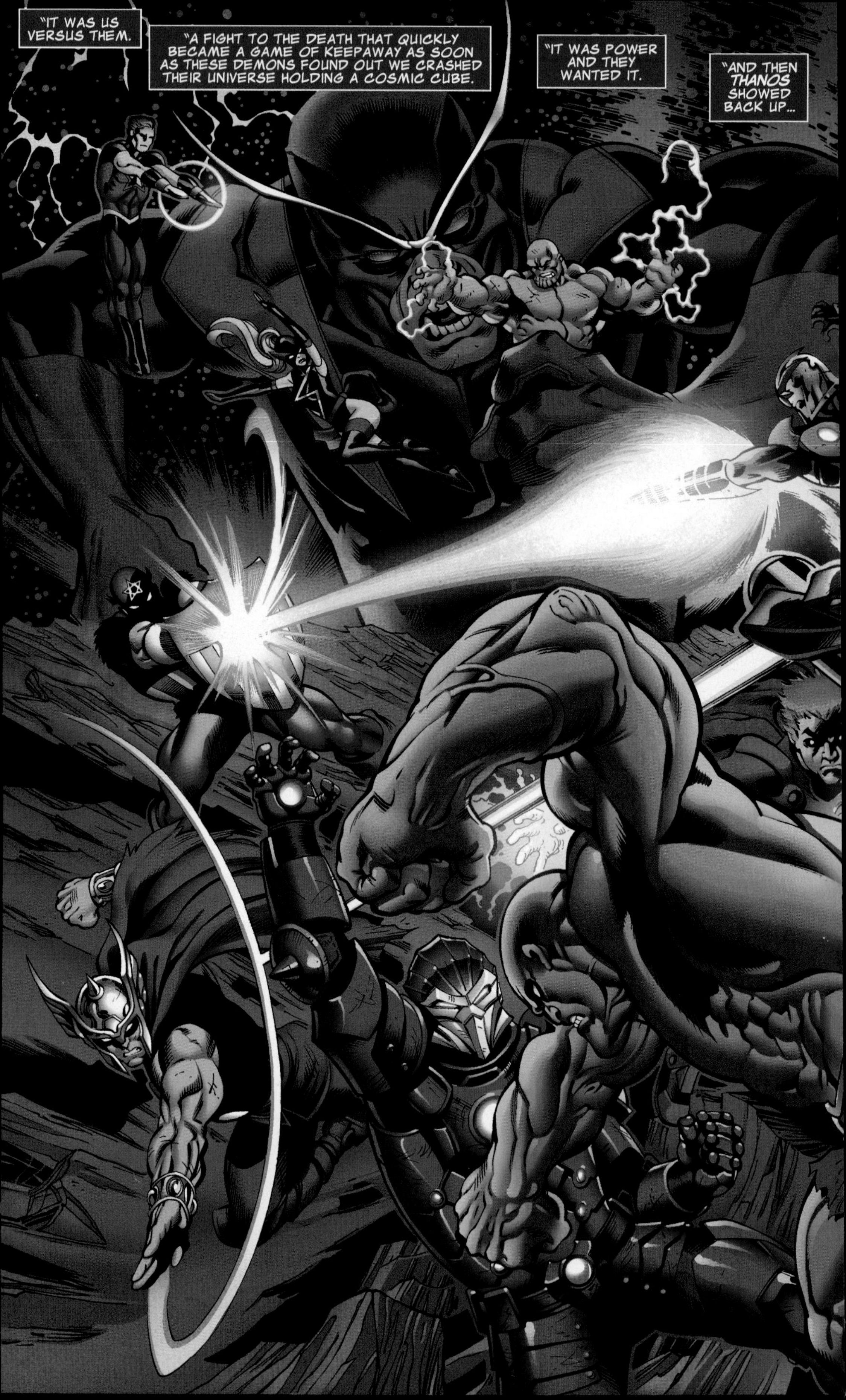
"IT WAS US VERSUS THEM.
"A FIGHT TO THE DEATH THAT QUICKLY BECAME A GAME OF KEEPAWAY AS SOON AS THESE DEMONS FOUND OUT WE CRASHED THEIR UNIVERSE HOLDING A COSMIC CUBE.
"IT WAS POWER AND THEY WANTED IT.
"AND THEN *THANOS* SHOWED BACK UP...

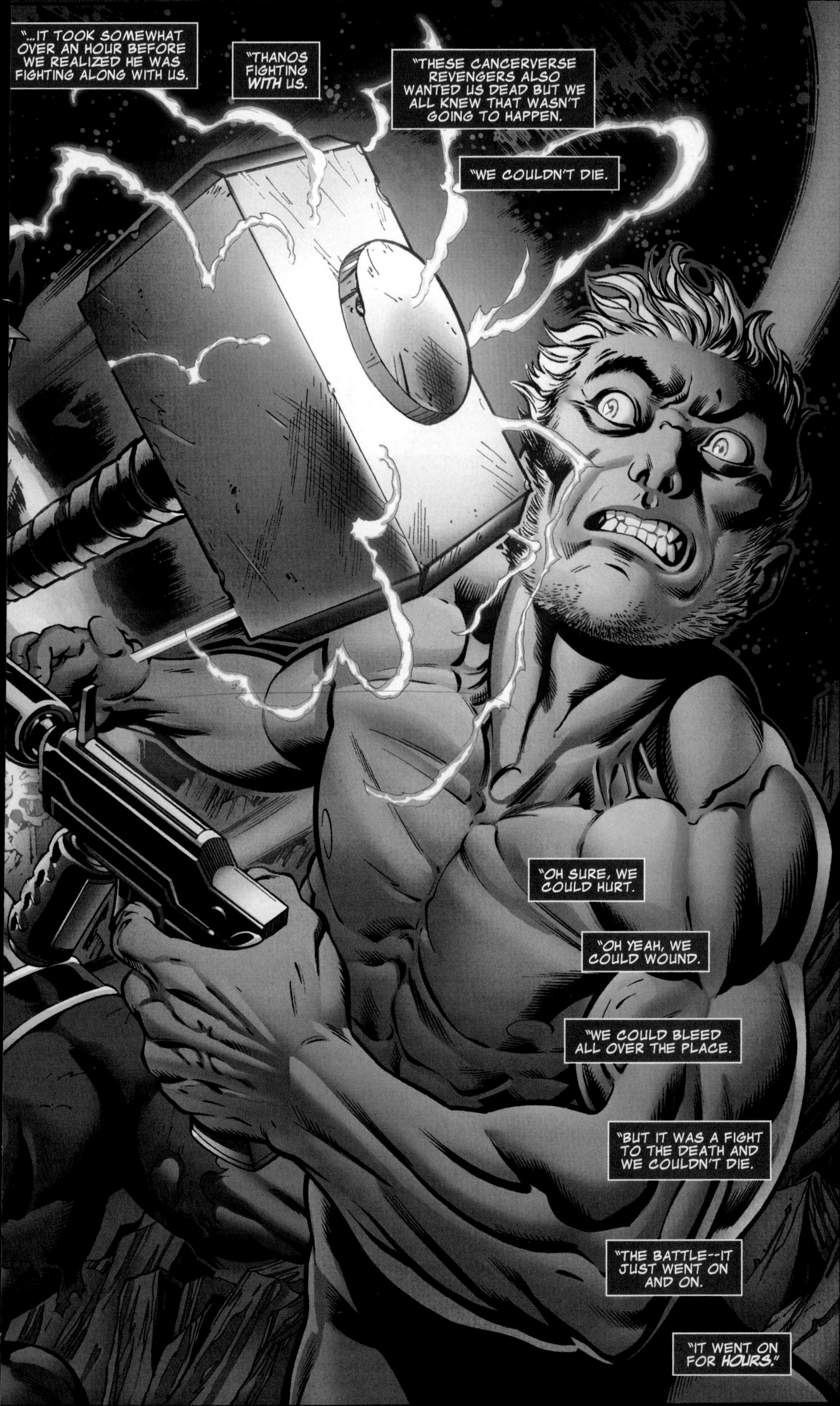
"...IT TOOK SOMEWHAT OVER AN HOUR BEFORE WE REALIZED HE WAS FIGHTING ALONG WITH US.
"THANOS FIGHTING *WITH* US.
"THESE CANCERVERSE REVENGERS ALSO WANTED US DEAD BUT WE ALL KNEW THAT WASN'T GOING TO HAPPEN.
"WE COULDN'T DIE.
"OH SURE, WE COULD HURT.
"OH YEAH, WE COULD WOUND.
"WE COULD BLEED ALL OVER THE PLACE.
"BUT IT WAS A FIGHT TO THE DEATH AND WE COULDN'T DIE.
"THE BATTLE--IT JUST WENT ON AND ON.
"IT WENT ON FOR *HOURS*."

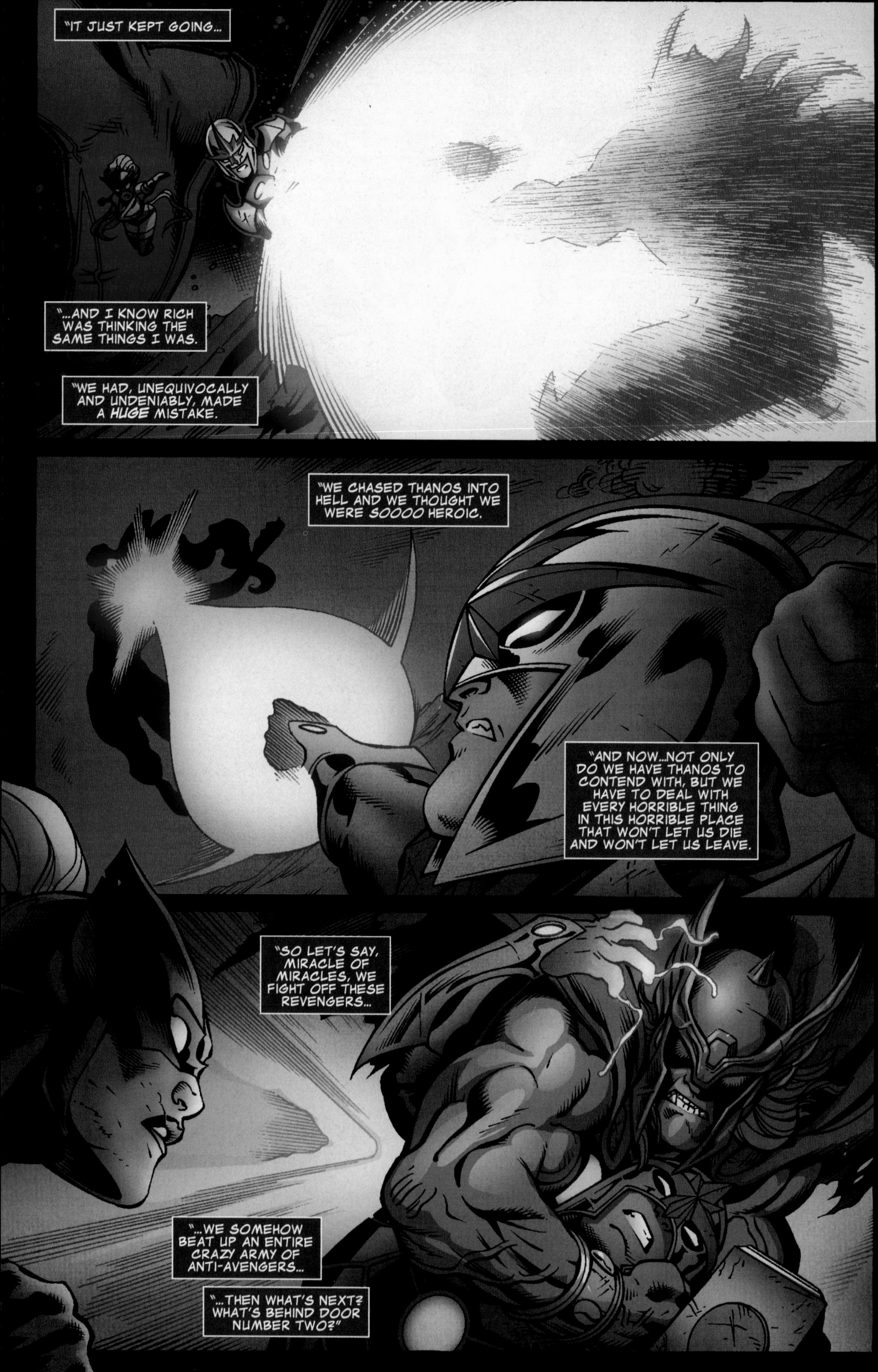
"IT JUST KEPT GOING...
"...AND I KNOW RICH WAS THINKING THE SAME THINGS I WAS.
"WE HAD, UNEQUIVOCALLY AND UNDENIABLY, MADE A *HUGE* MISTAKE.
"WE CHASED THANOS INTO HELL AND WE THOUGHT WE WERE *SOOOO* HEROIC.
"AND NOW...NOT ONLY DO WE HAVE THANOS TO CONTEND WITH, BUT WE HAVE TO DEAL WITH EVERY HORRIBLE THING IN THIS HORRIBLE PLACE THAT WON'T LET US DIE AND WON'T LET US LEAVE.
"SO LET'S SAY, MIRACLE OF MIRACLES, WE FIGHT OFF THESE REVENGERS...
"...WE SOMEHOW BEAT UP AN ENTIRE CRAZY ARMY OF ANTI-AVENGERS...
"...THEN WHAT'S NEXT? WHAT'S BEHIND DOOR NUMBER TWO?"

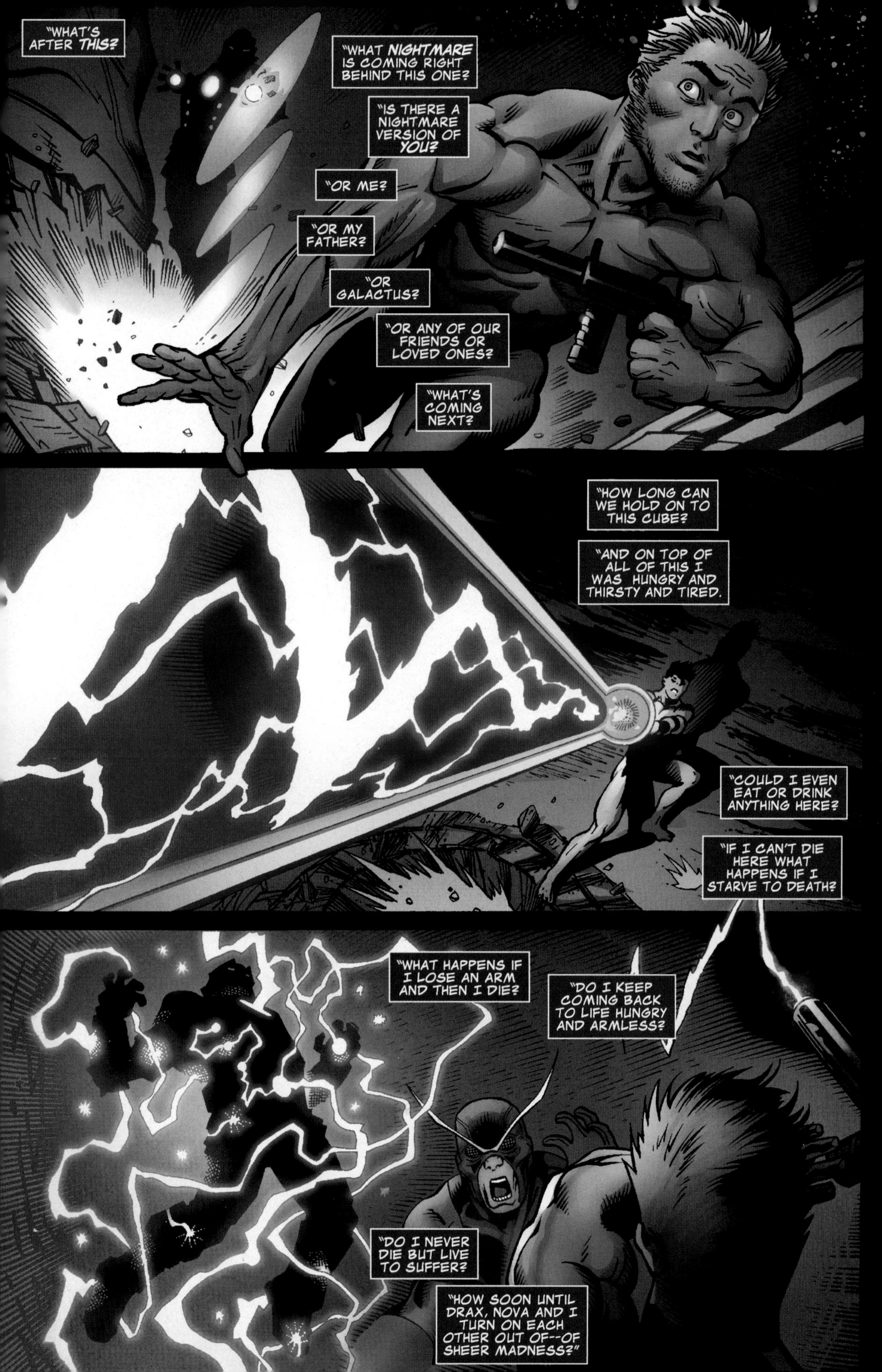
"WHAT'S AFTER THIS?
"WHAT NIGHTMARE IS COMING RIGHT BEHIND THIS ONE?
"IS THERE A NIGHTMARE VERSION OF YOU?
"OR ME?
"OR MY FATHER?
"OR GALACTUS?
"OR ANY OF OUR FRIENDS OR LOVED ONES?
"WHAT'S COMING NEXT?
"HOW LONG CAN WE HOLD ON TO THIS CUBE?
"AND ON TOP OF ALL OF THIS I WAS HUNGRY AND THIRSTY AND TIRED.
"COULD I EVEN EAT OR DRINK ANYTHING HERE?
"IF I CAN'T DIE HERE WHAT HAPPENS IF I STARVE TO DEATH?
"WHAT HAPPENS IF I LOSE AN ARM AND THEN I DIE?
"DO I KEEP COMING BACK TO LIFE HUNGRY AND ARMLESS?
"DO I NEVER DIE BUT LIVE TO SUFFER?
"HOW SOON UNTIL DRAX, NOVA AND I TURN ON EACH OTHER OUT OF--OF SHEER MADNESS?"

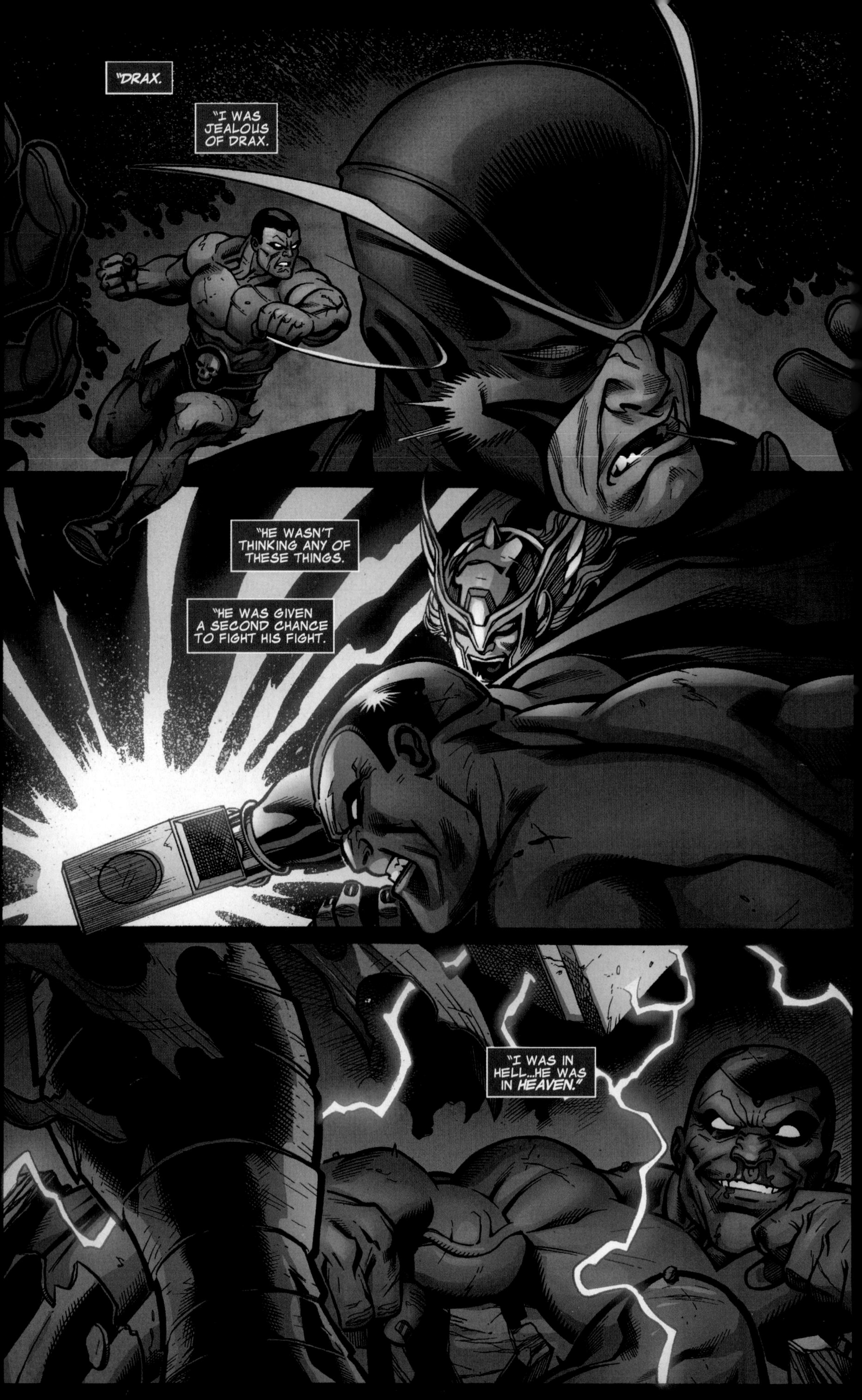
"DRAX.
"I WAS JEALOUS OF DRAX.
"HE WASN'T THINKING ANY OF THESE THINGS.
"HE WAS GIVEN A SECOND CHANCE TO FIGHT HIS FIGHT.
"I WAS IN HELL...HE WAS IN HEAVEN."

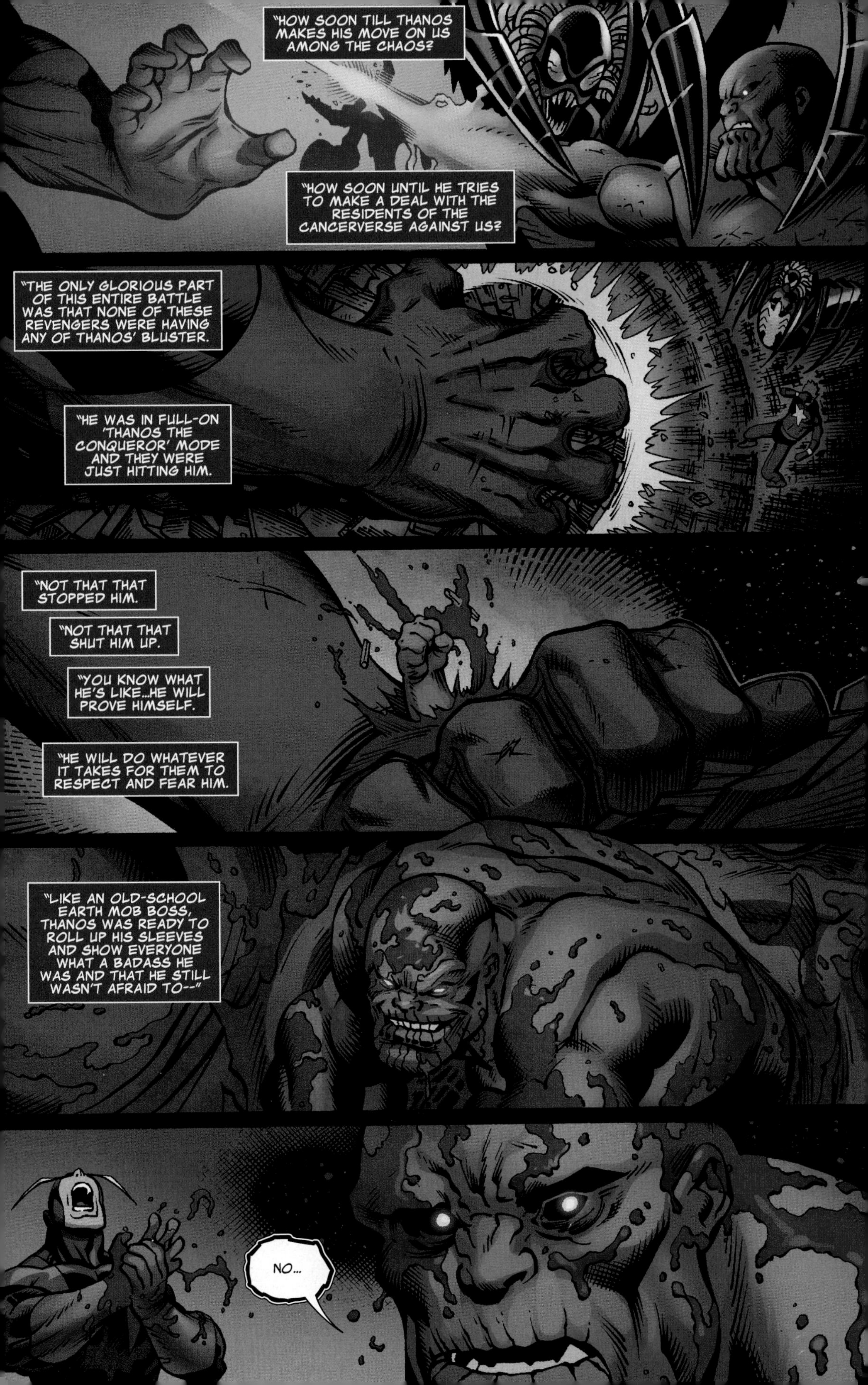
"HOW SOON TILL THANOS MAKES HIS MOVE ON US AMONG THE CHAOS?
"HOW SOON UNTIL HE TRIES TO MAKE A DEAL WITH THE RESIDENTS OF THE CANCERVERSE AGAINST US?
"THE ONLY GLORIOUS PART OF THIS ENTIRE BATTLE WAS THAT NONE OF THESE REVENGERS WERE HAVING ANY OF THANOS' BLUSTER.
"HE WAS IN FULL-ON 'THANOS THE CONQUEROR' MODE AND THEY WERE JUST HITTING HIM.
"NOT THAT THAT STOPPED HIM.
"NOT THAT THAT SHUT HIM UP.
"YOU KNOW WHAT HE'S LIKE...HE WILL PROVE HIMSELF.
"HE WILL DO WHATEVER IT TAKES FOR THEM TO RESPECT AND FEAR HIM.
"LIKE AN OLD-SCHOOL EARTH MOB BOSS, THANOS WAS READY TO ROLL UP HIS SLEEVES AND SHOW EVERYONE WHAT A BADASS HE WAS AND THAT HE STILL WASN'T AFRAID TO--"
NO...

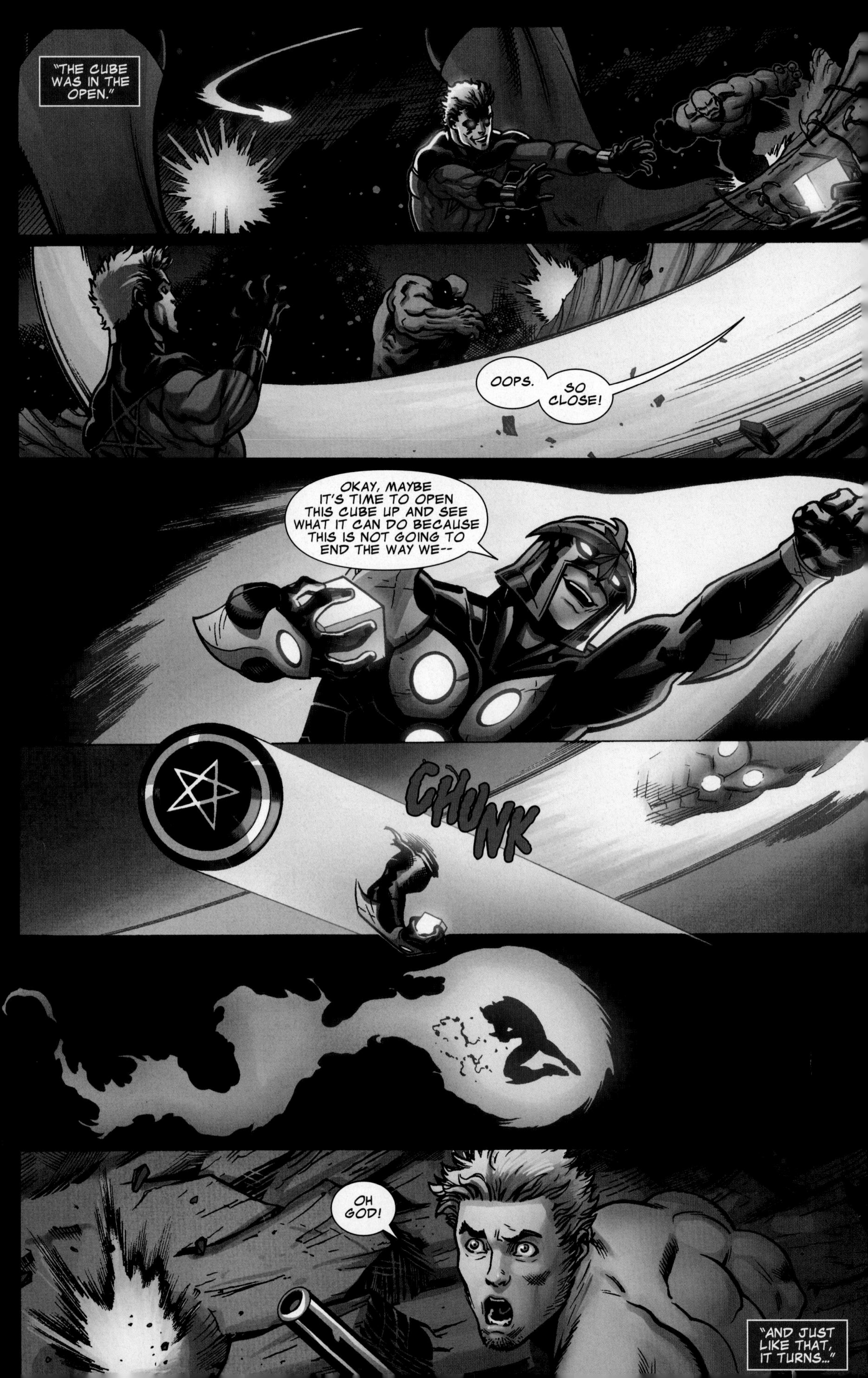
"THE CUBE WAS IN THE OPEN."
OOPS.
SO CLOSE!
OKAY, MAYBE IT'S TIME TO OPEN THIS CUBE UP AND SEE WHAT IT CAN DO BECAUSE THIS IS NOT GOING TO END THE WAY WE--
CHUNK
OH GOD!
"AND JUST LIKE THAT, IT TURNS..."

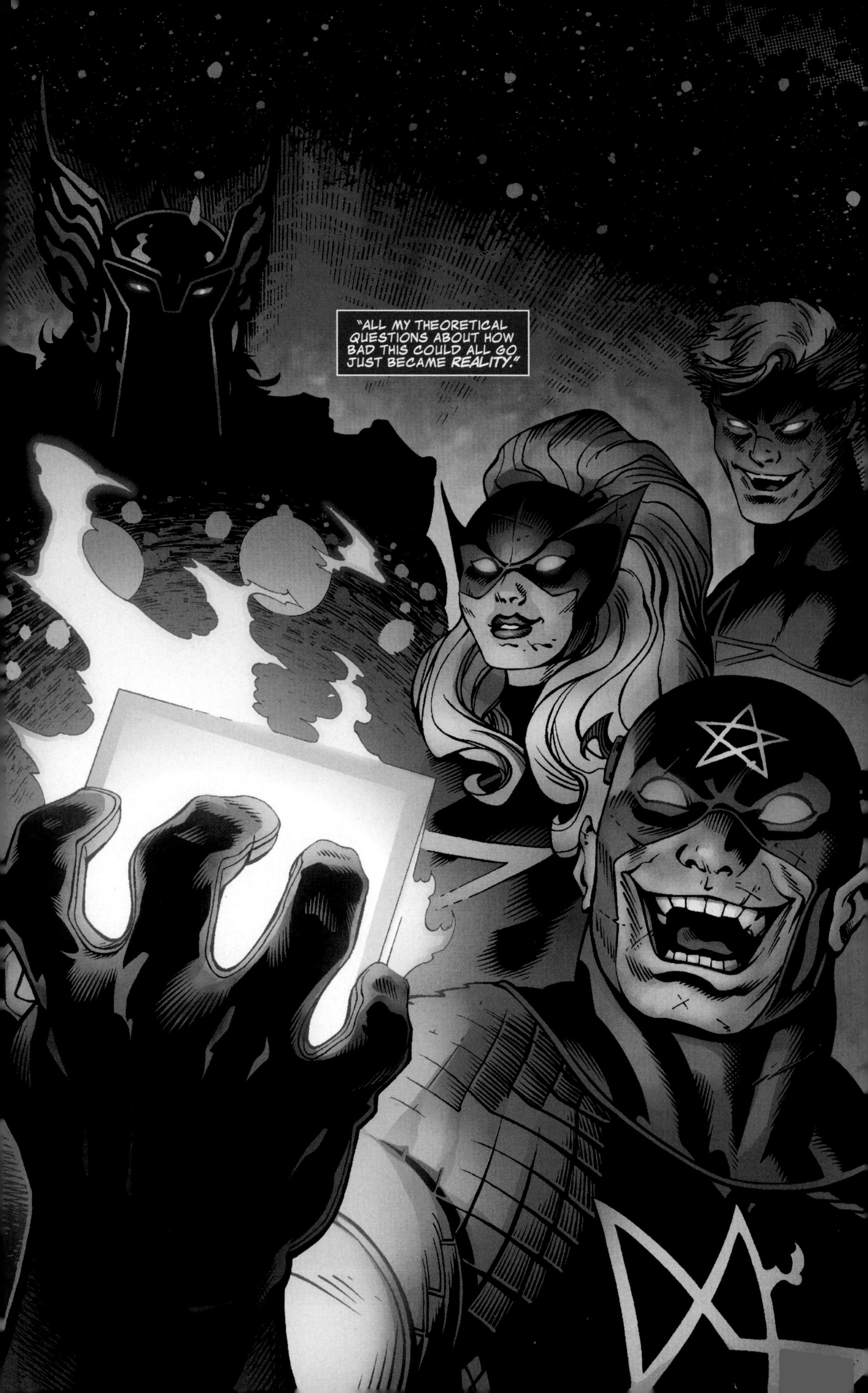
"ALL MY THEORETICAL QUESTIONS ABOUT HOW BAD THIS COULD ALL GO JUST BECAME *REALITY*."

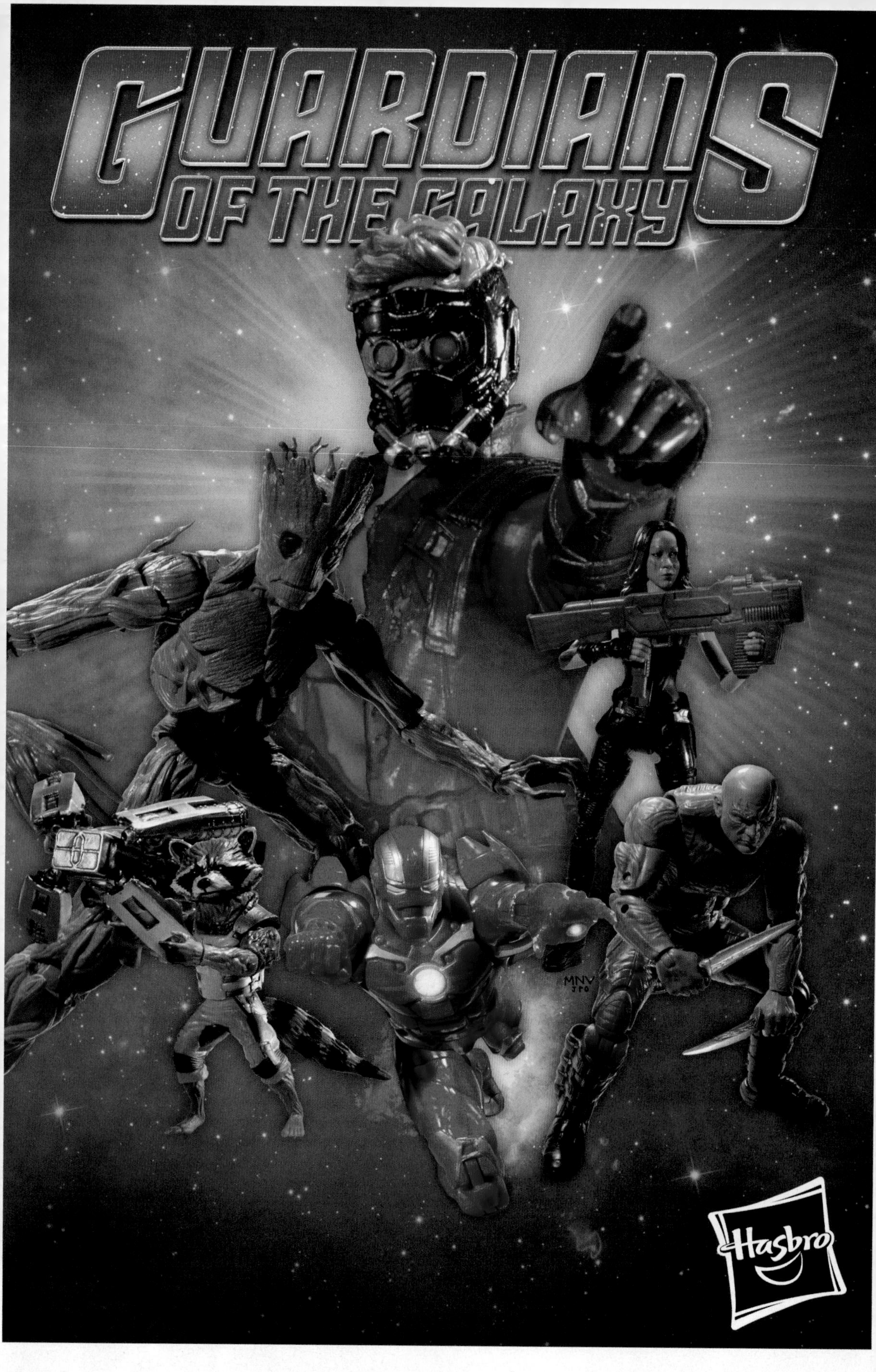
GUARDIANS
OF THE GALAXY
MNV
Hasbro

#20 HASBRO VARIANT

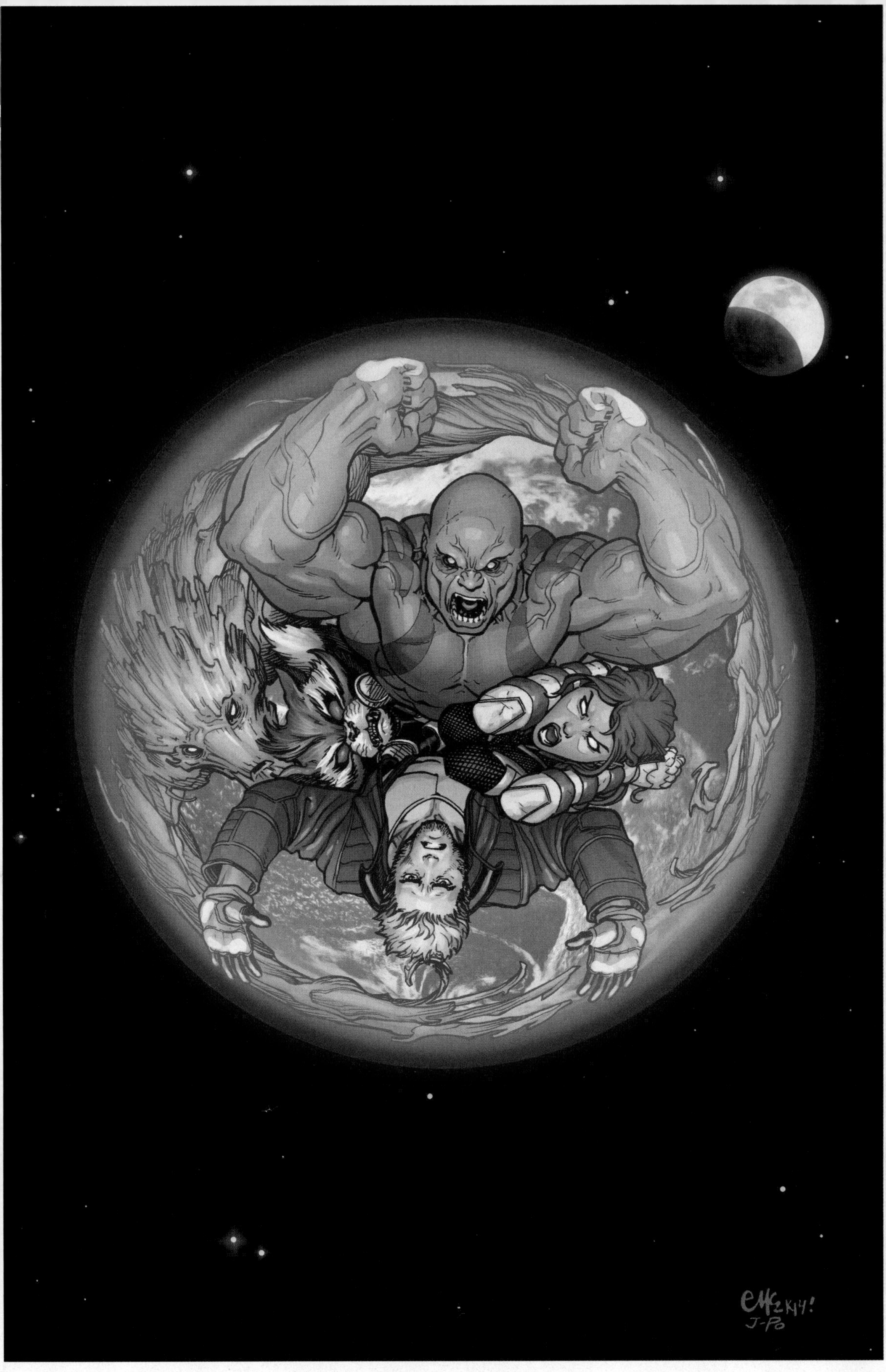

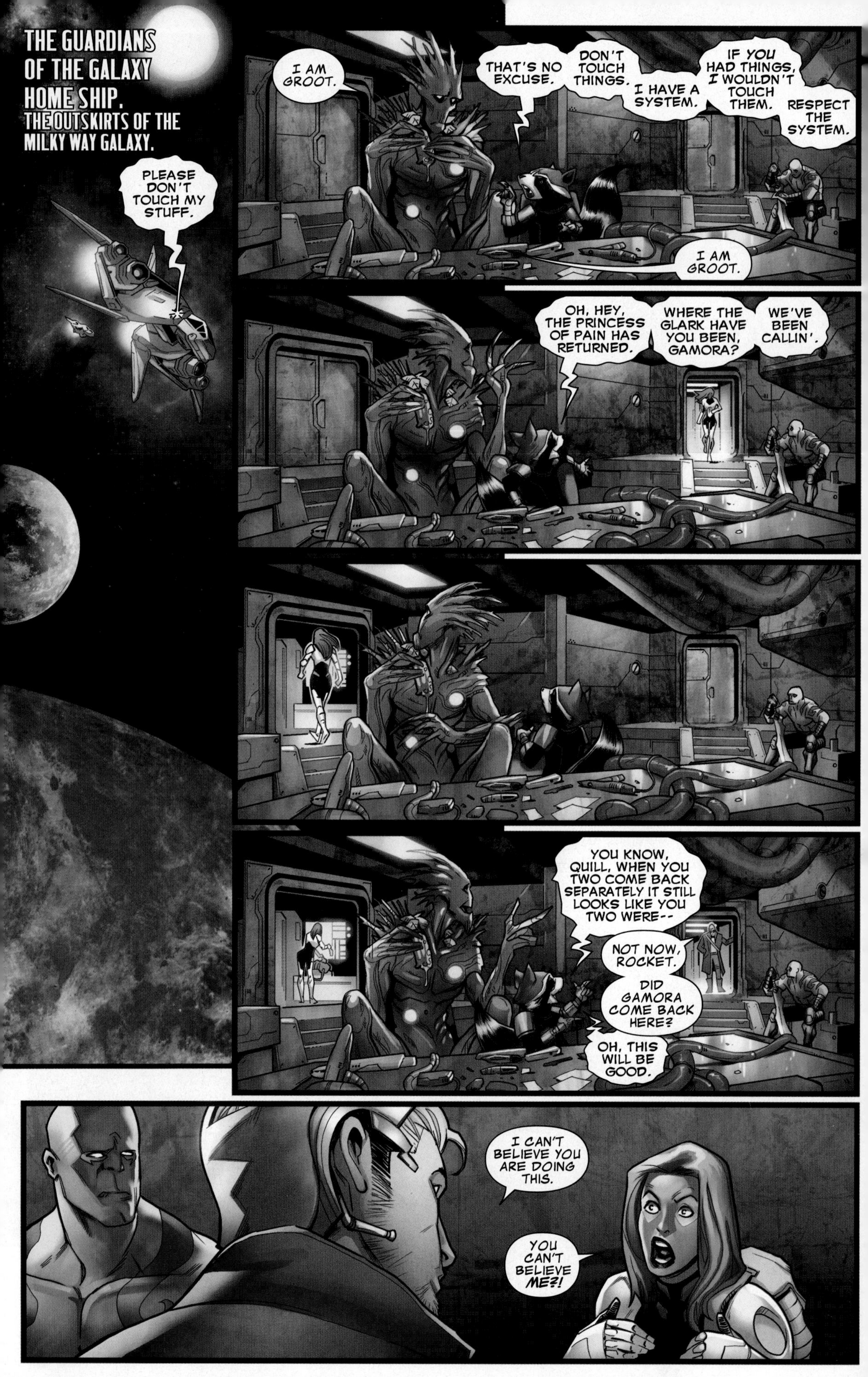
THE GUARDIANS OF THE GALAXY HOME SHIP.
THE OUTSKIRTS OF THE MILKY WAY GALAXY.
PLEASE DON'T TOUCH MY STUFF.
I AM GROOT.
THAT'S NO EXCUSE.
DON'T TOUCH THINGS.
I HAVE A SYSTEM.
IF YOU HAD THINGS, I WOULDN'T TOUCH THEM.
RESPECT THE SYSTEM.
I AM GROOT.
OH, HEY, THE PRINCESS OF PAIN HAS RETURNED.
WHERE THE GLARK HAVE YOU BEEN, GAMORA?
WE'VE BEEN CALLIN'.
YOU KNOW, QUILL, WHEN YOU TWO COME BACK SEPARATELY IT STILL LOOKS LIKE YOU TWO WERE--
NOT NOW, ROCKET.
DID GAMORA COME BACK HERE?
OH, THIS WILL BE GOOD.
I CAN'T BELIEVE YOU ARE DOING THIS.
YOU CAN'T BELIEVE ME?!

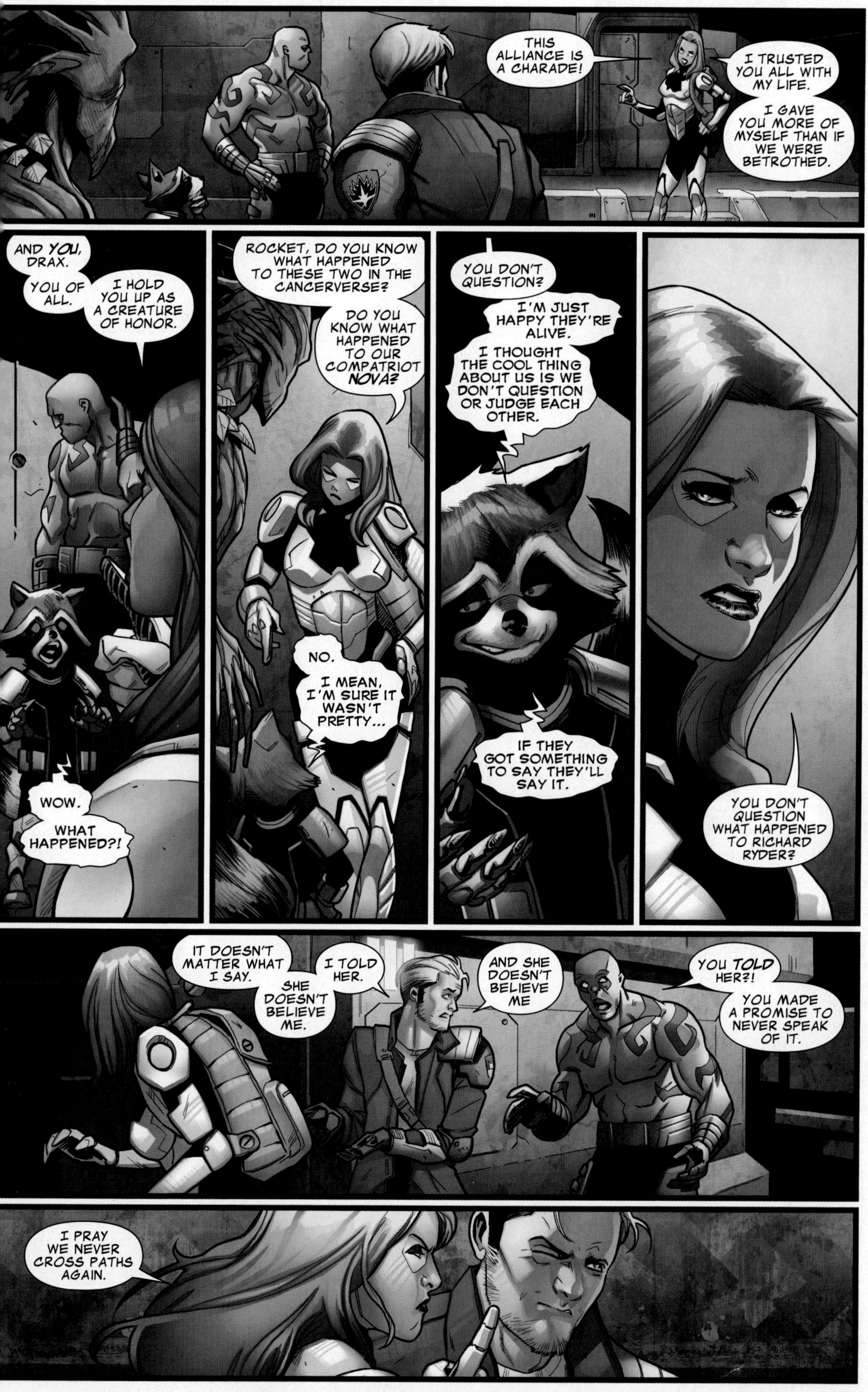
THIS ALLIANCE IS A CHARADE!
I TRUSTED YOU ALL WITH MY LIFE.
I GAVE YOU MORE OF MYSELF THAN IF WE WERE BETROTHED.
AND YOU, DRAX.
YOU OF ALL.
I HOLD YOU UP AS A CREATURE OF HONOR.
WOW.
WHAT HAPPENED?!
ROCKET, DO YOU KNOW WHAT HAPPENED TO THESE TWO IN THE CANCERVERSE?
DO YOU KNOW WHAT HAPPENED TO OUR COMPATRIOT NOVA?
NO.
I MEAN, I'M SURE IT WASN'T PRETTY...
YOU DON'T QUESTION?
I'M JUST HAPPY THEY'RE ALIVE.
I THOUGHT THE COOL THING ABOUT US IS WE DON'T QUESTION OR JUDGE EACH OTHER.
IF THEY GOT SOMETHING TO SAY THEY'LL SAY IT.
YOU DON'T QUESTION WHAT HAPPENED TO RICHARD RYDER?
IT DOESN'T MATTER WHAT I SAY.
I TOLD HER.
SHE DOESN'T BELIEVE ME.
AND SHE DOESN'T BELIEVE ME
YOU TOLD HER?!
YOU MADE A PROMISE TO NEVER SPEAK OF IT.
I PRAY WE NEVER CROSS PATHS AGAIN.

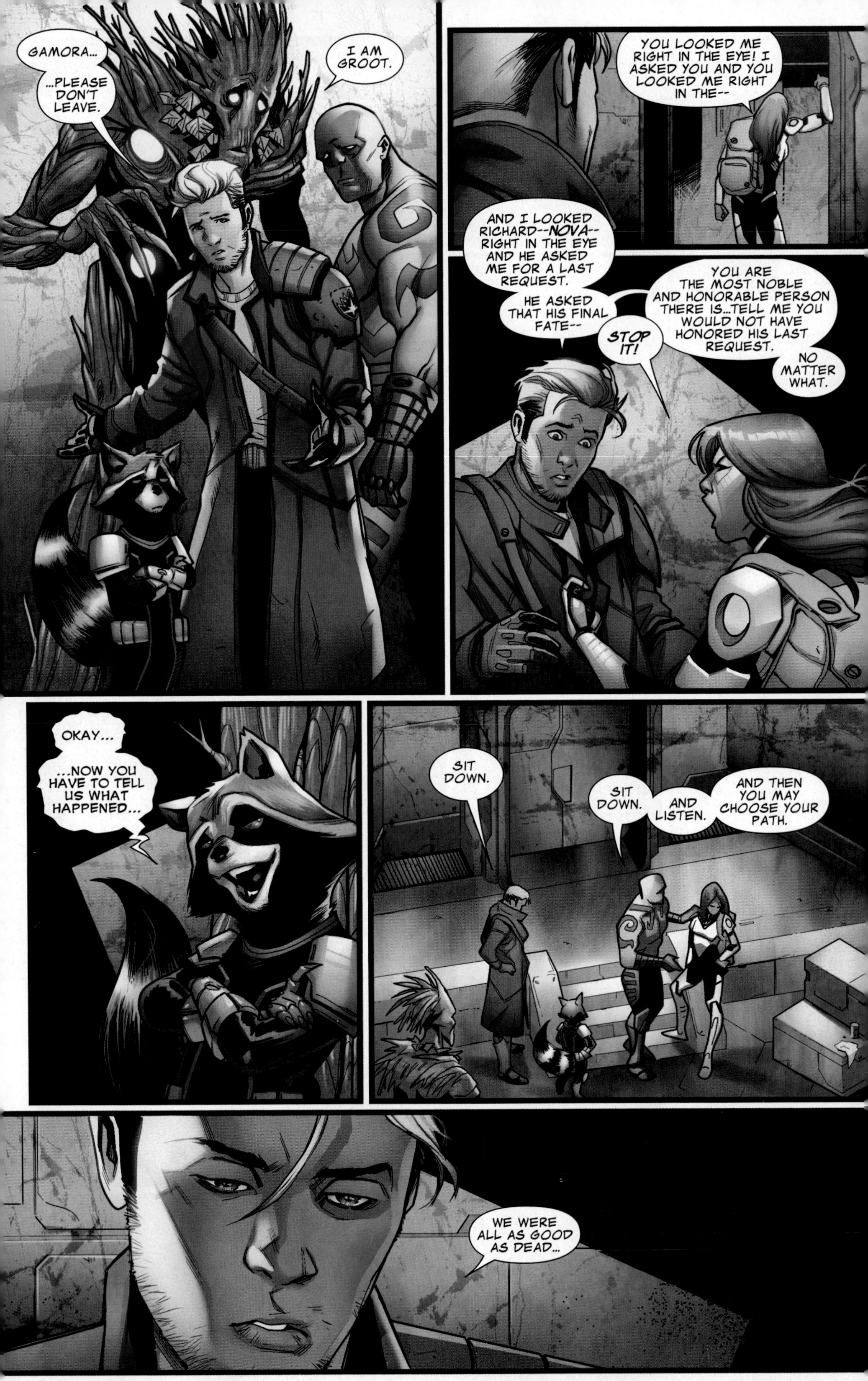
GAMORA...
...PLEASE DON'T LEAVE.
I AM GROOT.
YOU LOOKED ME RIGHT IN THE EYE! I ASKED YOU AND YOU LOOKED ME RIGHT IN THE--
AND I LOOKED RICHARD--NOVA--RIGHT IN THE EYE AND HE ASKED ME FOR A LAST REQUEST.
HE ASKED THAT HIS FINAL FATE--
STOP IT!
YOU ARE THE MOST NOBLE AND HONORABLE PERSON THERE IS...TELL ME YOU WOULD NOT HAVE HONORED HIS LAST REQUEST.
NO MATTER WHAT.
OKAY...
...NOW YOU HAVE TO TELL US WHAT HAPPENED...
SIT DOWN.
SIT DOWN.
AND LISTEN.
AND THEN YOU MAY CHOOSE YOUR PATH.
WE WERE ALL AS GOOD AS DEAD...

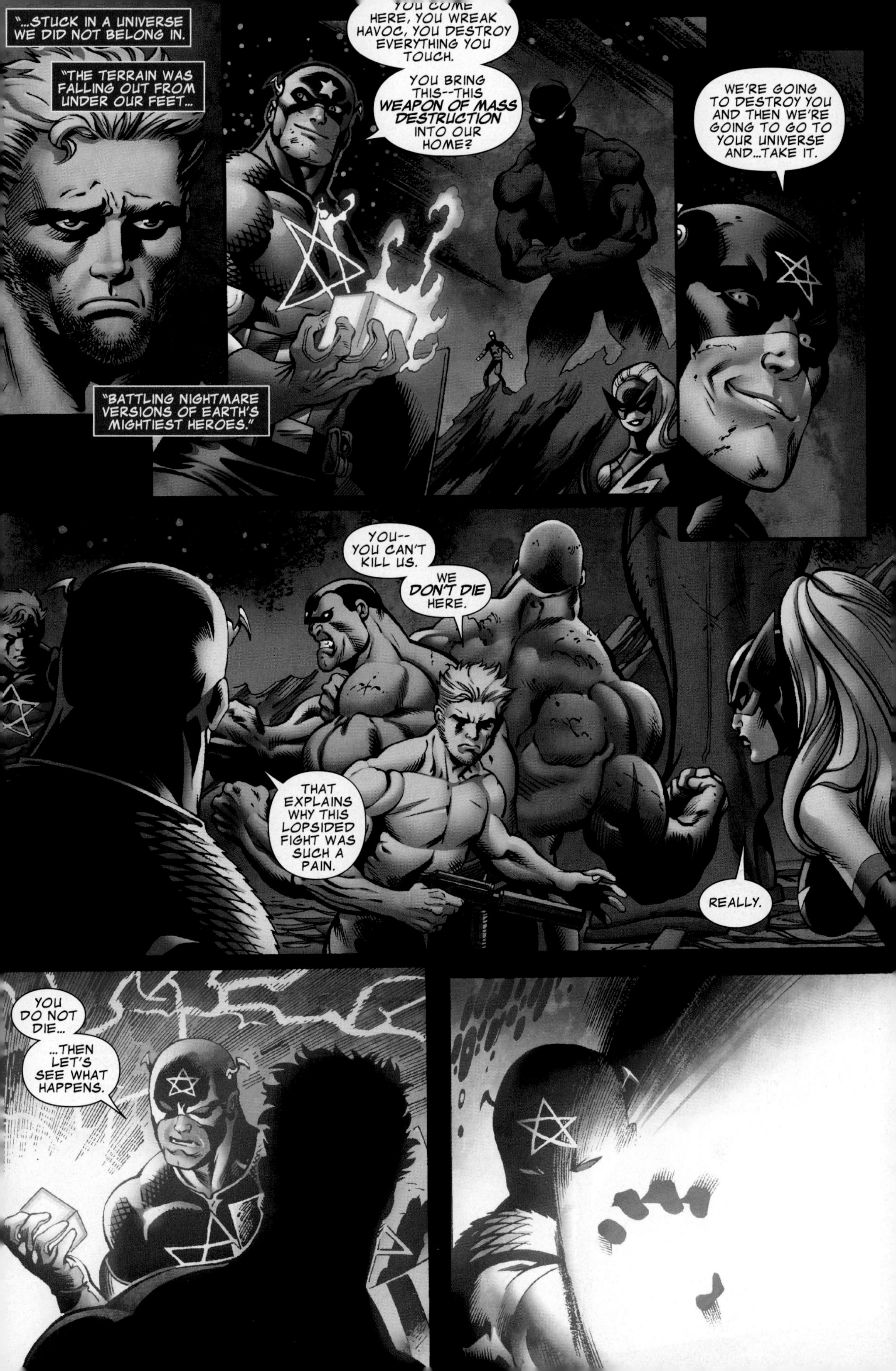
"...STUCK IN A UNIVERSE WE DID NOT BELONG IN.
"THE TERRAIN WAS FALLING OUT FROM UNDER OUR FEET...
"BATTLING NIGHTMARE VERSIONS OF EARTH'S MIGHTIEST HEROES."
YOU COME HERE, YOU WREAK HAVOC, YOU DESTROY EVERYTHING YOU TOUCH.
YOU BRING THIS--THIS WEAPON OF MASS DESTRUCTION INTO OUR HOME?
WE'RE GOING TO DESTROY YOU AND THEN WE'RE GOING TO GO TO YOUR UNIVERSE AND...TAKE IT.
YOU-- YOU CAN'T KILL US.
WE DON'T DIE HERE.
THAT EXPLAINS WHY THIS LOPSIDED FIGHT WAS SUCH A PAIN.
REALLY.
YOU DO NOT DIE...
...THEN LET'S SEE WHAT HAPPENS.

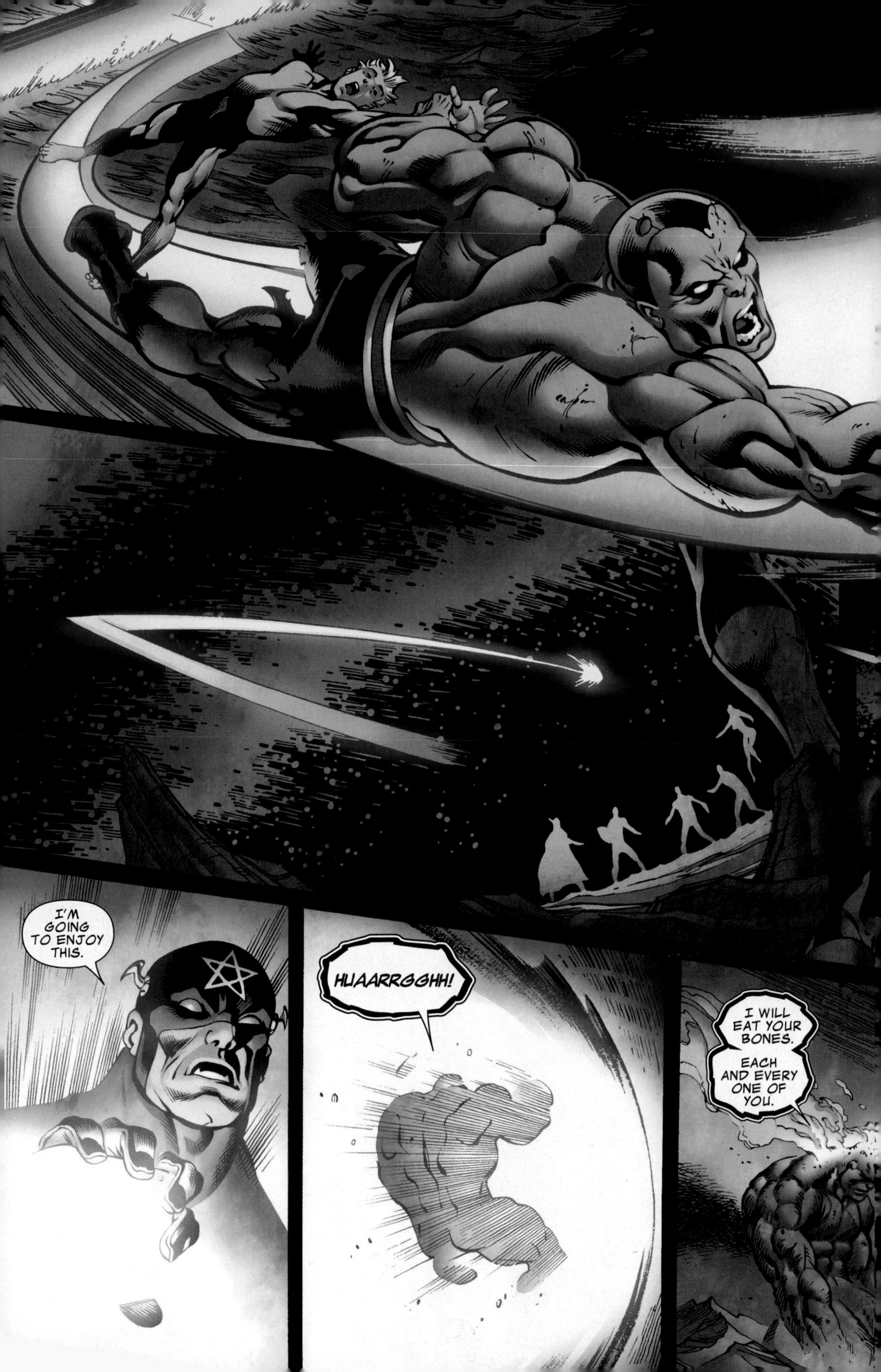
I'M GOING TO ENJOY THIS.
HUAARRGGHH!
I WILL EAT YOUR BONES.
EACH AND EVERY ONE OF YOU.

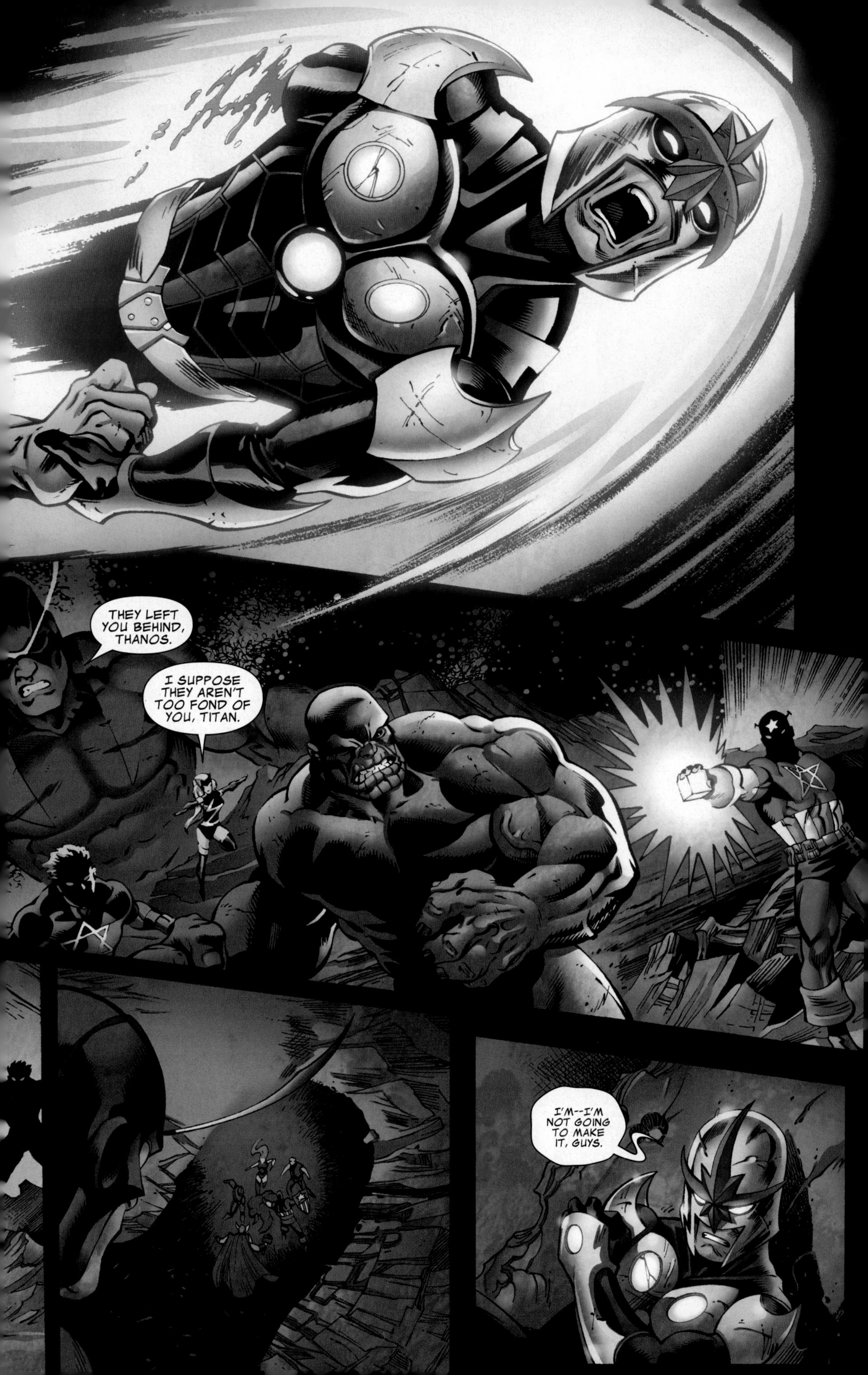
THEY LEFT YOU BEHIND, THANOS.
I SUPPOSE THEY AREN'T TOO FOND OF YOU, TITAN.
I'M--I'M NOT GOING TO MAKE IT, GUYS.

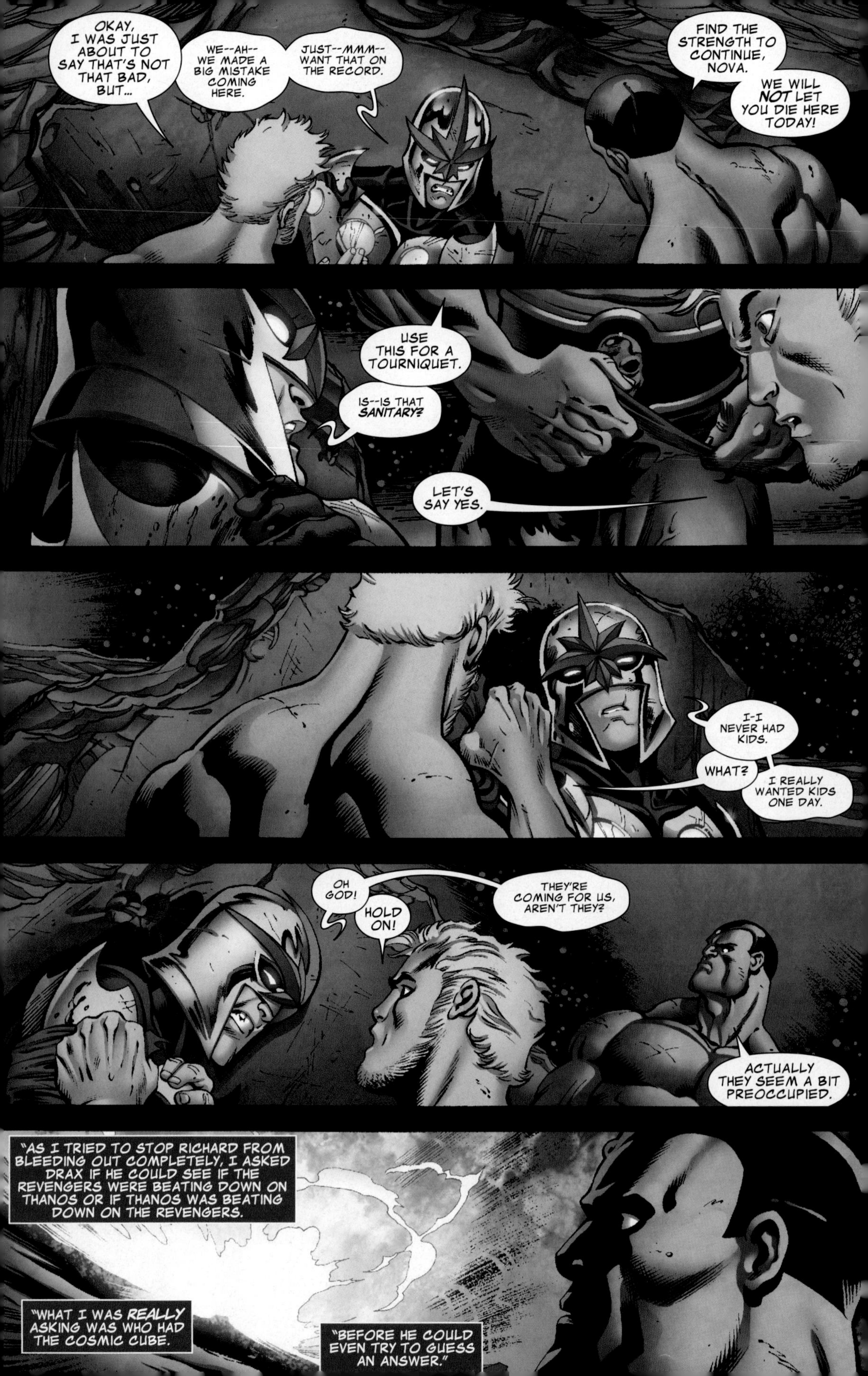
OKAY, I WAS JUST ABOUT TO SAY THAT'S NOT THAT BAD, BUT...
WE--AH-- WE MADE A BIG MISTAKE COMING HERE.
JUST--MMM-- WANT THAT ON THE RECORD.
FIND THE STRENGTH TO CONTINUE, NOVA.
WE WILL NOT LET YOU DIE HERE TODAY!
USE THIS FOR A TOURNIQUET.
IS--IS THAT SANITARY?
LET'S SAY YES.
I-I NEVER HAD KIDS.
WHAT?
I REALLY WANTED KIDS ONE DAY.
OH GOD!
HOLD ON!
THEY'RE COMING FOR US, AREN'T THEY?
ACTUALLY THEY SEEM A BIT PREOCCUPIED.
"AS I TRIED TO STOP RICHARD FROM BLEEDING OUT COMPLETELY, I ASKED DRAX IF HE COULD SEE IF THE REVENGERS WERE BEATING DOWN ON THANOS OR IF THANOS WAS BEATING DOWN ON THE REVENGERS.
"WHAT I WAS REALLY ASKING WAS WHO HAD THE COSMIC CUBE.
"BEFORE HE COULD EVEN TRY TO GUESS AN ANSWER."

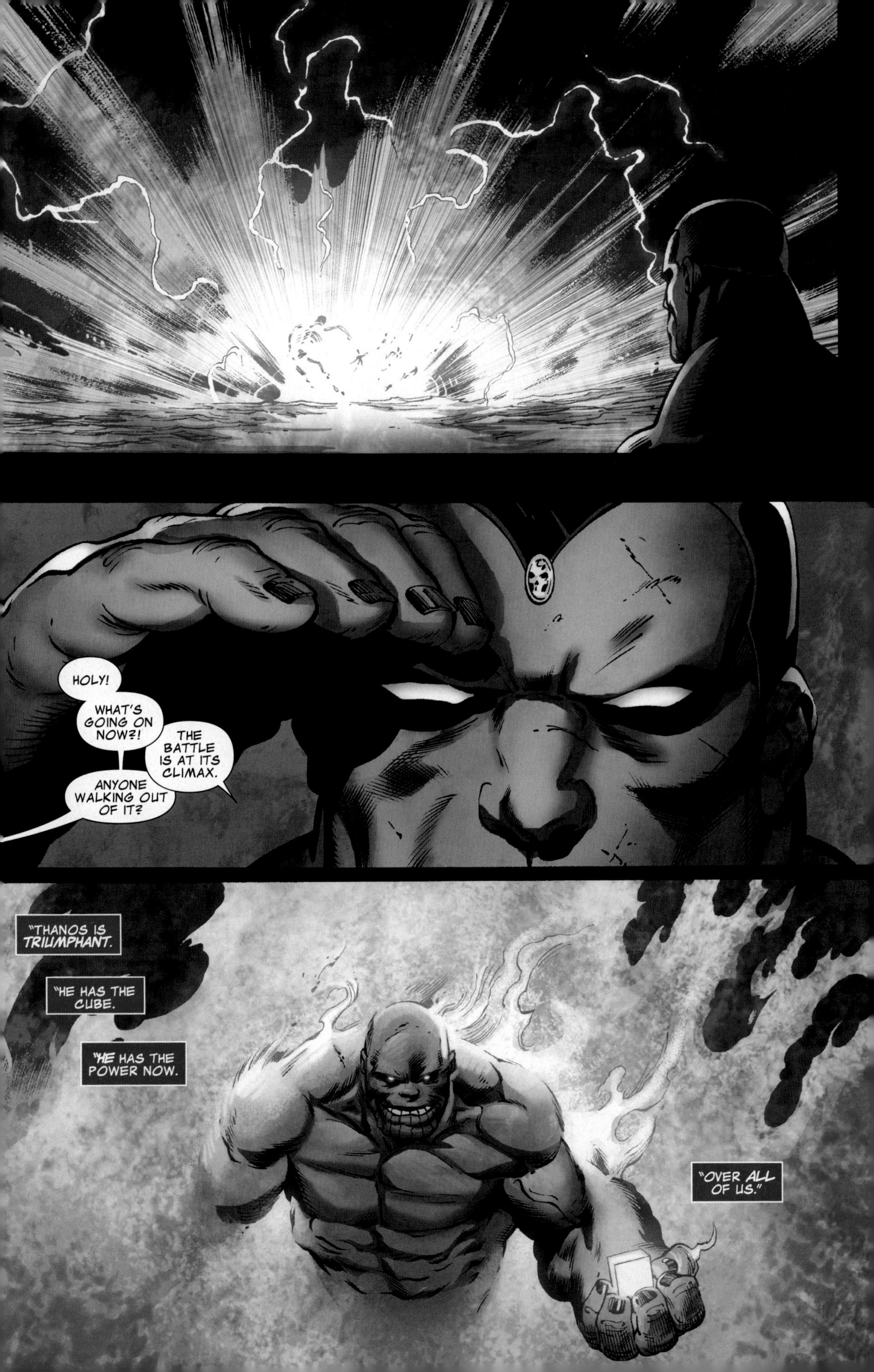

HOLY!
WHAT'S GOING ON NOW?!
ANYONE WALKING OUT OF IT?
THE BATTLE IS AT ITS CLIMAX.
"THANOS IS TRIUMPHANT.
"HE HAS THE CUBE.
"HE HAS THE POWER NOW.
"OVER ALL OF US."

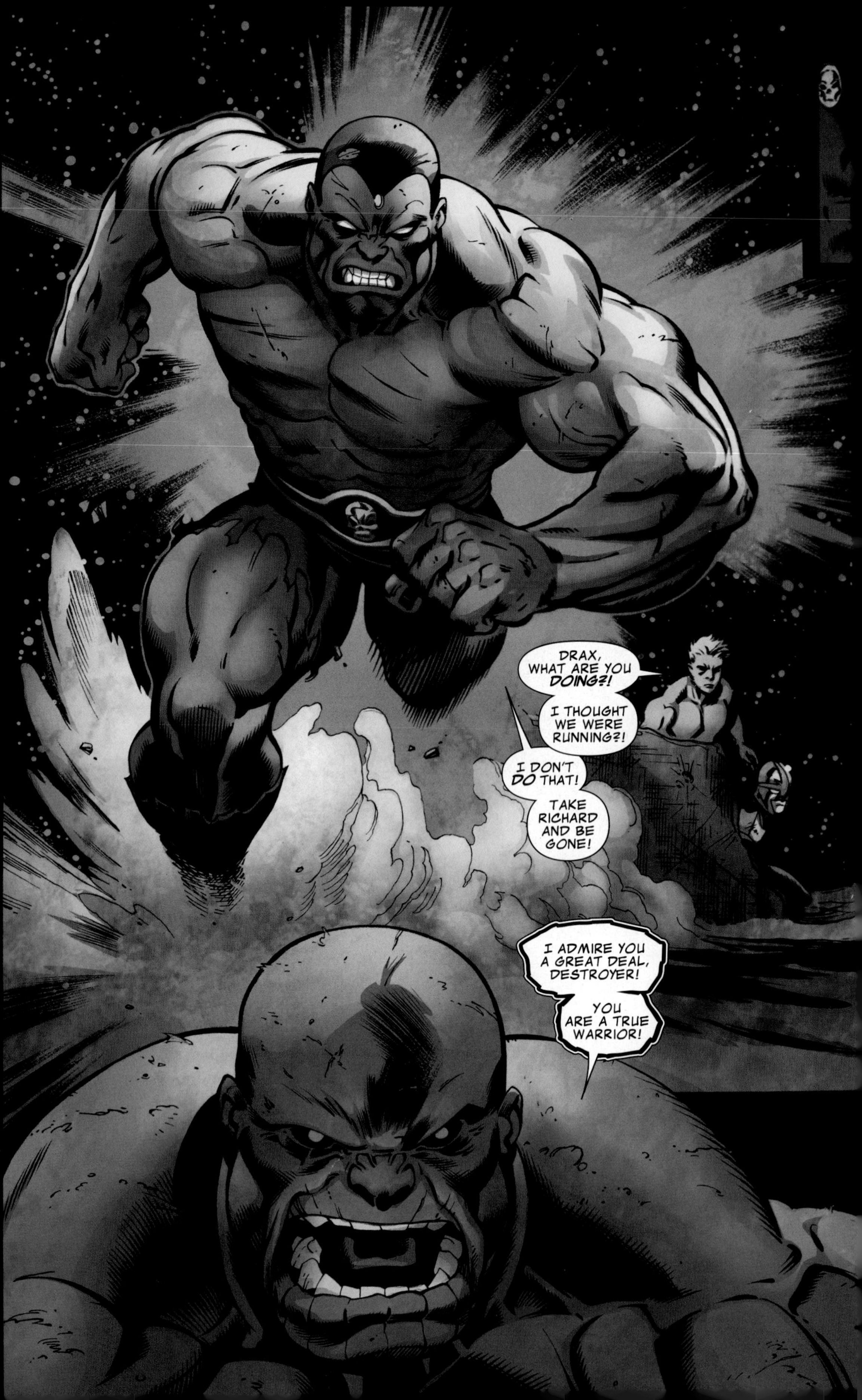
DRAX, WHAT ARE YOU DOING?!
I THOUGHT WE WERE RUNNING?!
I DON'T DO THAT!
TAKE RICHARD AND BE GONE!
I ADMIRE YOU A GREAT DEAL, DESTROYER!
YOU ARE A TRUE WARRIOR!

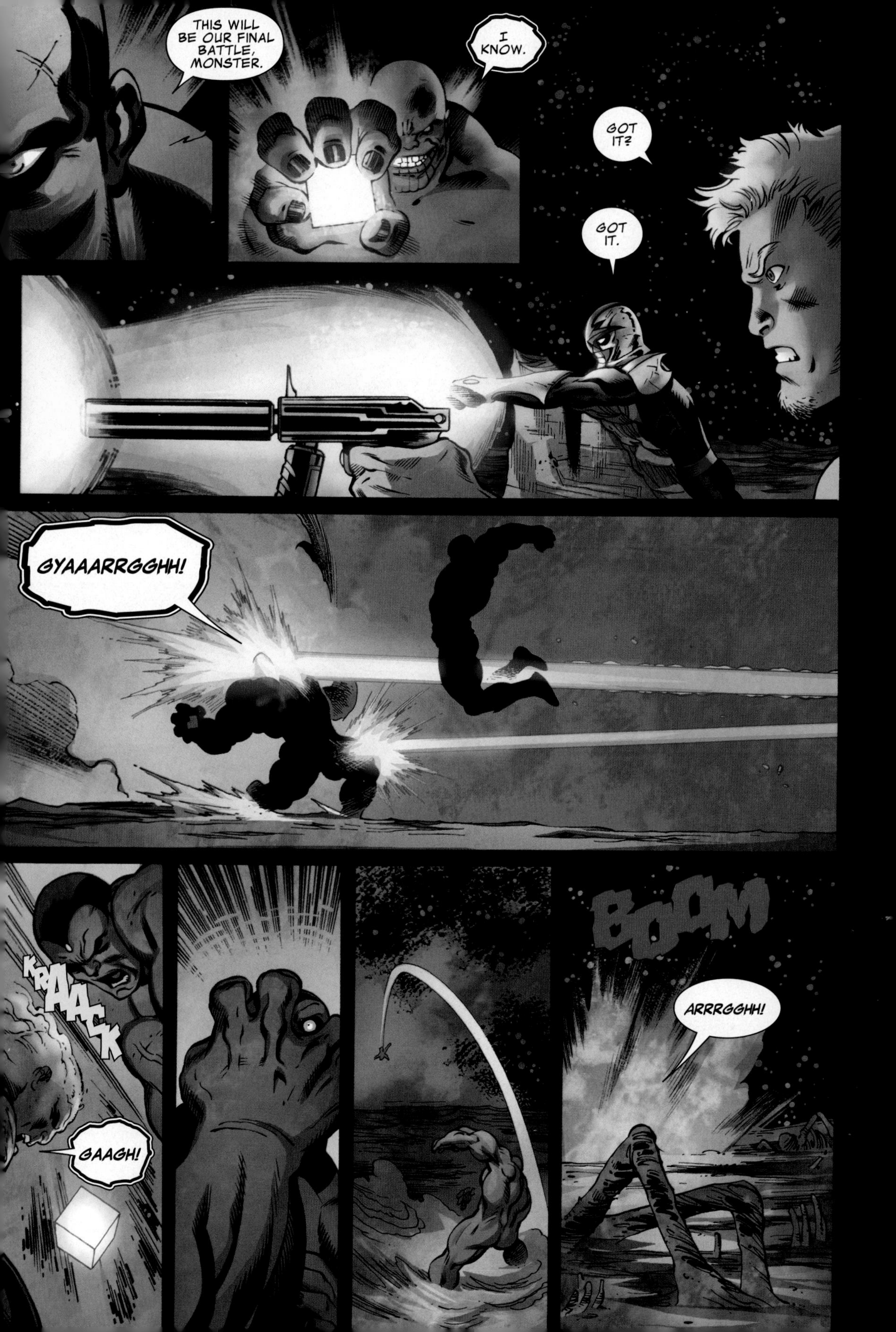
THIS WILL BE OUR FINAL BATTLE, MONSTER.
I KNOW.
GOT IT?
GOT IT.
GYAAARRGGHH!
KRAAACK
GAAGH!
BOOM
ARRRGGHH!

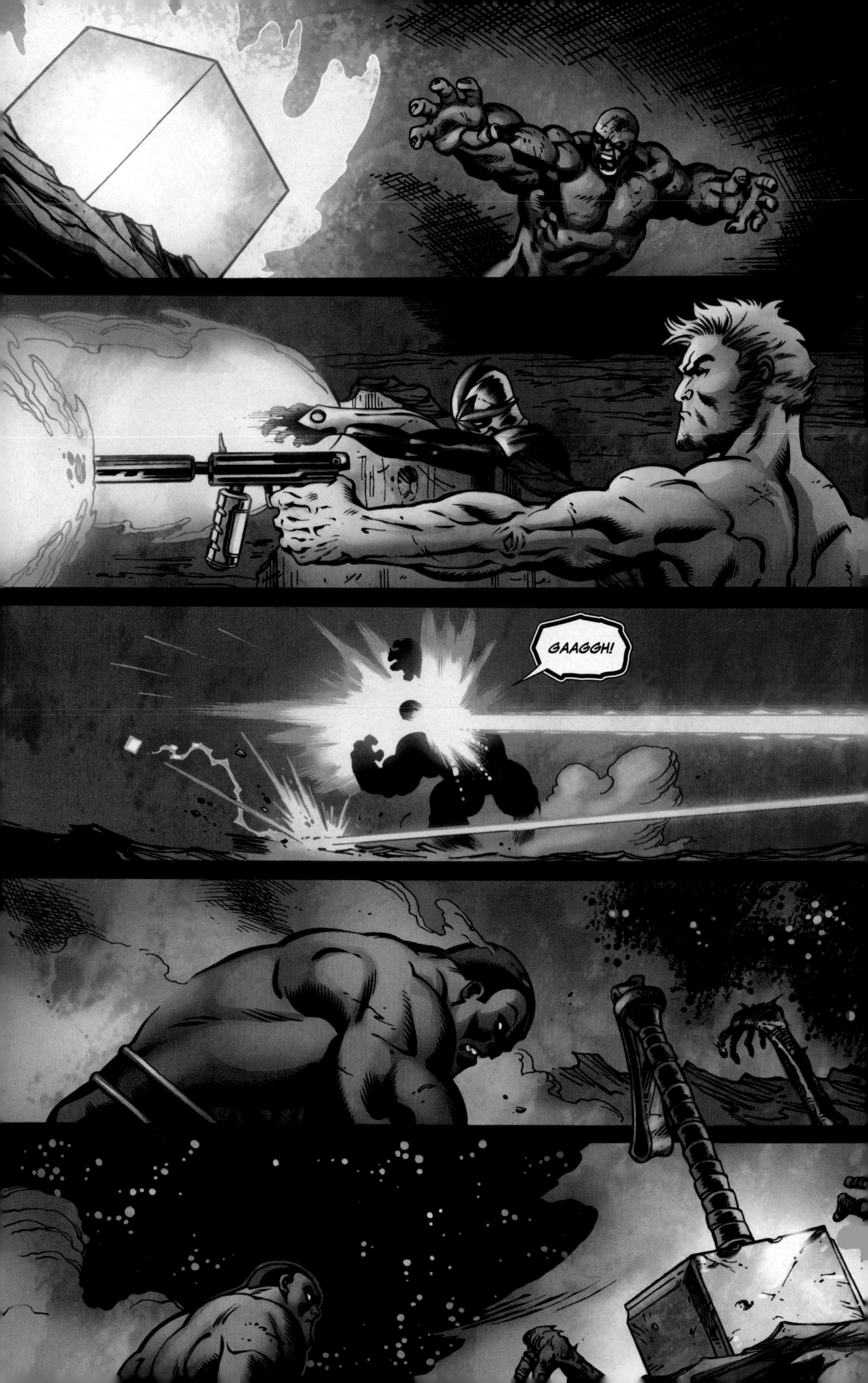
GAAGGH!

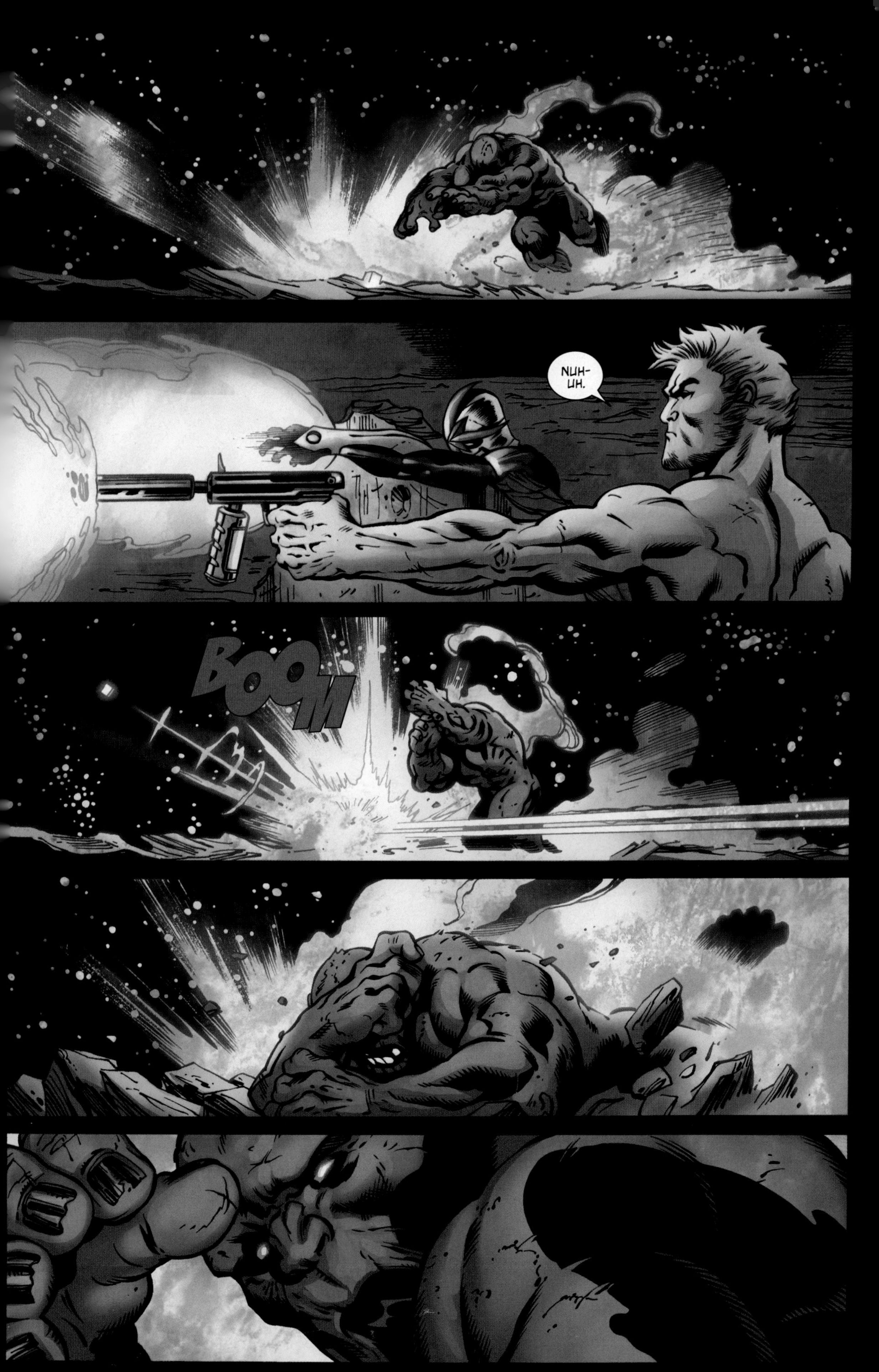
NUH-UH.
BOOM

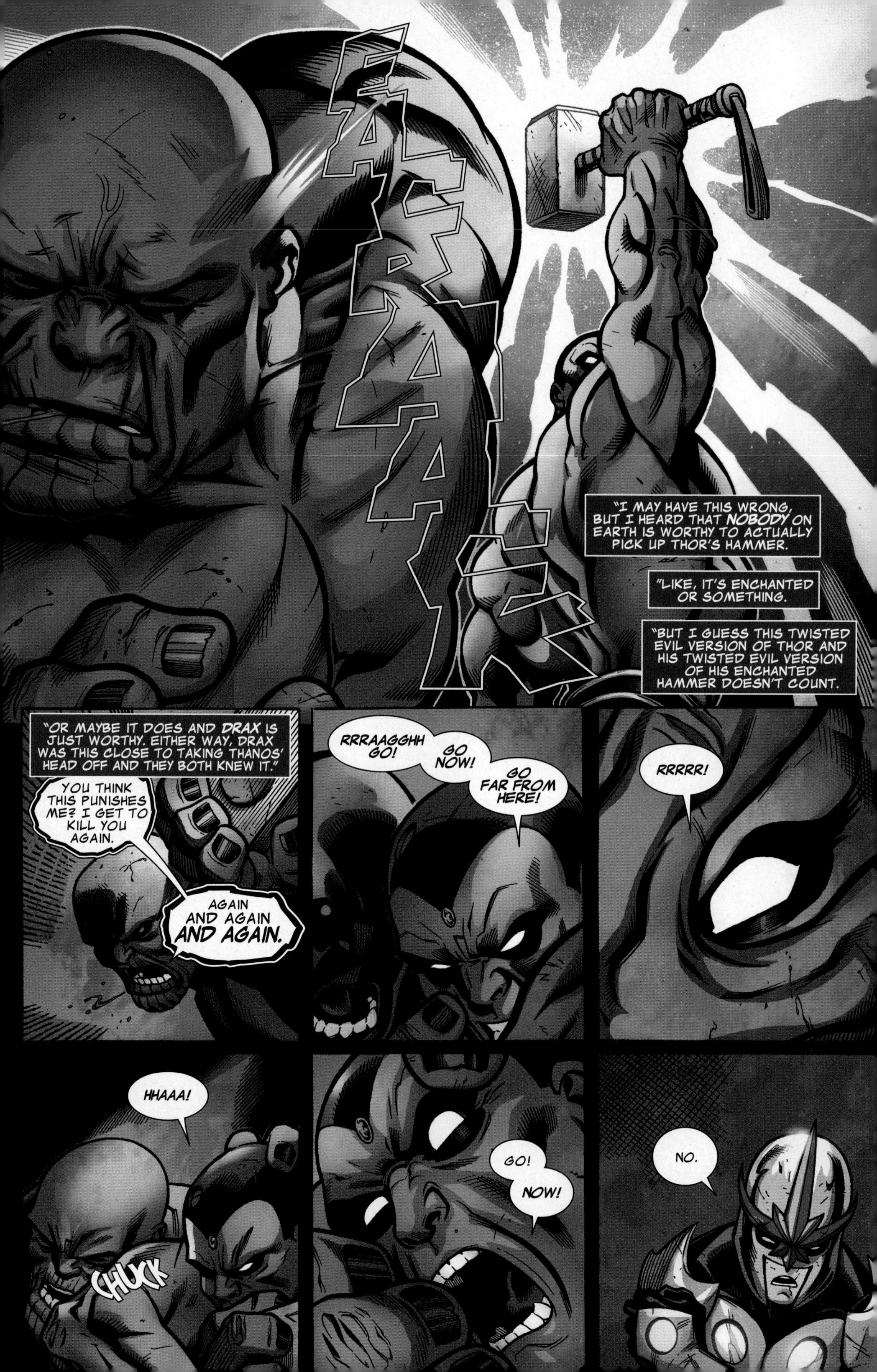
KRAKAKAKOOM
"I MAY HAVE THIS WRONG, BUT I HEARD THAT NOBODY ON EARTH IS WORTHY TO ACTUALLY PICK UP THOR'S HAMMER.
"LIKE, IT'S ENCHANTED OR SOMETHING.
"BUT I GUESS THIS TWISTED EVIL VERSION OF THOR AND HIS TWISTED EVIL VERSION OF HIS ENCHANTED HAMMER DOESN'T COUNT.
"OR MAYBE IT DOES AND DRAX IS JUST WORTHY. EITHER WAY, DRAX WAS THIS CLOSE TO TAKING THANOS' HEAD OFF AND THEY BOTH KNEW IT."
YOU THINK THIS PUNISHES ME? I GET TO KILL YOU AGAIN.
AGAIN AND AGAIN AND AGAIN.
RRRAAGGHH GO!
GO NOW!
GO FAR FROM HERE!
RRRRR!
HHAAA!
CHUCK
GO!
NOW!
NO.

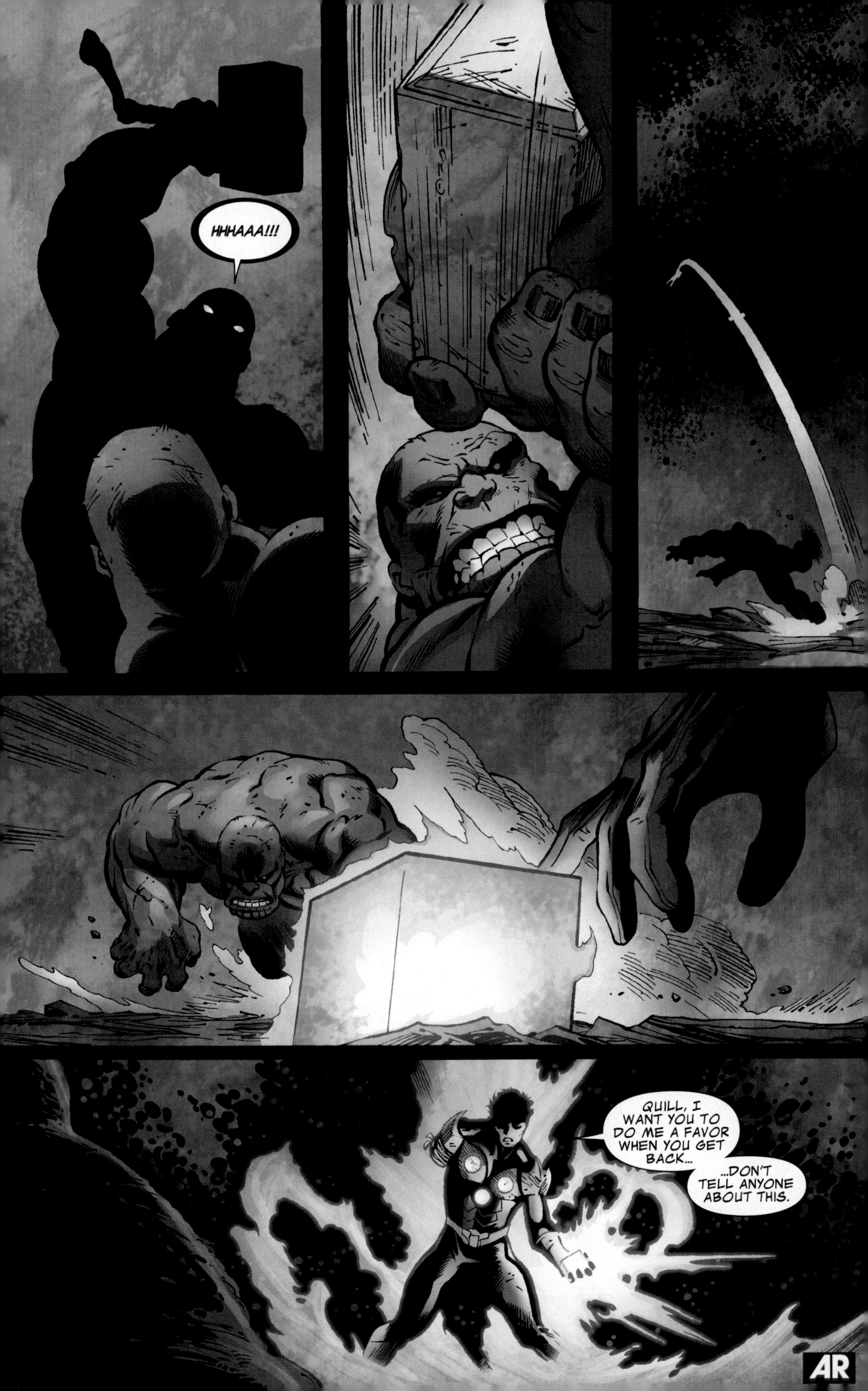
HHHAAA!!!
QUILL, I WANT YOU TO DO ME A FAVOR WHEN YOU GET BACK...
...DON'T TELL ANYONE ABOUT THIS.
AR

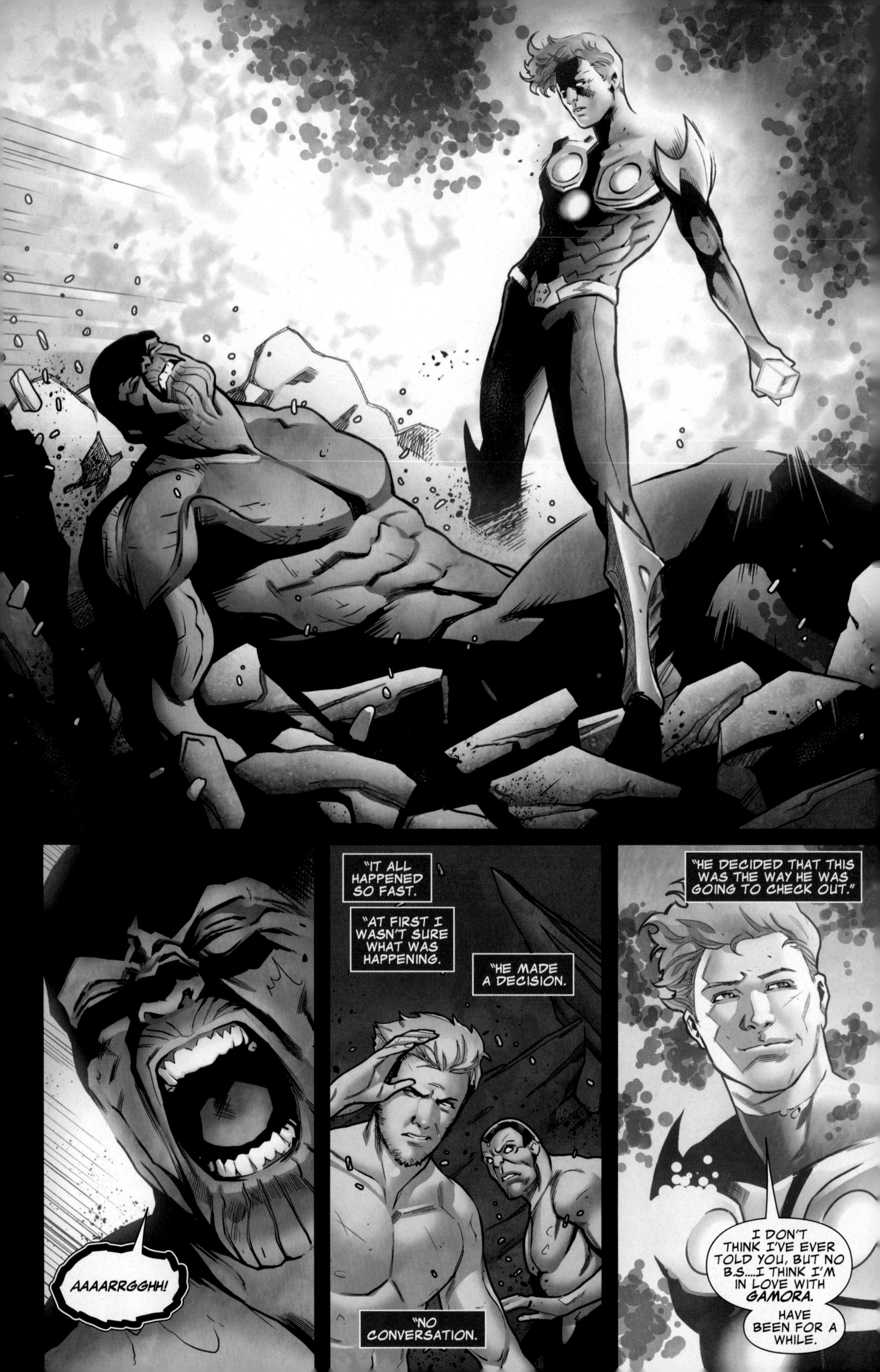
AAAARRGGHH!
"IT ALL HAPPENED SO FAST.
"AT FIRST I WASN'T SURE WHAT WAS HAPPENING.
"HE MADE A DECISION.
"NO CONVERSATION.
"HE DECIDED THAT THIS WAS THE WAY HE WAS GOING TO CHECK OUT."
I DON'T THINK I'VE EVER TOLD YOU, BUT NO B.S....I THINK I'M IN LOVE WITH GAMORA.
HAVE BEEN FOR A WHILE.

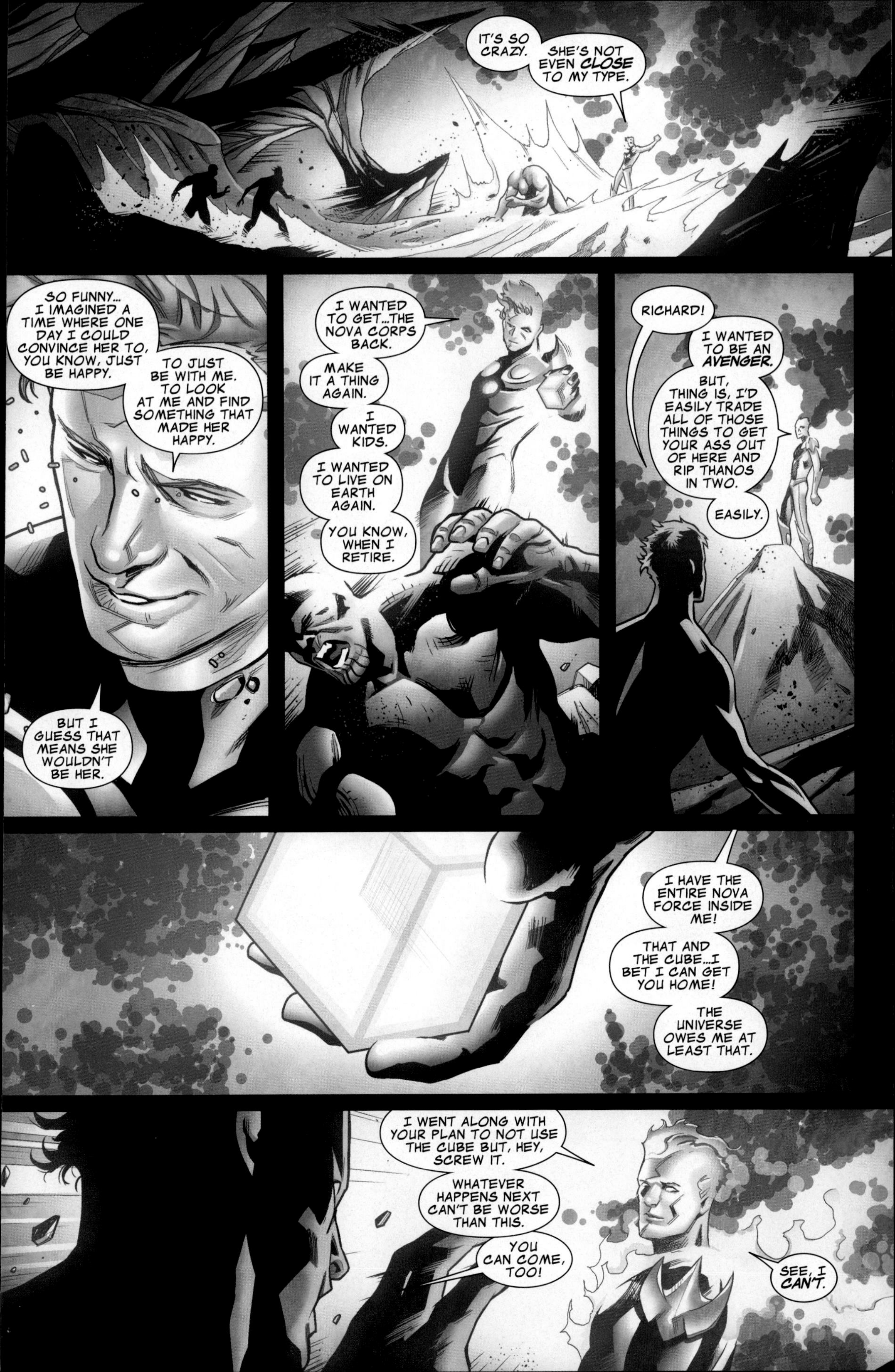
IT'S SO CRAZY.
SHE'S NOT EVEN CLOSE TO MY TYPE.
SO FUNNY... I IMAGINED A TIME WHERE ONE DAY I COULD CONVINCE HER TO, YOU KNOW, JUST BE HAPPY.
TO JUST BE WITH ME. TO LOOK AT ME AND FIND SOMETHING THAT MADE HER HAPPY.
BUT I GUESS THAT MEANS SHE WOULDN'T BE HER.
I WANTED TO GET...THE NOVA CORPS BACK.
MAKE IT A THING AGAIN.
I WANTED KIDS.
I WANTED TO LIVE ON EARTH AGAIN.
YOU KNOW, WHEN I RETIRE.
RICHARD!
I WANTED TO BE AN AVENGER.
BUT, THING IS, I'D EASILY TRADE ALL OF THOSE THINGS TO GET YOUR ASS OUT OF HERE AND RIP THANOS IN TWO.
EASILY.
I HAVE THE ENTIRE NOVA FORCE INSIDE ME!
THAT AND THE CUBE...I BET I CAN GET YOU HOME!
THE UNIVERSE OWES ME AT LEAST THAT.
I WENT ALONG WITH YOUR PLAN TO NOT USE THE CUBE BUT, HEY, SCREW IT.
WHATEVER HAPPENS NEXT CAN'T BE WORSE THAN THIS.
YOU CAN COME, TOO!
SEE, I CAN'T.

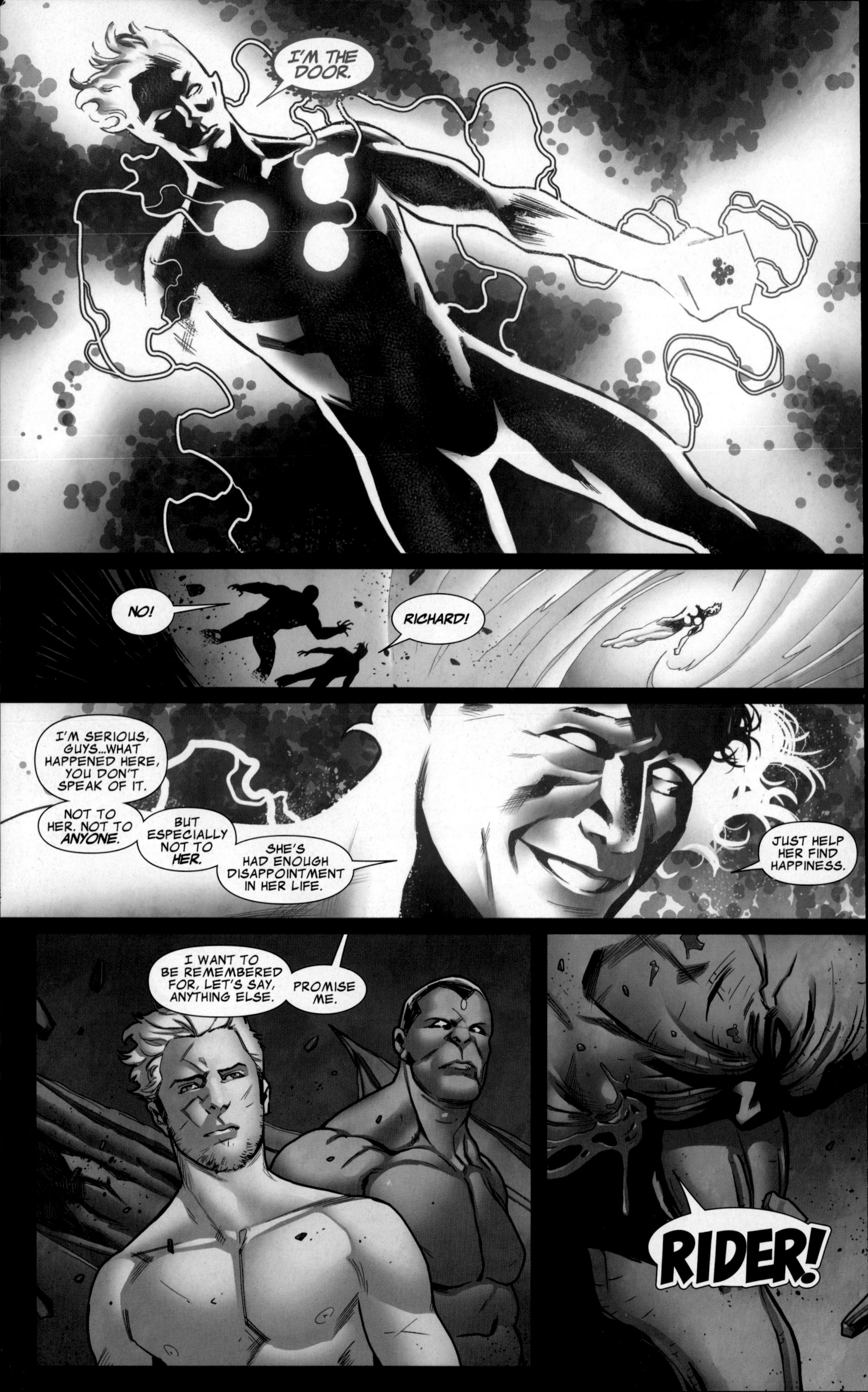
I'M THE DOOR.
NO!
RICHARD!
I'M SERIOUS, GUYS...WHAT HAPPENED HERE, YOU DON'T SPEAK OF IT.
NOT TO HER. NOT TO ANYONE.
BUT ESPECIALLY NOT TO HER.
SHE'S HAD ENOUGH DISAPPOINTMENT IN HER LIFE.
JUST HELP HER FIND HAPPINESS.
I WANT TO BE REMEMBERED FOR, LET'S SAY, ANYTHING ELSE.
PROMISE ME.
RIDER!

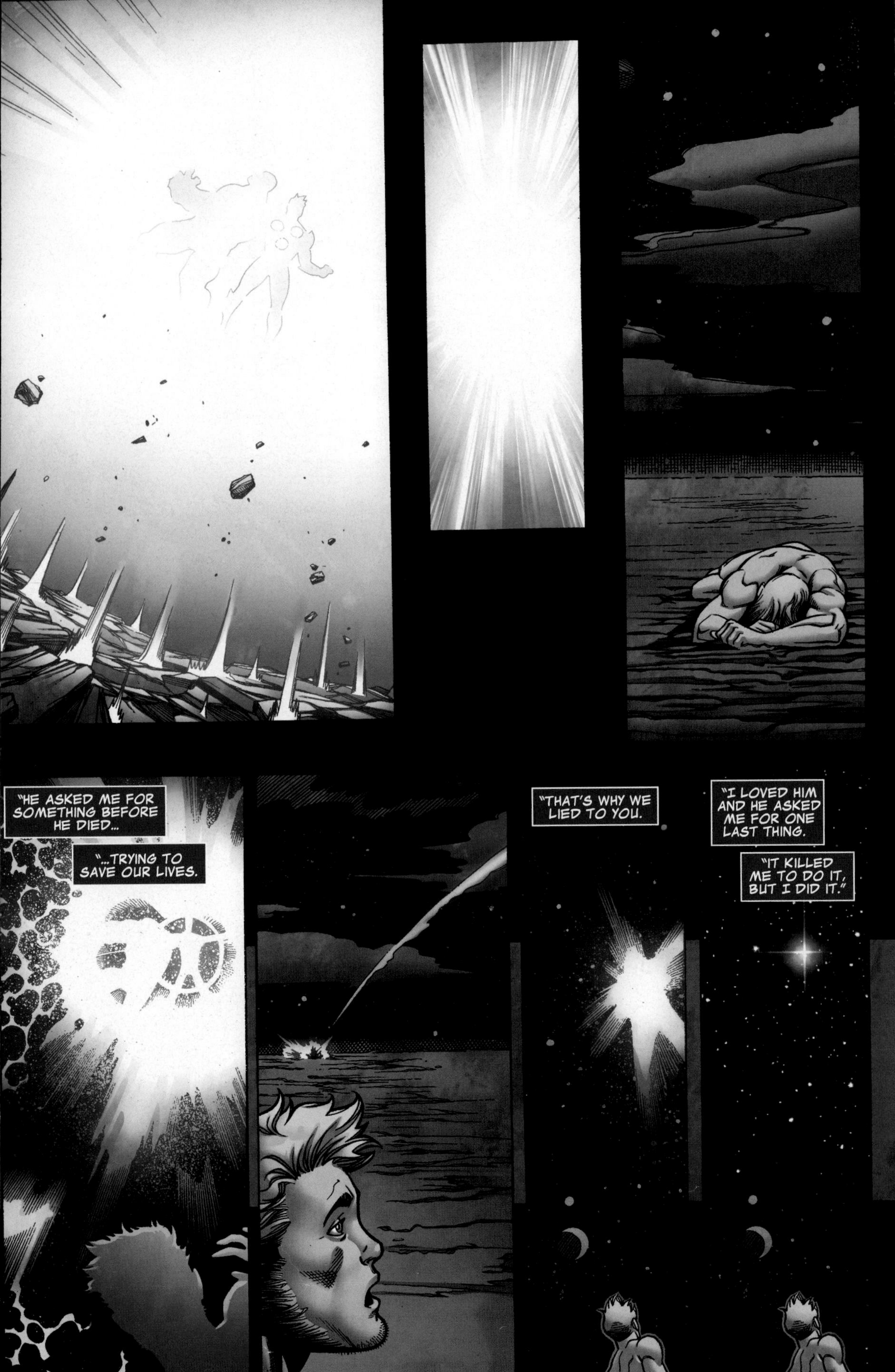
"HE ASKED ME FOR SOMETHING BEFORE HE DIED...
"...TRYING TO SAVE OUR LIVES.
"THAT'S WHY WE LIED TO YOU.
"I LOVED HIM AND HE ASKED ME FOR ONE LAST THING.
"IT KILLED ME TO DO IT, BUT I DID IT."

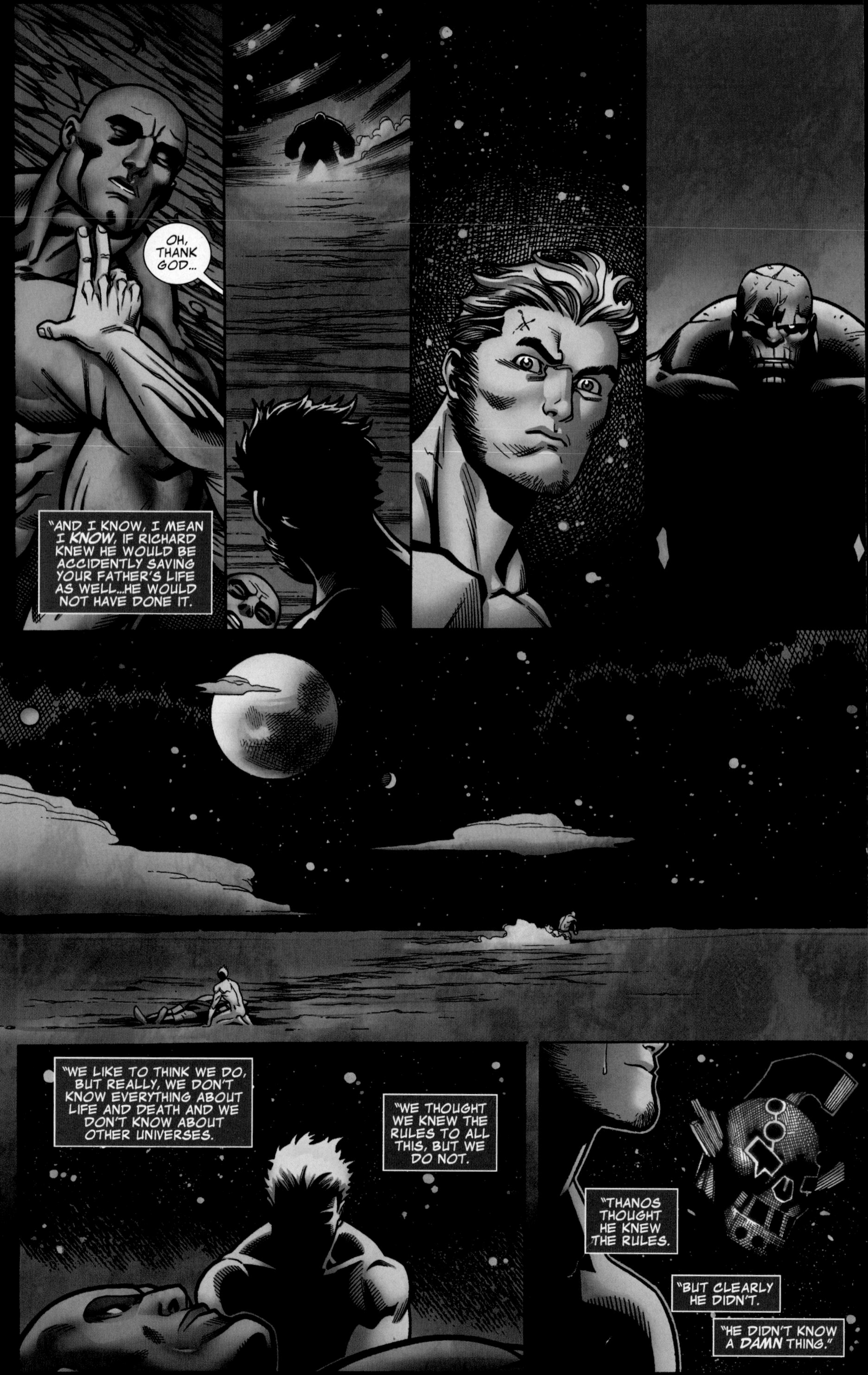
OH, THANK GOD...
"AND I KNOW, I MEAN I KNOW, IF RICHARD KNEW HE WOULD BE ACCIDENTLY SAVING YOUR FATHER'S LIFE AS WELL...HE WOULD NOT HAVE DONE IT.
"WE LIKE TO THINK WE DO, BUT REALLY, WE DON'T KNOW EVERYTHING ABOUT LIFE AND DEATH AND WE DON'T KNOW ABOUT OTHER UNIVERSES.
"WE THOUGHT WE KNEW THE RULES TO ALL THIS, BUT WE DO NOT.
"THANOS THOUGHT HE KNEW THE RULES.
"BUT CLEARLY HE DIDN'T.
"HE DIDN'T KNOW A DAMN THING."

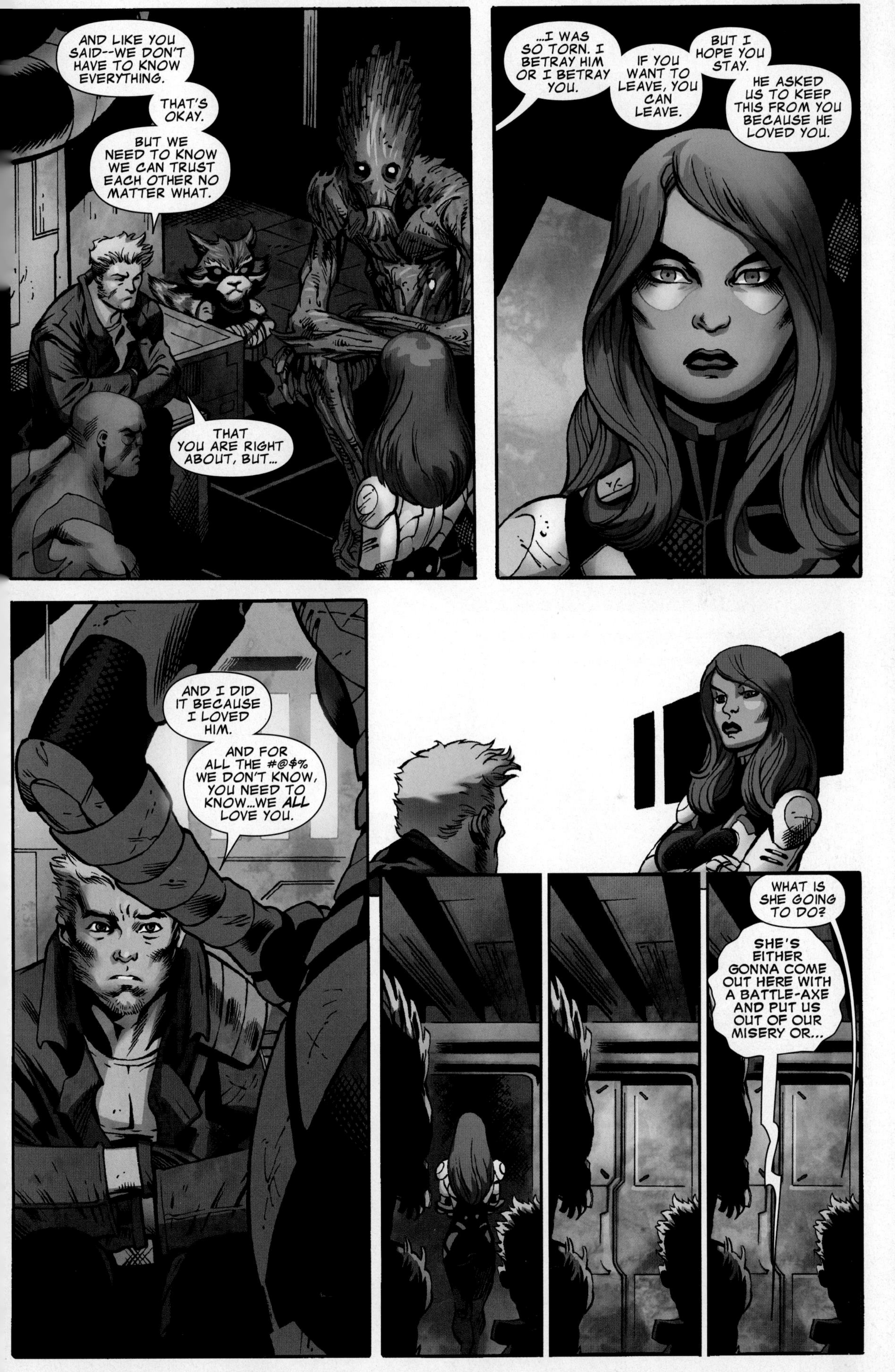

AND LIKE YOU SAID--WE DON'T HAVE TO KNOW EVERYTHING.
THAT'S OKAY.
BUT WE NEED TO KNOW WE CAN TRUST EACH OTHER NO MATTER WHAT.
THAT YOU ARE RIGHT ABOUT, BUT...
...I WAS SO TORN. I BETRAY HIM OR I BETRAY YOU.
IF YOU WANT TO LEAVE, YOU CAN LEAVE.
BUT I HOPE YOU STAY.
HE ASKED US TO KEEP THIS FROM YOU BECAUSE HE LOVED YOU.
AND I DID IT BECAUSE I LOVED HIM.
AND FOR ALL THE #@$% WE DON'T KNOW, YOU NEED TO KNOW...WE ALL LOVE YOU.
WHAT IS SHE GOING TO DO?
SHE'S EITHER GONNA COME OUT HERE WITH A BATTLE-AXE AND PUT US OUT OF OUR MISERY OR...

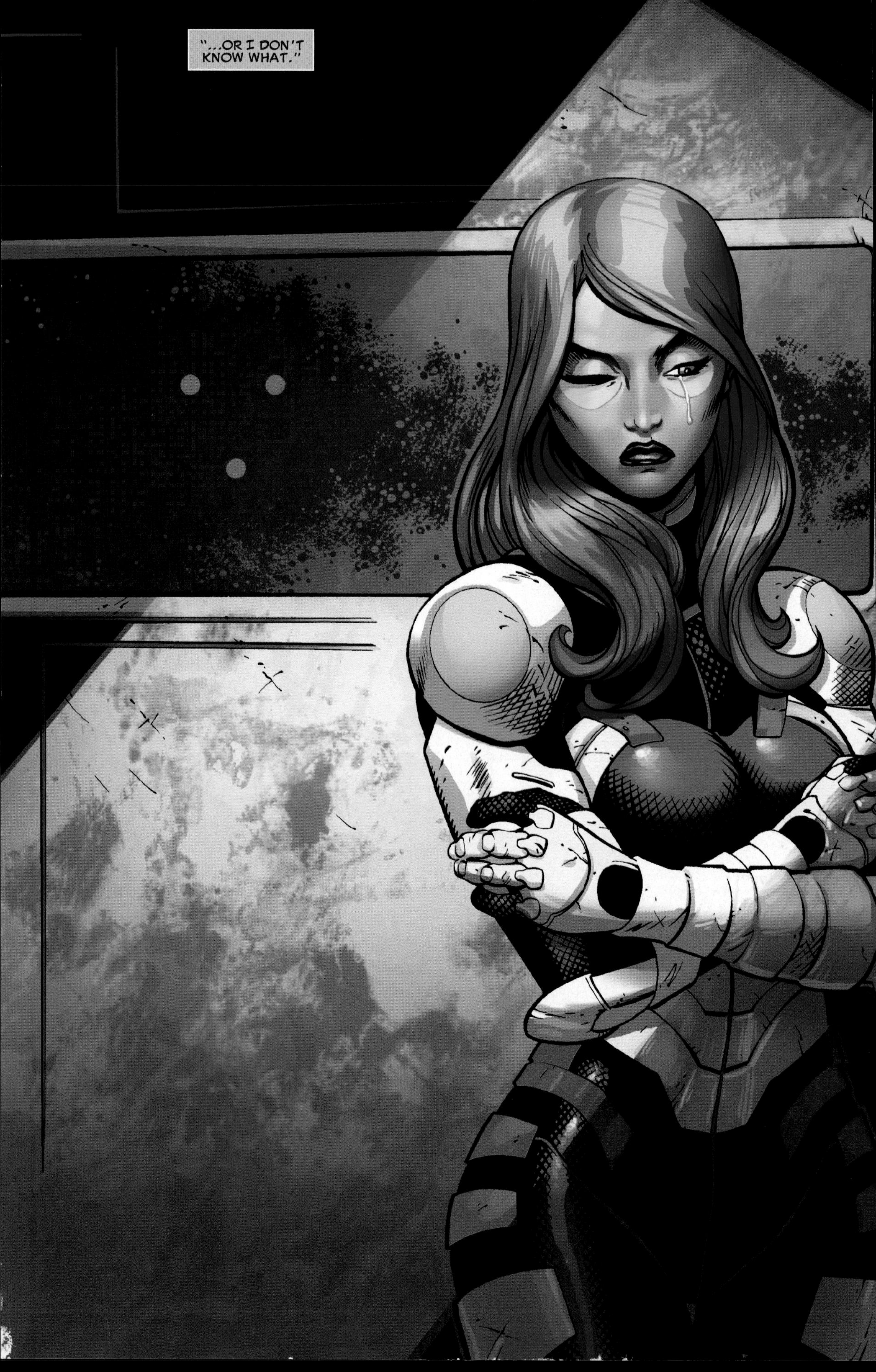
"...OR I DON'T KNOW WHAT."

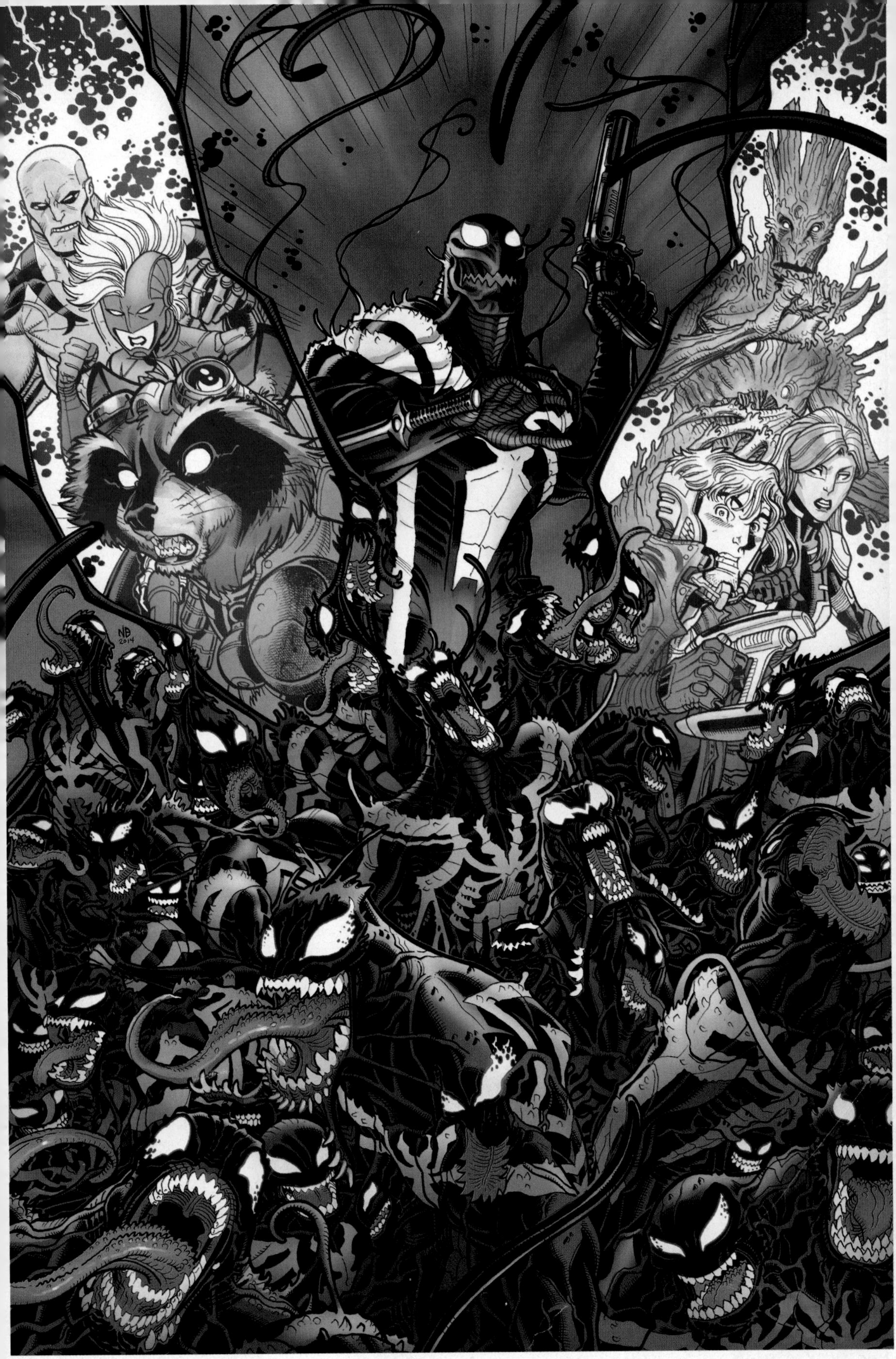
NB
2014

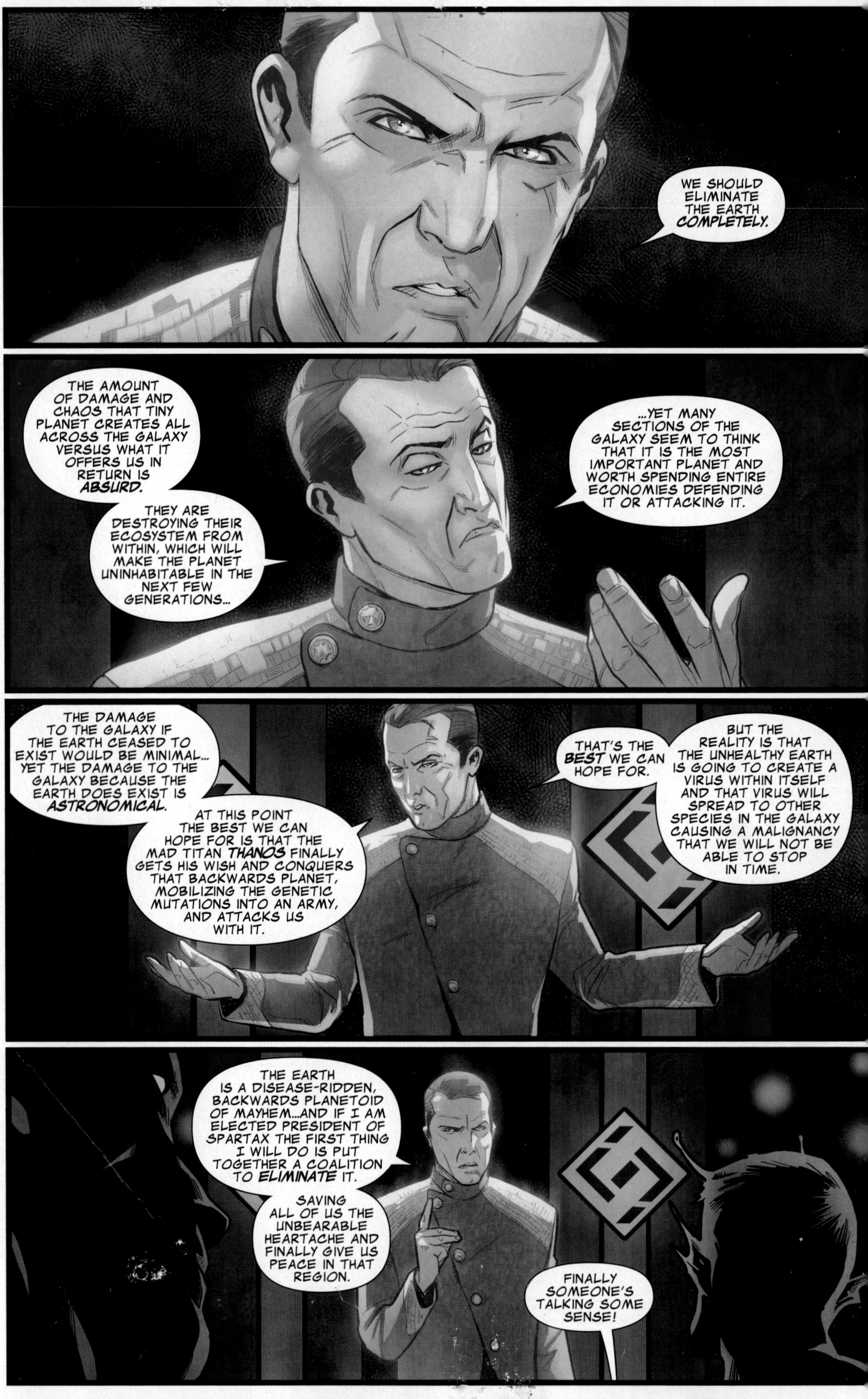
WE SHOULD ELIMINATE THE EARTH COMPLETELY.
THE AMOUNT OF DAMAGE AND CHAOS THAT TINY PLANET CREATES ALL ACROSS THE GALAXY VERSUS WHAT IT OFFERS US IN RETURN IS ABSURD.
THEY ARE DESTROYING THEIR ECOSYSTEM FROM WITHIN, WHICH WILL MAKE THE PLANET UNINHABITABLE IN THE NEXT FEW GENERATIONS...
...YET MANY SECTIONS OF THE GALAXY SEEM TO THINK THAT IT IS THE MOST IMPORTANT PLANET AND WORTH SPENDING ENTIRE ECONOMIES DEFENDING IT OR ATTACKING IT.
THE DAMAGE TO THE GALAXY IF THE EARTH CEASED TO EXIST WOULD BE MINIMAL... YET THE DAMAGE TO THE GALAXY BECAUSE THE EARTH DOES EXIST IS ASTRONOMICAL.
AT THIS POINT THE BEST WE CAN HOPE FOR IS THAT THE MAD TITAN THANOS FINALLY GETS HIS WISH AND CONQUERS THAT BACKWARDS PLANET, MOBILIZING THE GENETIC MUTATIONS INTO AN ARMY, AND ATTACKS US WITH IT.
THAT'S THE BEST WE CAN HOPE FOR.
BUT THE REALITY IS THAT THE UNHEALTHY EARTH IS GOING TO CREATE A VIRUS WITHIN ITSELF AND THAT VIRUS WILL SPREAD TO OTHER SPECIES IN THE GALAXY CAUSING A MALIGNANCY THAT WE WILL NOT BE ABLE TO STOP IN TIME.
THE EARTH IS A DISEASE-RIDDEN, BACKWARDS PLANETOID OF MAYHEM...AND IF I AM ELECTED PRESIDENT OF SPARTAX THE FIRST THING I WILL DO IS PUT TOGETHER A COALITION TO ELIMINATE IT.
SAVING ALL OF US THE UNBEARABLE HEARTACHE AND FINALLY GIVE US PEACE IN THAT REGION.
FINALLY SOMEONE'S TALKING SOME SENSE!

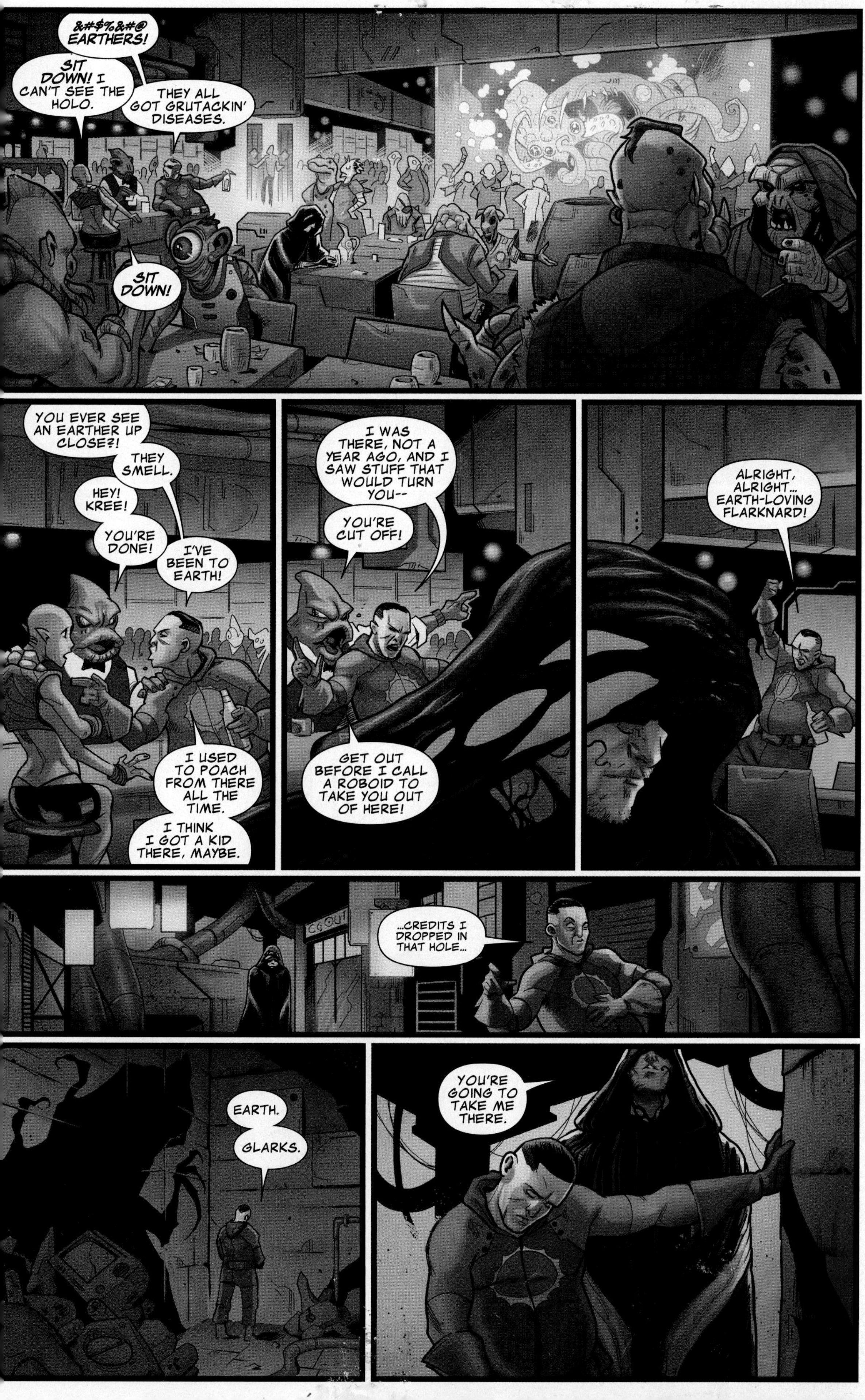
&#$%&#@ EARTHERS!
SIT DOWN! I CAN'T SEE THE HOLO.
THEY ALL GOT GRUTACKIN' DISEASES.
SIT DOWN!
YOU EVER SEE AN EARTHER UP CLOSE?!
THEY SMELL.
HEY! KREE!
YOU'RE DONE!
I'VE BEEN TO EARTH!
I USED TO POACH FROM THERE ALL THE TIME.
I THINK I GOT A KID THERE, MAYBE.
I WAS THERE, NOT A YEAR AGO, AND I SAW STUFF THAT WOULD TURN YOU--
YOU'RE CUT OFF!
GET OUT BEFORE I CALL A ROBOID TO TAKE YOU OUT OF HERE!
ALRIGHT, ALRIGHT... EARTH-LOVING FLARKNARD!
...CREDITS I DROPPED IN THAT HOLE...
EARTH.
GLARKS.
YOU'RE GOING TO TAKE ME THERE.

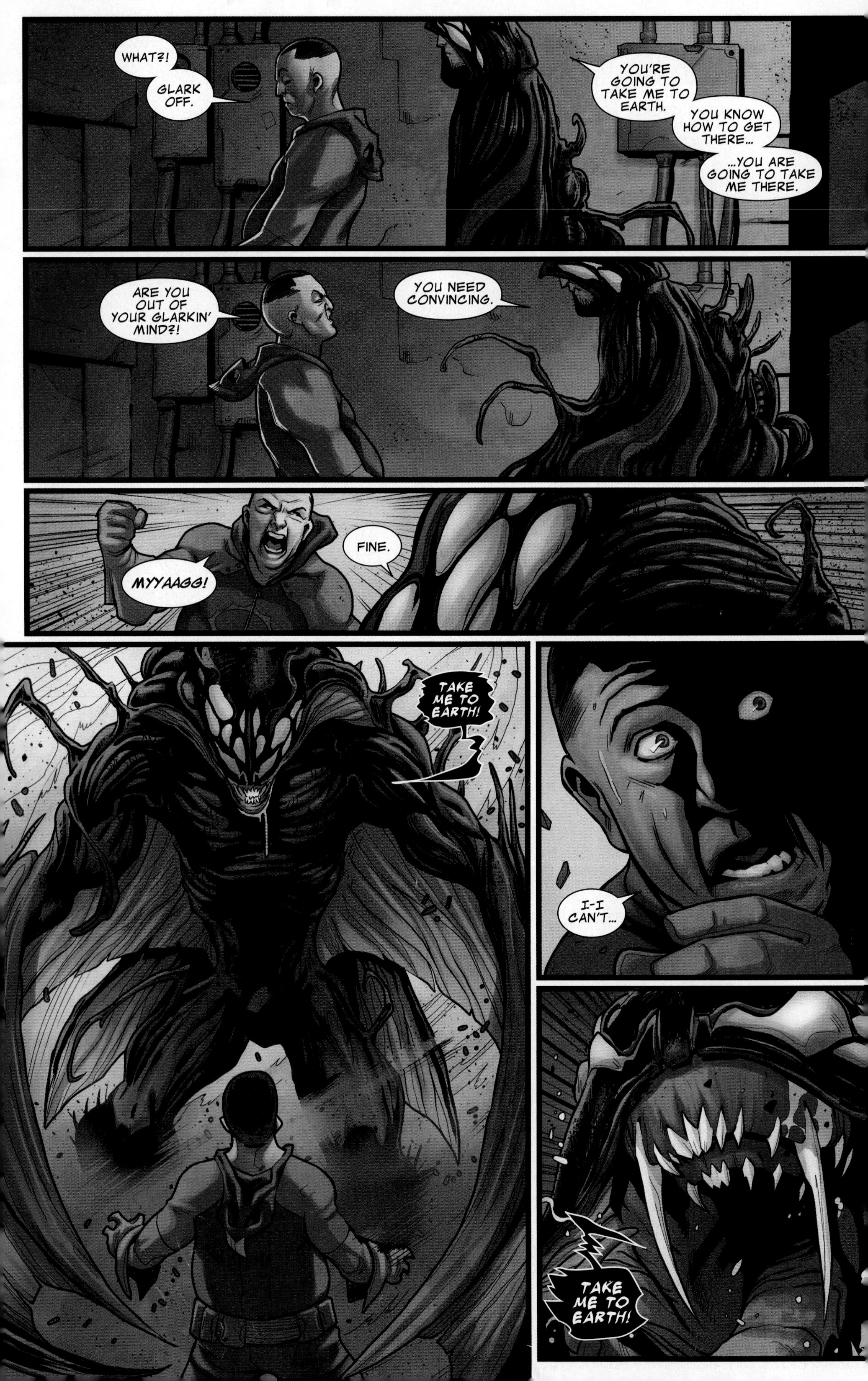
WHAT?!
GLARK OFF.
YOU'RE GOING TO TAKE ME TO EARTH.
YOU KNOW HOW TO GET THERE...
...YOU ARE GOING TO TAKE ME THERE.
ARE YOU OUT OF YOUR GLARKIN' MIND?!
YOU NEED CONVINCING.
MYYAAGG!
FINE.
TAKE ME TO EARTH!
I-I CAN'T...
TAKE ME TO EARTH!

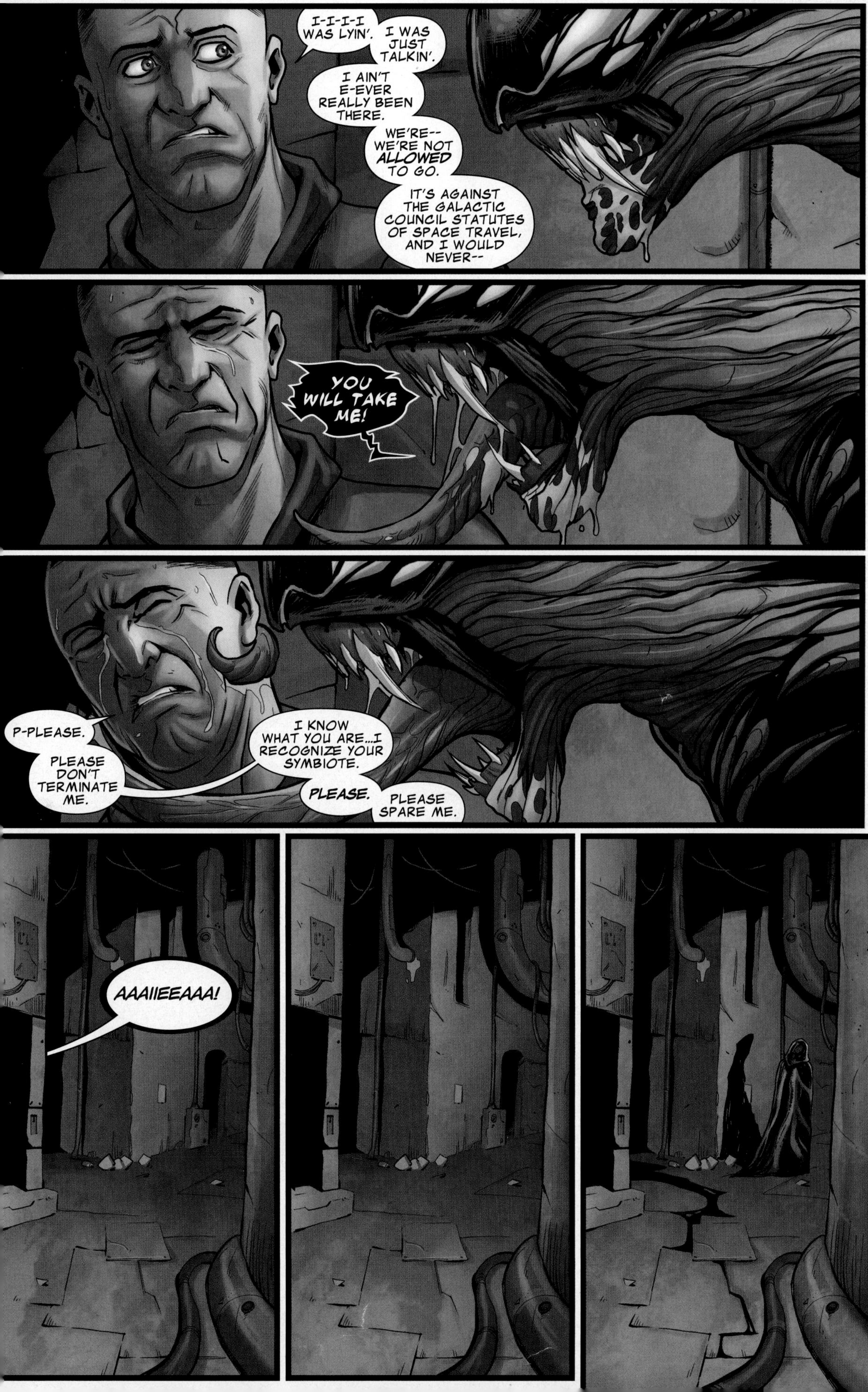
I-I-I-I WAS LYIN'.
I WAS JUST TALKIN'.
I AIN'T E-EVER REALLY BEEN THERE.
WE'RE-- WE'RE NOT ALLOWED TO GO.
IT'S AGAINST THE GALACTIC COUNCIL STATUTES OF SPACE TRAVEL, AND I WOULD NEVER--
YOU WILL TAKE ME!
P-PLEASE.
PLEASE DON'T TERMINATE ME.
I KNOW WHAT YOU ARE...I RECOGNIZE YOUR SYMBIOTE.
PLEASE.
PLEASE SPARE ME.
AAAIIEEAAA!

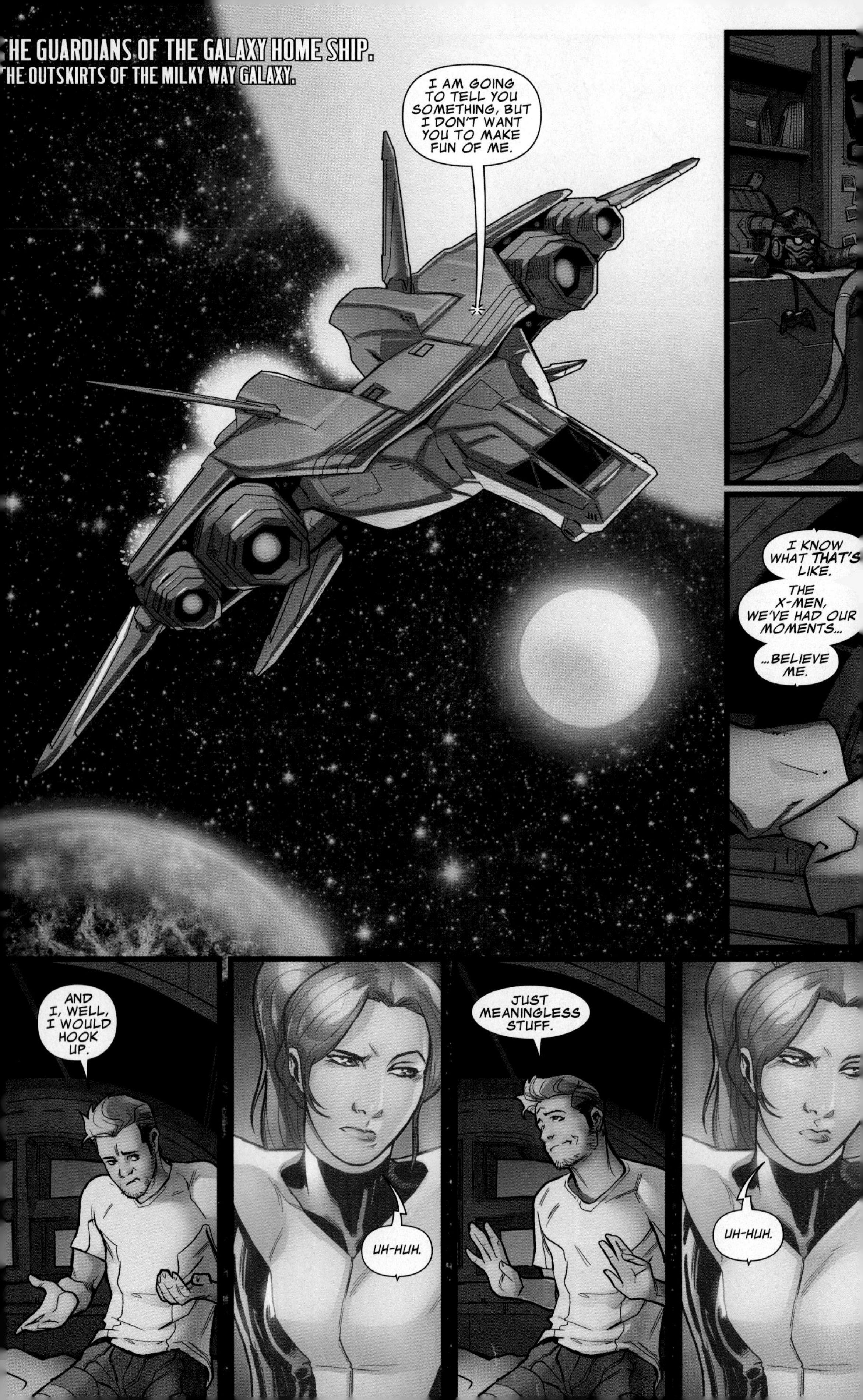
THE GUARDIANS OF THE GALAXY HOME SHIP.
THE OUTSKIRTS OF THE MILKY WAY GALAXY.
I AM GOING TO TELL YOU SOMETHING, BUT I DON'T WANT YOU TO MAKE FUN OF ME.
I KNOW WHAT THAT'S LIKE.
THE X-MEN, WE'VE HAD OUR MOMENTS...
...BELIEVE ME.
AND I, WELL, I WOULD HOOK UP.
UH-HUH.
JUST MEANINGLESS STUFF.
UH-HUH.

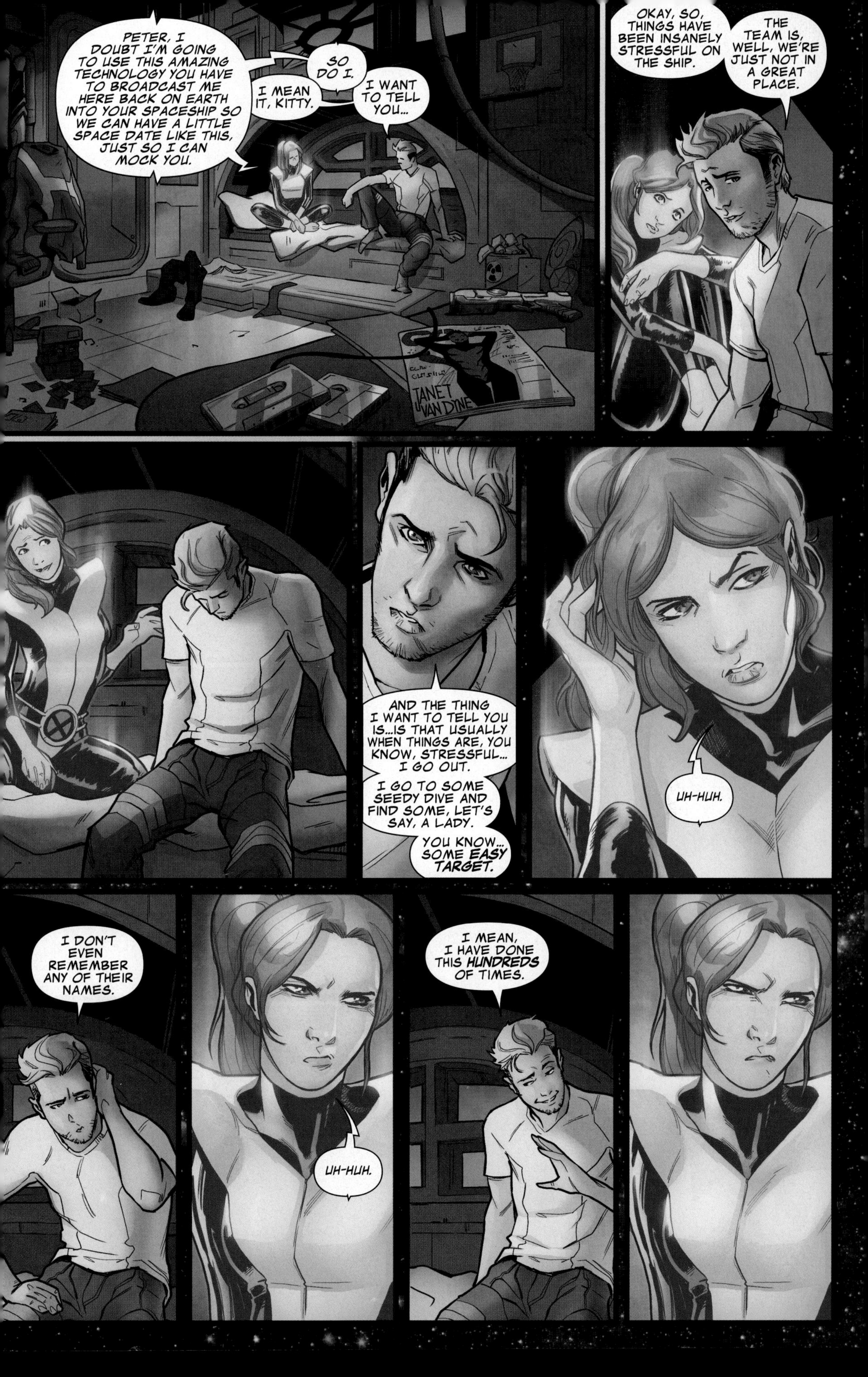
PETER, I DOUBT I'M GOING TO USE THIS AMAZING TECHNOLOGY YOU HAVE TO BROADCAST ME HERE BACK ON EARTH INTO YOUR SPACESHIP SO WE CAN HAVE A LITTLE SPACE DATE LIKE THIS, JUST SO I CAN MOCK YOU.
SO DO I.
I MEAN IT, KITTY.
I WANT TO TELL YOU...
JANET VAN DYNE
OKAY, SO, THINGS HAVE BEEN INSANELY STRESSFUL ON THE SHIP.
THE TEAM IS, WELL, WE'RE JUST NOT IN A GREAT PLACE.
AND THE THING I WANT TO TELL YOU IS...IS THAT USUALLY WHEN THINGS ARE, YOU KNOW, STRESSFUL... I GO OUT.
I GO TO SOME SEEDY DIVE AND FIND SOME, LET'S SAY, A LADY.
YOU KNOW... SOME EASY TARGET.
UH-HUH.
I DON'T EVEN REMEMBER ANY OF THEIR NAMES.
UH-HUH.
I MEAN, I HAVE DONE THIS HUNDREDS OF TIMES.

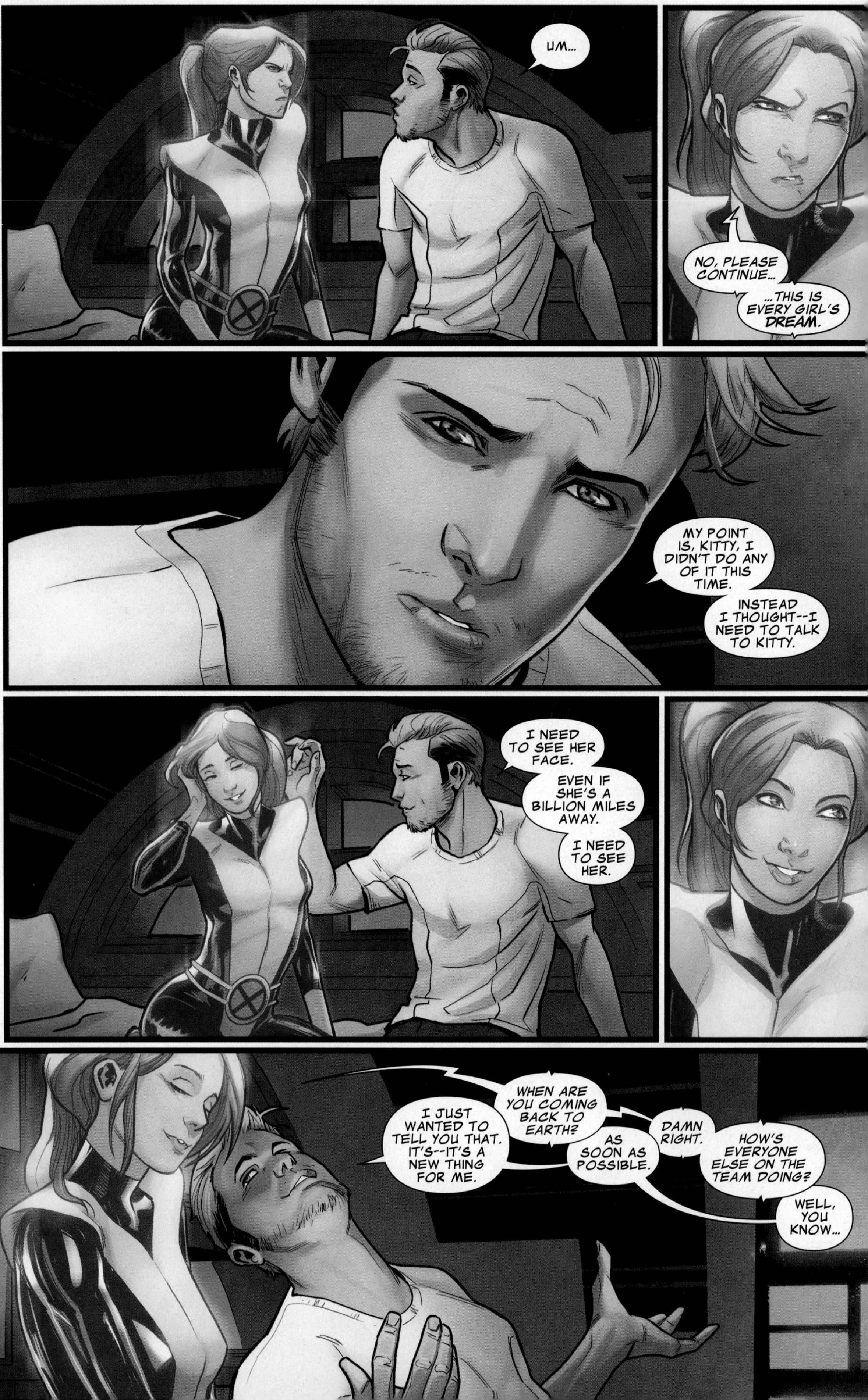
UM...
NO, PLEASE CONTINUE...
...THIS IS EVERY GIRL'S DREAM.
MY POINT IS, KITTY, I DIDN'T DO ANY OF IT THIS TIME.
INSTEAD I THOUGHT--I NEED TO TALK TO KITTY.
I NEED TO SEE HER FACE.
EVEN IF SHE'S A BILLION MILES AWAY.
I NEED TO SEE HER.
I JUST WANTED TO TELL YOU THAT. IT'S--IT'S A NEW THING FOR ME.
WHEN ARE YOU COMING BACK TO EARTH?
AS SOON AS POSSIBLE.
DAMN RIGHT.
HOW'S EVERYONE ELSE ON THE TEAM DOING?
WELL, YOU KNOW...

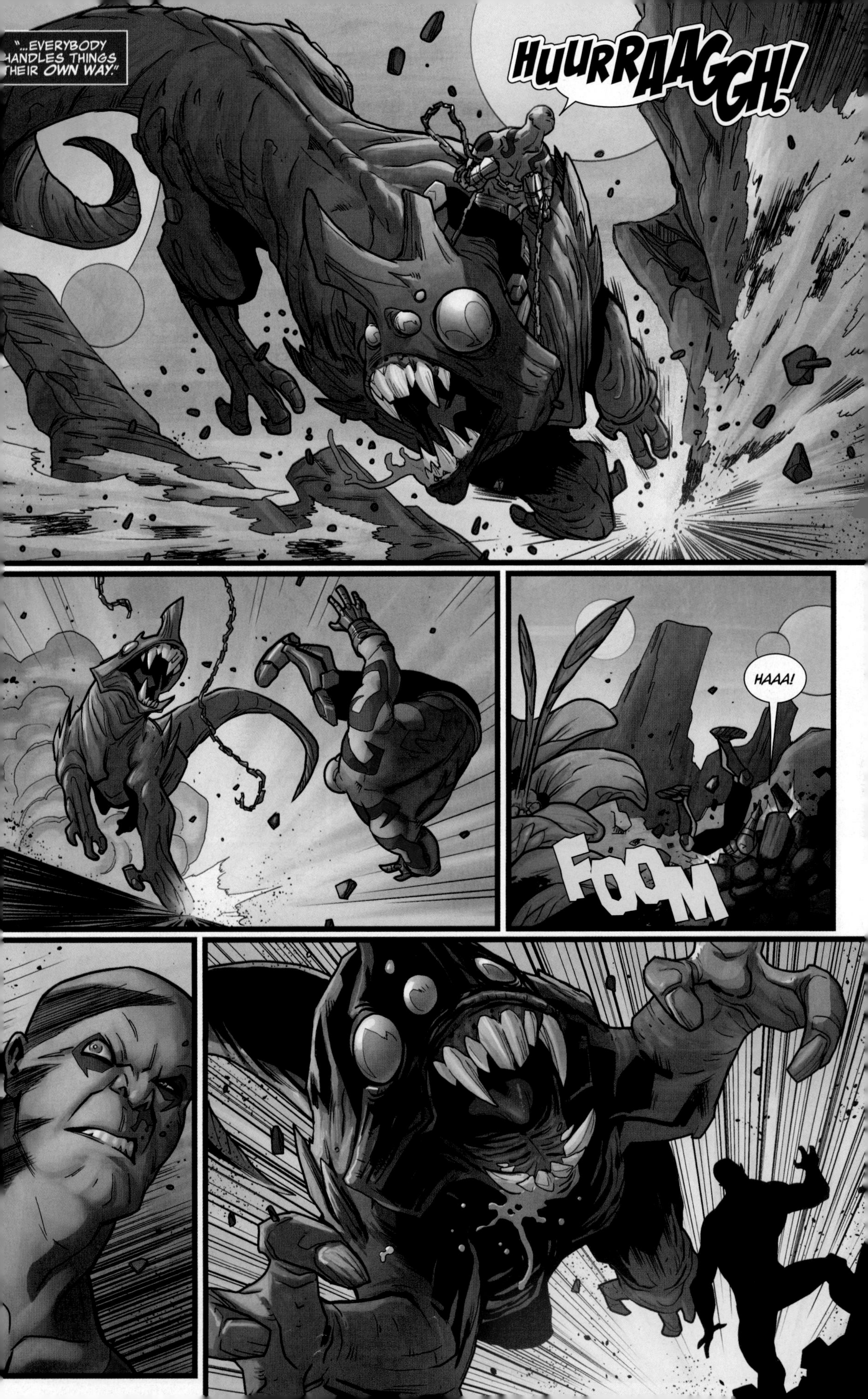
"...EVERYBODY HANDLES THINGS THEIR OWN WAY."
HUURRAAGGH!
HAAA!
FOOM

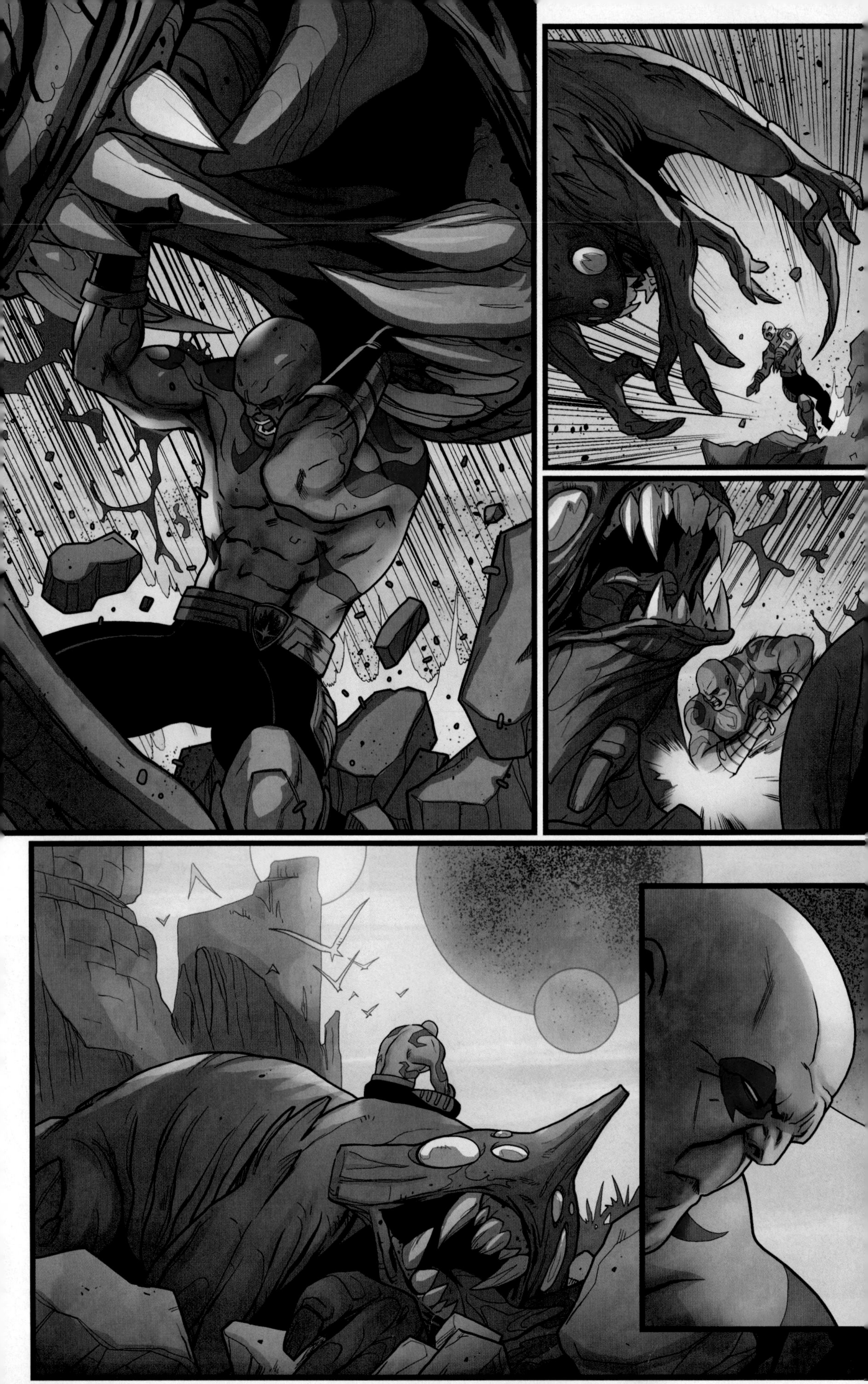

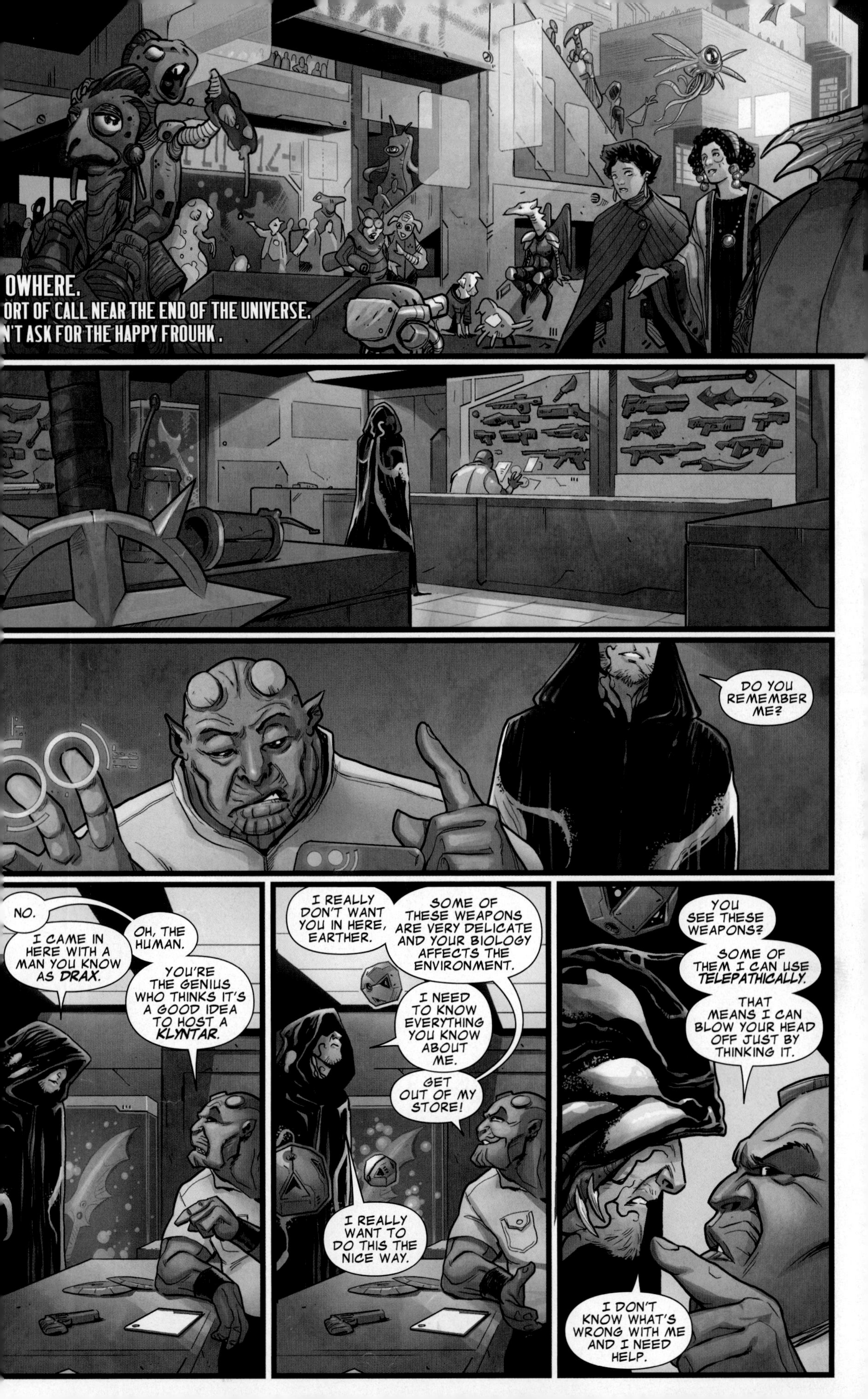
OWHERE.
ORT OF CALL NEAR THE END OF THE UNIVERSE.
N'T ASK FOR THE HAPPY FROUHK .
DO YOU REMEMBER ME?
NO.
I CAME IN HERE WITH A MAN YOU KNOW AS DRAX.
OH, THE HUMAN.
YOU'RE THE GENIUS WHO THINKS IT'S A GOOD IDEA TO HOST A KLYNTAR.
I REALLY DON'T WANT YOU IN HERE, EARTHER.
SOME OF THESE WEAPONS ARE VERY DELICATE AND YOUR BIOLOGY AFFECTS THE ENVIRONMENT.
I NEED TO KNOW EVERYTHING YOU KNOW ABOUT ME.
GET OUT OF MY STORE!
I REALLY WANT TO DO THIS THE NICE WAY.
YOU SEE THESE WEAPONS?
SOME OF THEM I CAN USE TELEPATHICALLY.
THAT MEANS I CAN BLOW YOUR HEAD OFF JUST BY THINKING IT.
I DON'T KNOW WHAT'S WRONG WITH ME AND I NEED HELP.

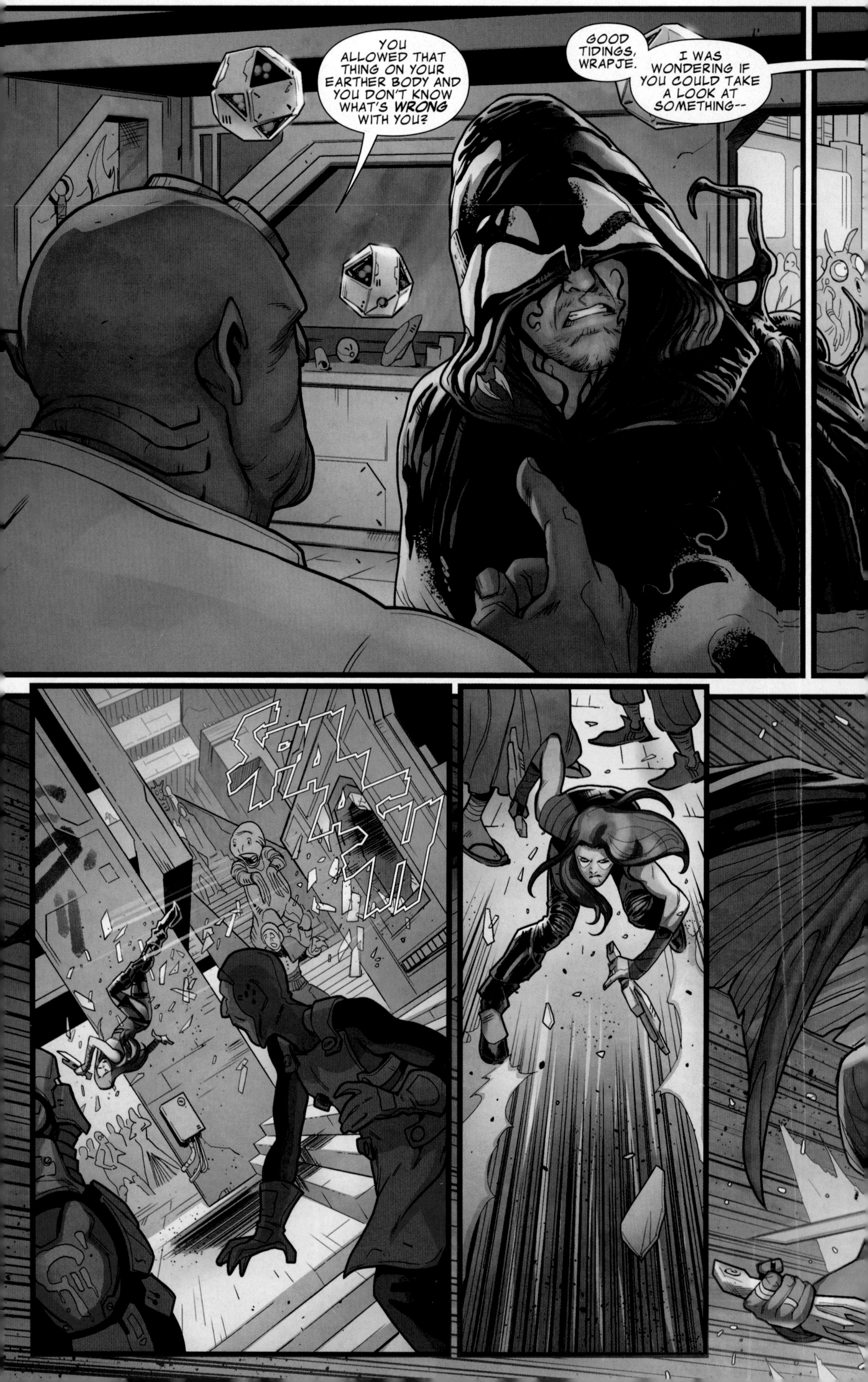
YOU ALLOWED THAT THING ON YOUR EARTHER BODY AND YOU DON'T KNOW WHAT'S WRONG WITH YOU?
GOOD TIDINGS, WRAPJE.
I WAS WONDERING IF YOU COULD TAKE A LOOK AT SOMETHING--

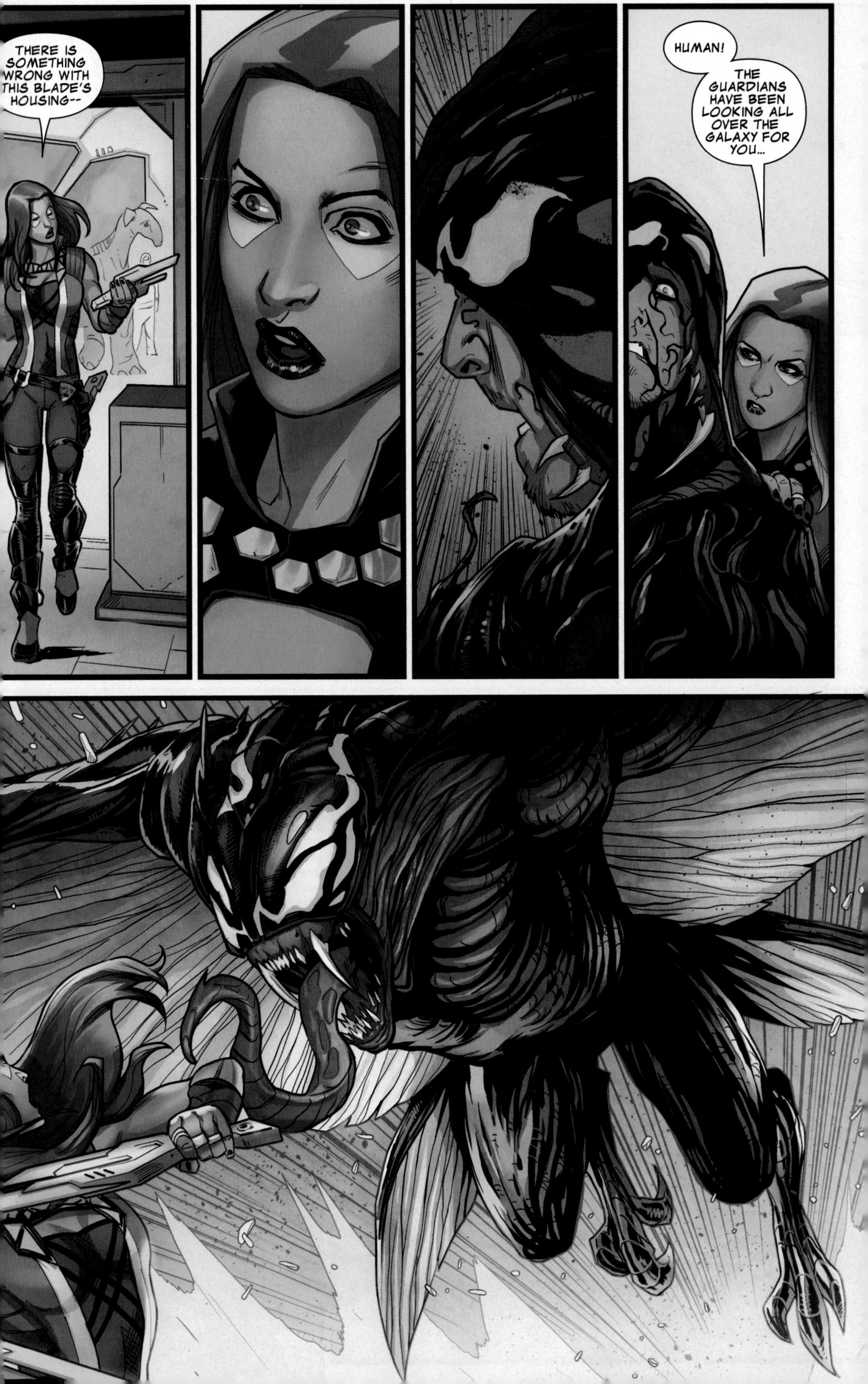
THERE IS SOMETHING WRONG WITH THIS BLADE'S HOUSING--
HUMAN!
THE GUARDIANS HAVE BEEN LOOKING ALL OVER THE GALAXY FOR YOU...

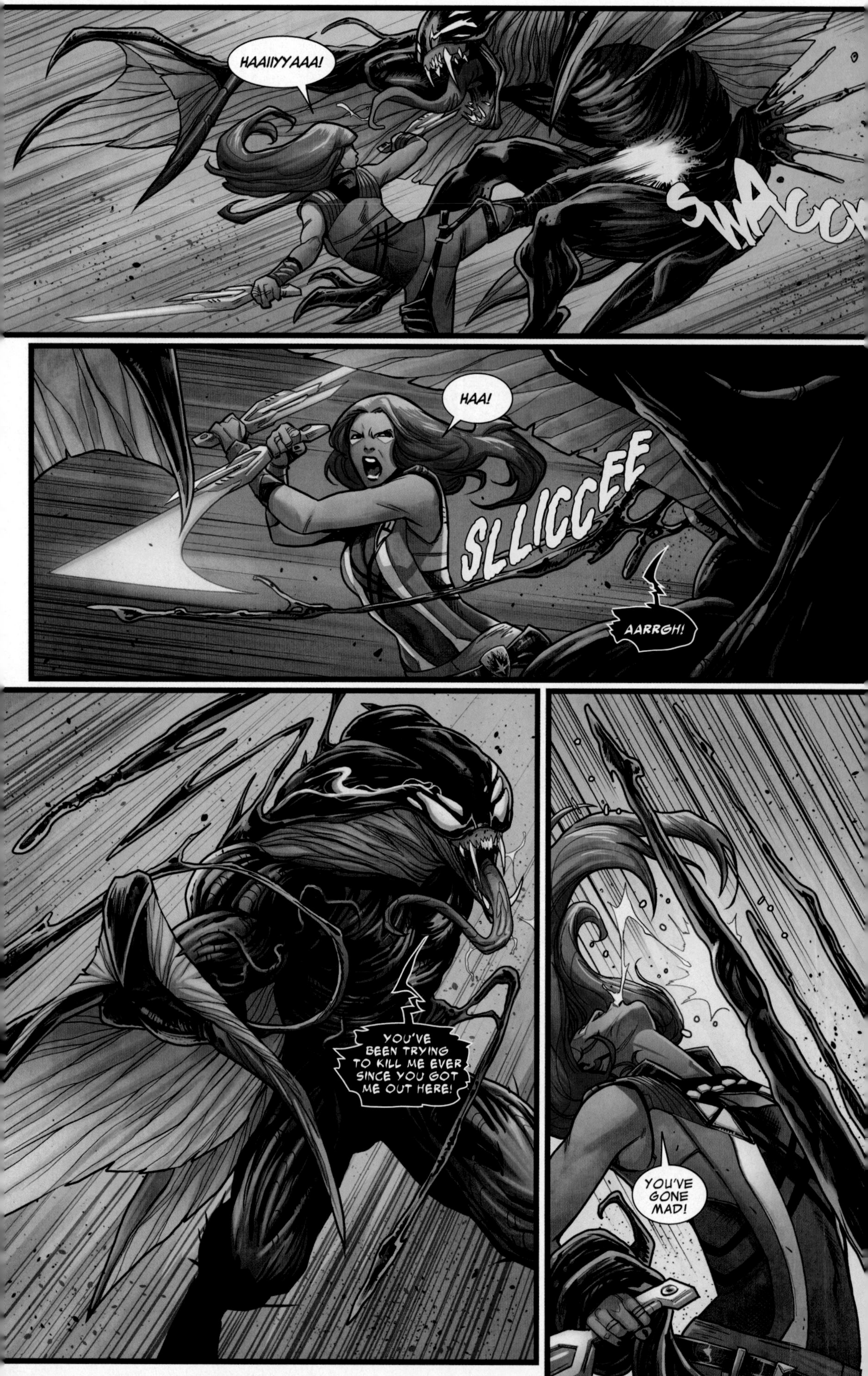
HAAIIYYAAA!
SWACCK
HAA!
SLLICCEE
AARRGH!
YOU'VE BEEN TRYING TO KILL ME EVER SINCE YOU GOT ME OUT HERE!
YOU'VE GONE MAD!

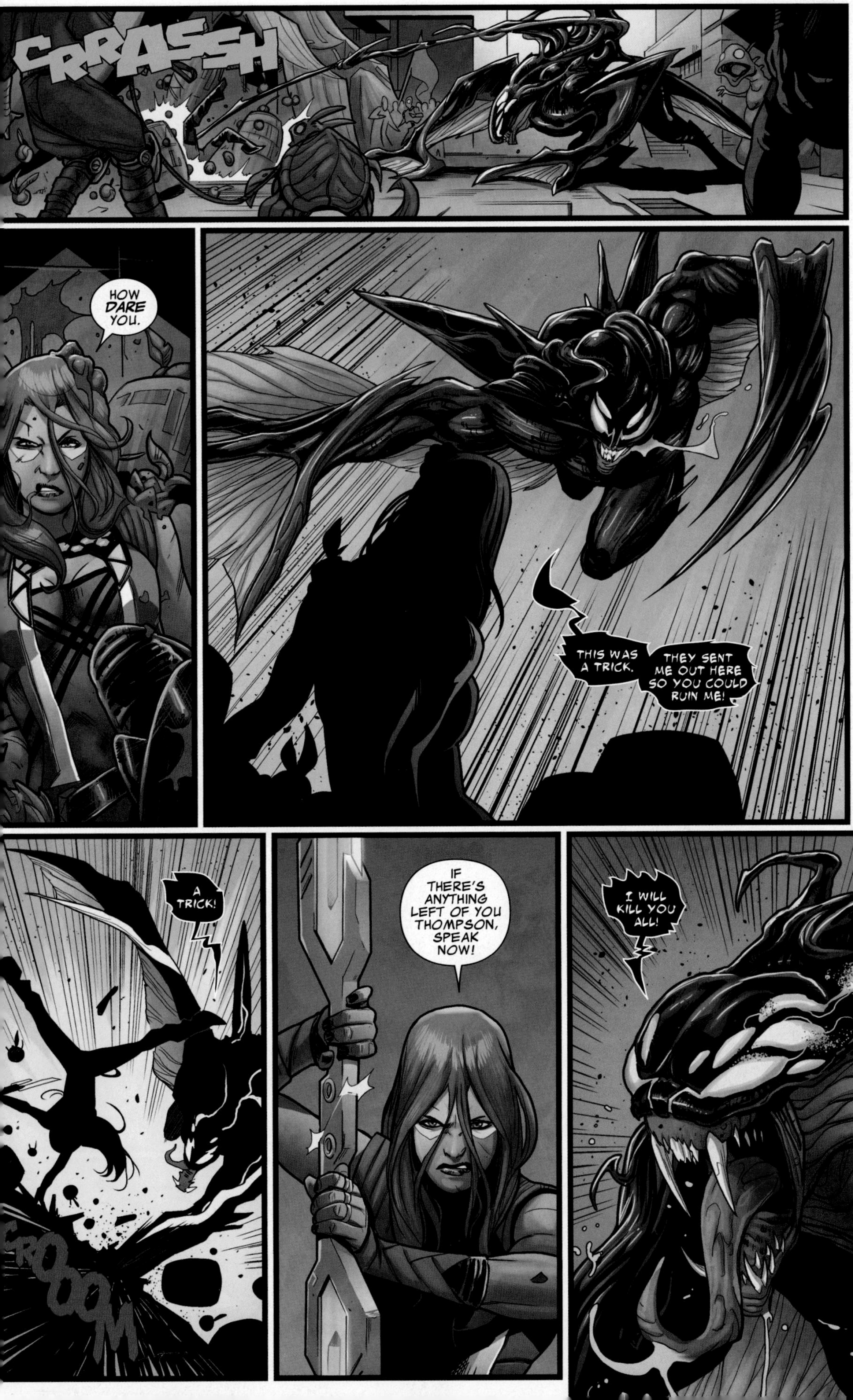
CRRASSH
HOW DARE YOU.
THIS WAS A TRICK.
THEY SENT ME OUT HERE SO YOU COULD RUIN ME!
A TRICK!
FROOOM
IF THERE'S ANYTHING LEFT OF YOU THOMPSON, SPEAK NOW!
I WILL KILL YOU ALL!

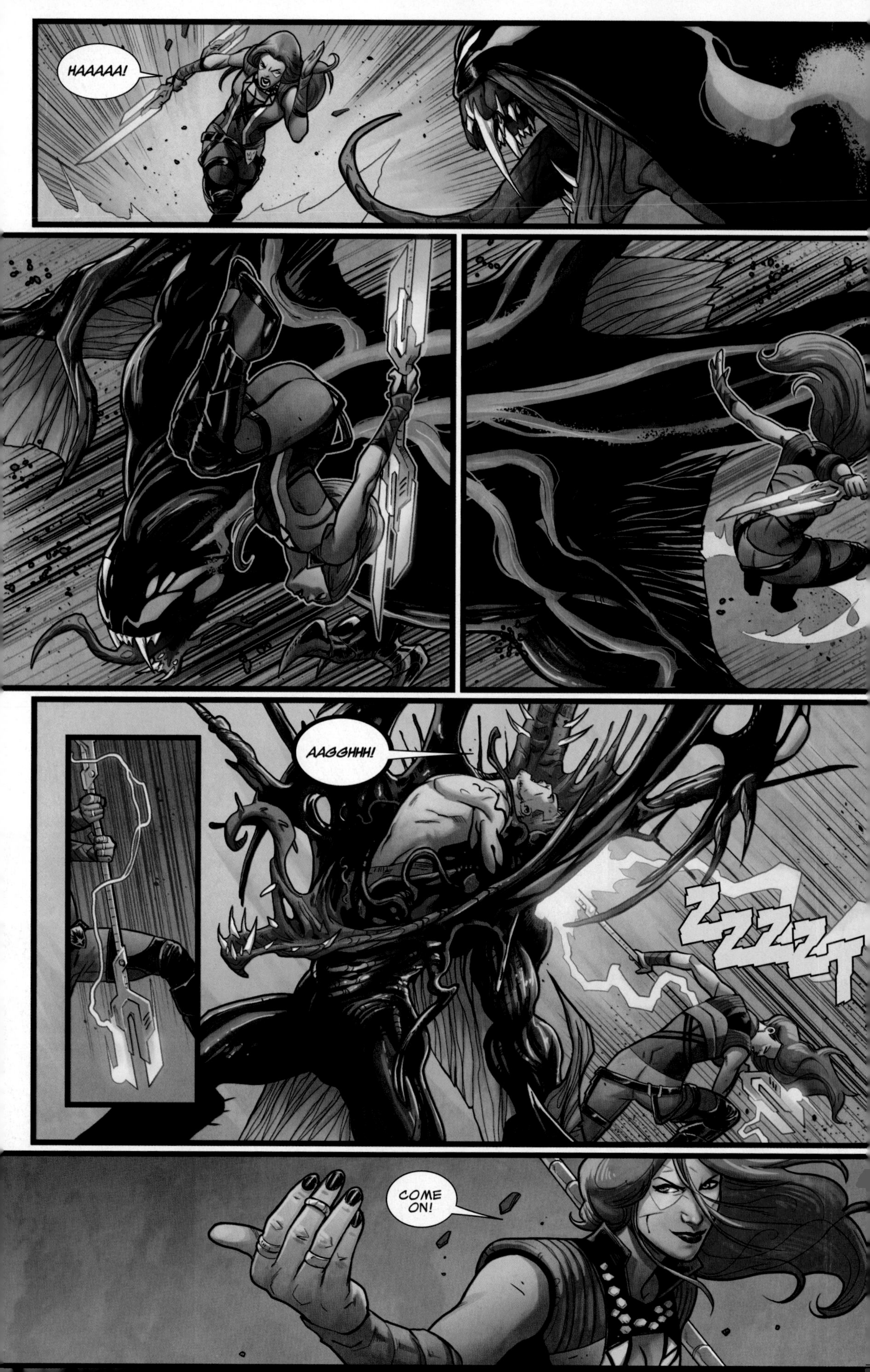
HAAAAA!
AAGGHHH!
ZZZZZT
COME ON!

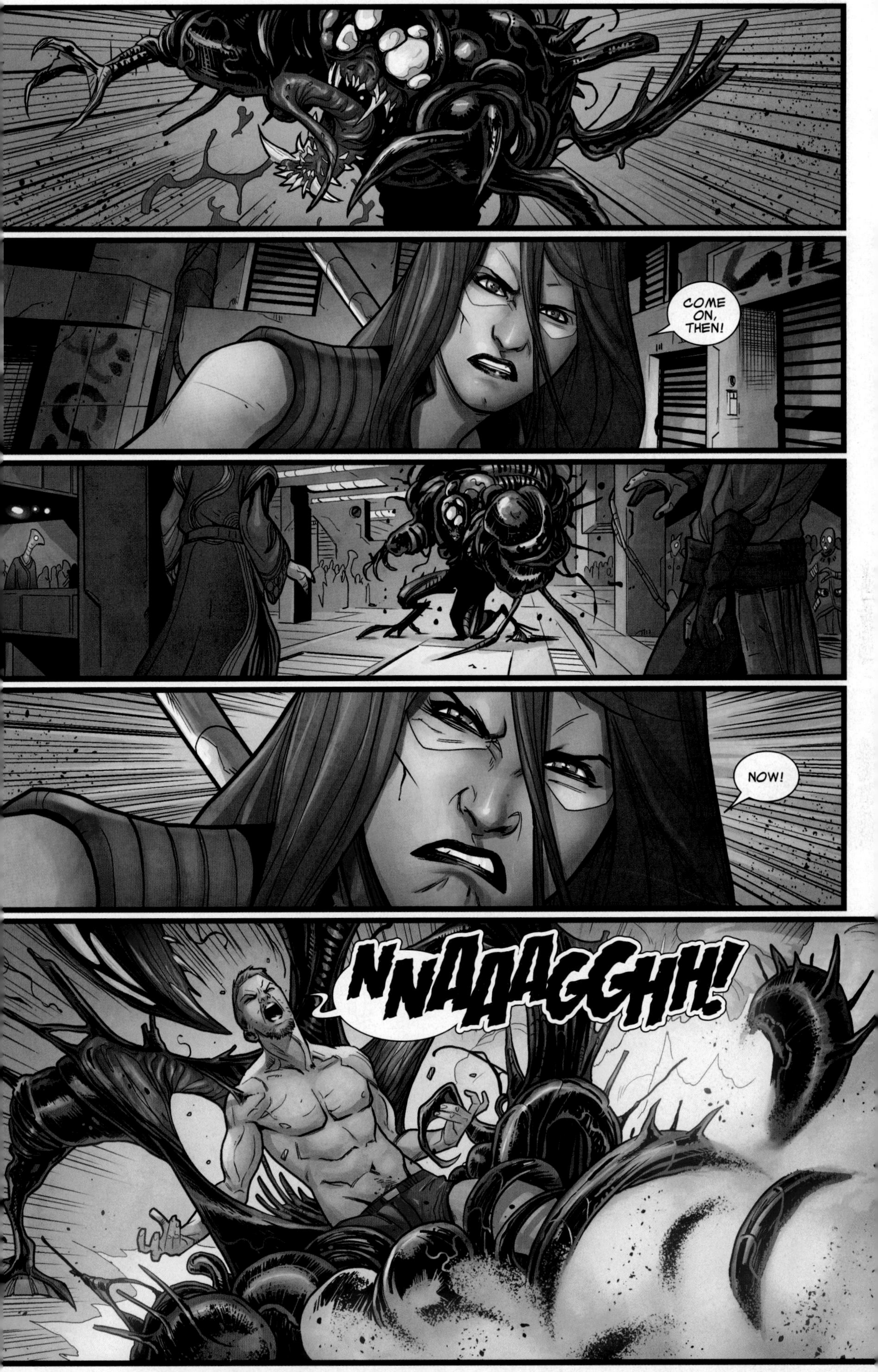
COME ON, THEN!
NOW!
NNAAAGGHH!

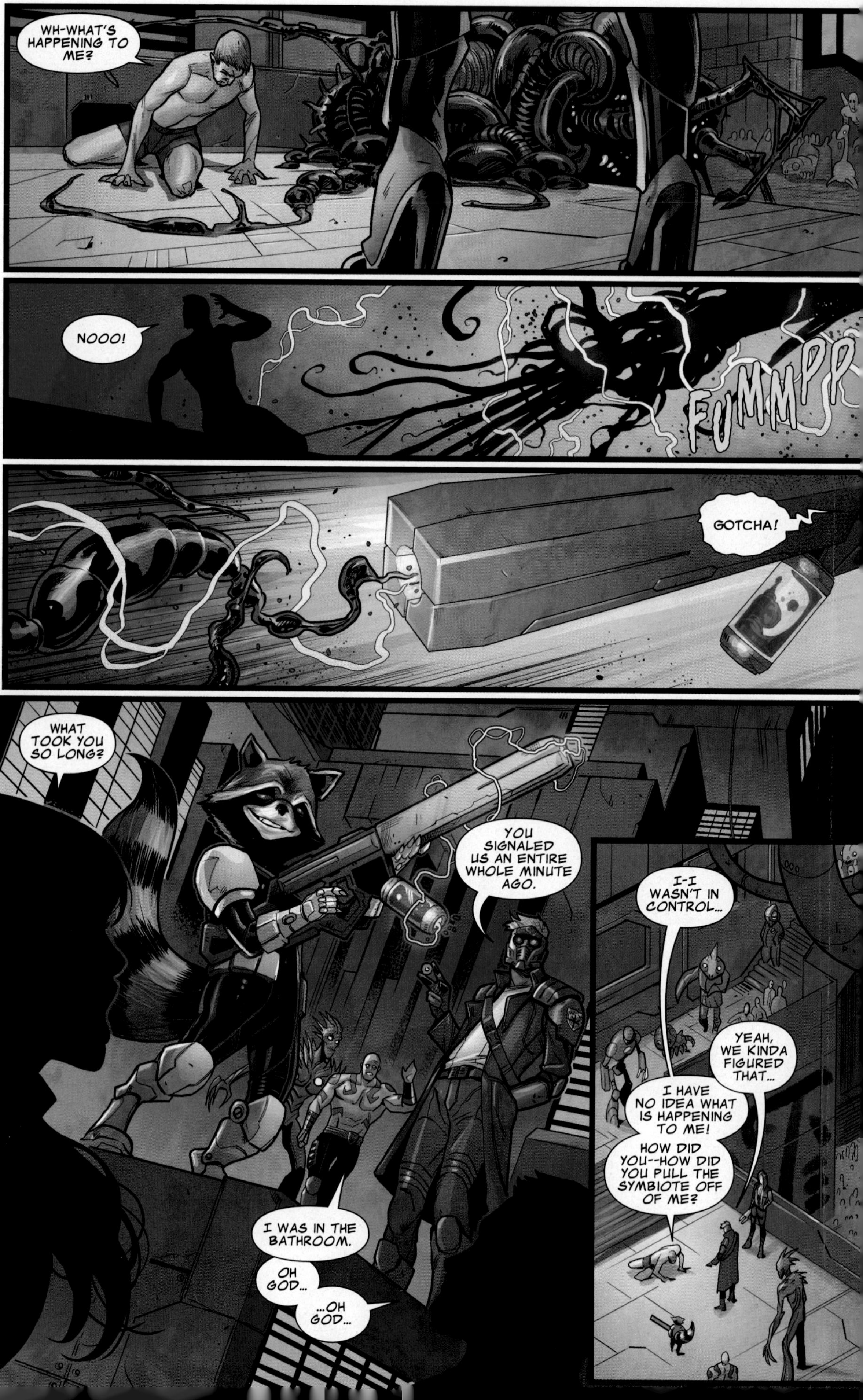
WH-WHAT'S HAPPENING TO ME?
NOOO!
FUMMPP
GOTCHA!
WHAT TOOK YOU SO LONG?
YOU SIGNALED US AN ENTIRE WHOLE MINUTE AGO.
I WAS IN THE BATHROOM.
OH GOD...
...OH GOD...
I-I WASN'T IN CONTROL...
YEAH, WE KINDA FIGURED THAT...
I HAVE NO IDEA WHAT IS HAPPENING TO ME!
HOW DID YOU--HOW DID YOU PULL THE SYMBIOTE OFF OF ME?

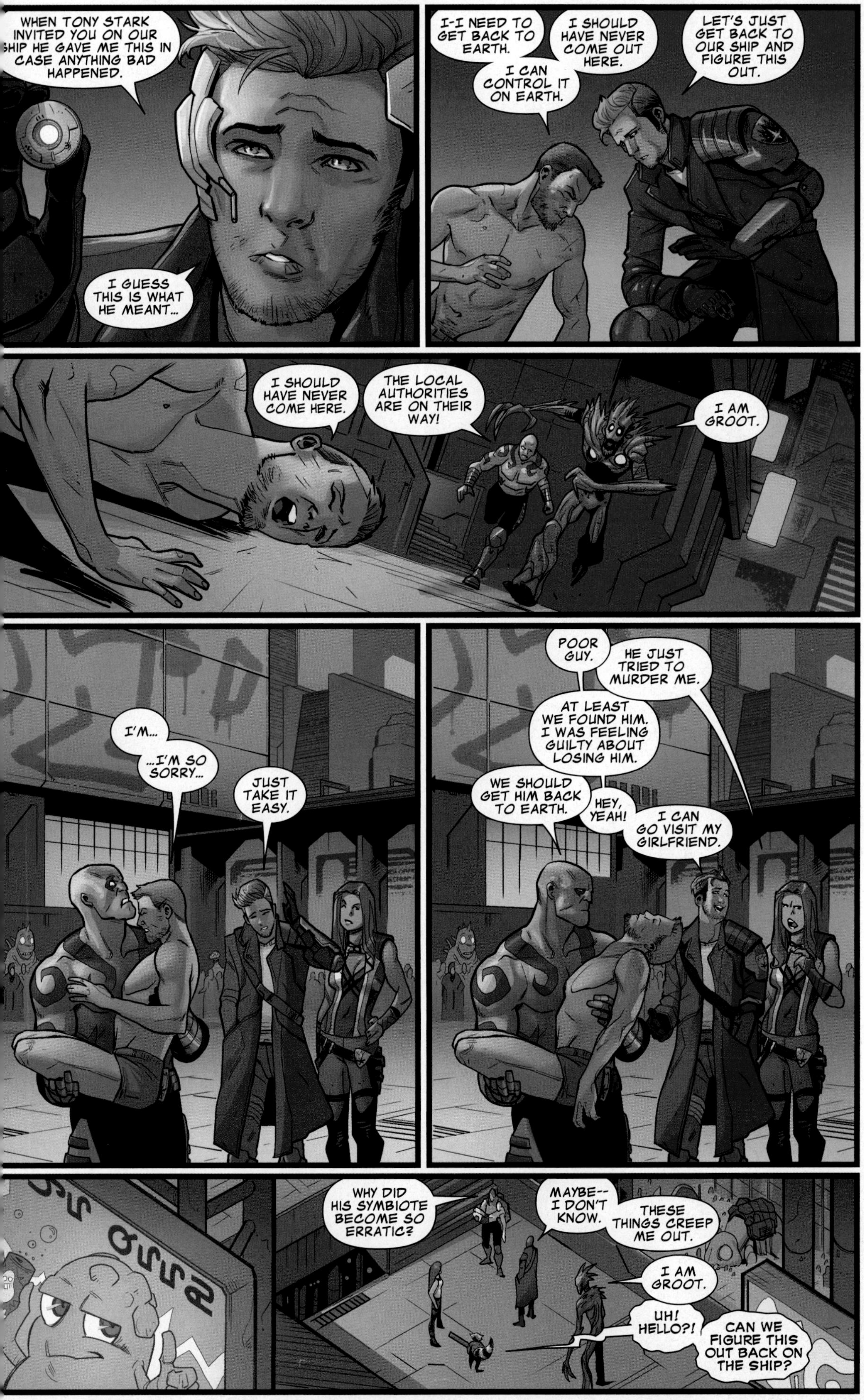
WHEN TONY STARK INVITED YOU ON OUR SHIP HE GAVE ME THIS IN CASE ANYTHING BAD HAPPENED.
I GUESS THIS IS WHAT HE MEANT...
I-I NEED TO GET BACK TO EARTH.
I SHOULD HAVE NEVER COME OUT HERE.
I CAN CONTROL IT ON EARTH.
LET'S JUST GET BACK TO OUR SHIP AND FIGURE THIS OUT.
I SHOULD HAVE NEVER COME HERE.
THE LOCAL AUTHORITIES ARE ON THEIR WAY!
I AM GROOT.
I'M...
...I'M SO SORRY...
JUST TAKE IT EASY.
POOR GUY.
HE JUST TRIED TO MURDER ME.
AT LEAST WE FOUND HIM. I WAS FEELING GUILTY ABOUT LOSING HIM.
WE SHOULD GET HIM BACK TO EARTH.
HEY, YEAH!
I CAN GO VISIT MY GIRLFRIEND.
WHY DID HIS SYMBIOTE BECOME SO ERRATIC?
MAYBE-- I DON'T KNOW.
THESE THINGS CREEP ME OUT.
I AM GROOT.
UH! HELLO?!
CAN WE FIGURE THIS OUT BACK ON THE SHIP?

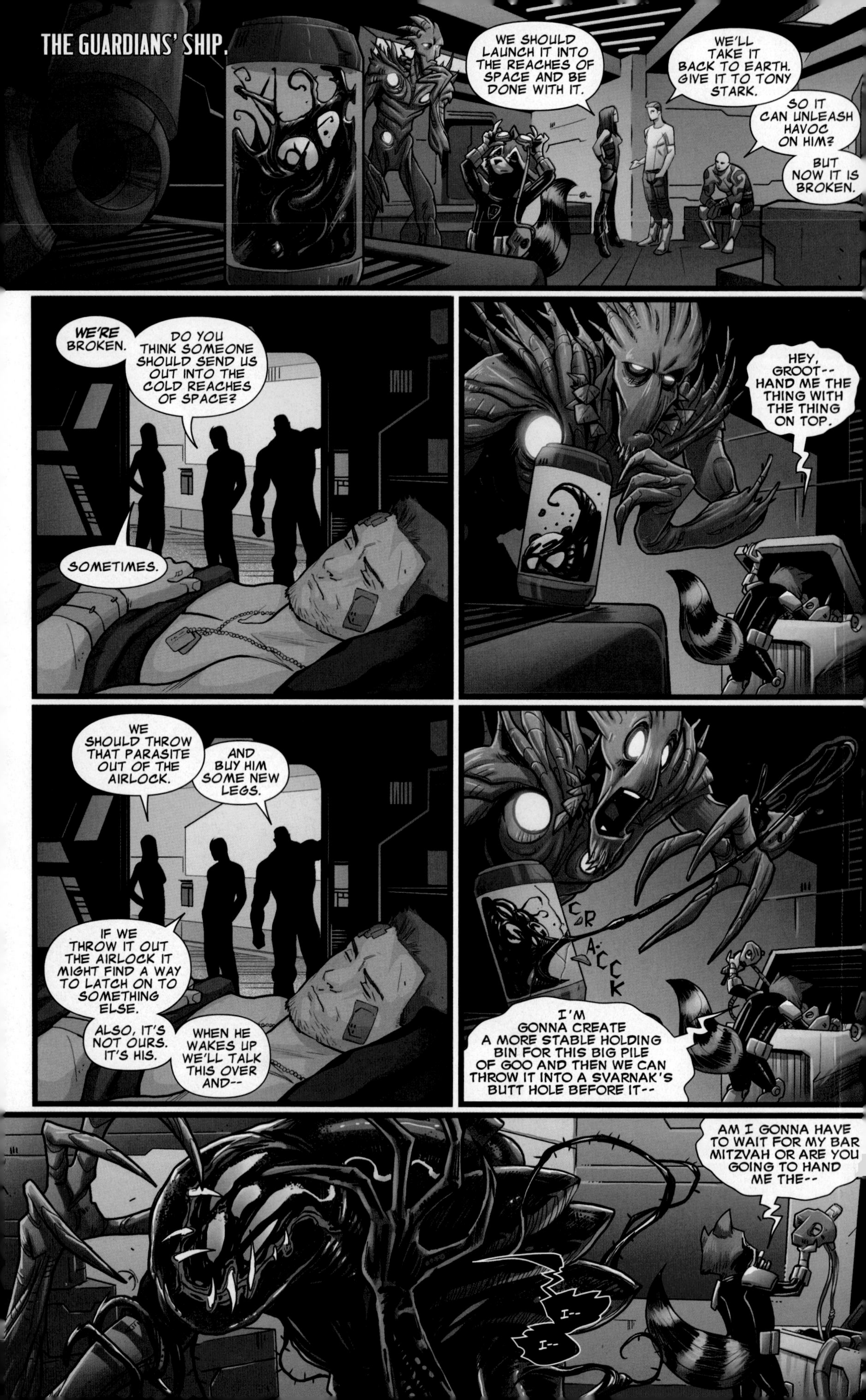
THE GUARDIANS' SHIP.
WE SHOULD LAUNCH IT INTO THE REACHES OF SPACE AND BE DONE WITH IT.
WE'LL TAKE IT BACK TO EARTH. GIVE IT TO TONY STARK.
SO IT CAN UNLEASH HAVOC ON HIM?
BUT NOW IT IS BROKEN.
WE'RE BROKEN.
DO YOU THINK SOMEONE SHOULD SEND US OUT INTO THE COLD REACHES OF SPACE?
SOMETIMES.
HEY, GROOT-- HAND ME THE THING WITH THE THING ON TOP.
WE SHOULD THROW THAT PARASITE OUT OF THE AIRLOCK.
AND BUY HIM SOME NEW LEGS.
IF WE THROW IT OUT THE AIRLOCK IT MIGHT FIND A WAY TO LATCH ON TO SOMETHING ELSE.
ALSO, IT'S NOT OURS. IT'S HIS.
WHEN HE WAKES UP WE'LL TALK THIS OVER AND--
CRACCK
I'M GONNA CREATE A MORE STABLE HOLDING BIN FOR THIS BIG PILE OF GOO AND THEN WE CAN THROW IT INTO A SVARNAK'S BUTT HOLE BEFORE IT--
AM I GONNA HAVE TO WAIT FOR MY BAR MITZVAH OR ARE YOU GOING TO HAND ME THE--
I--
I--

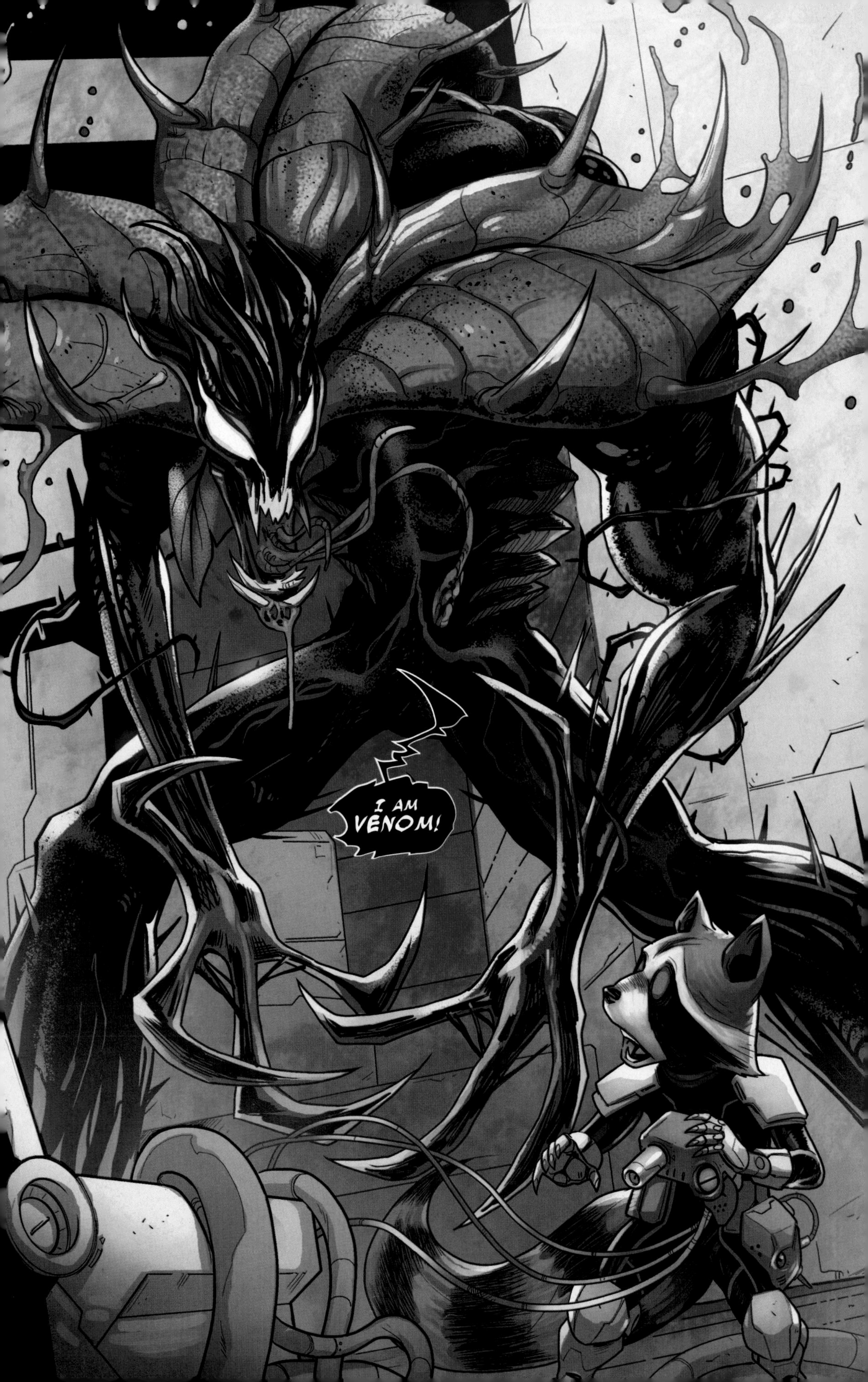
I AM VENOM!

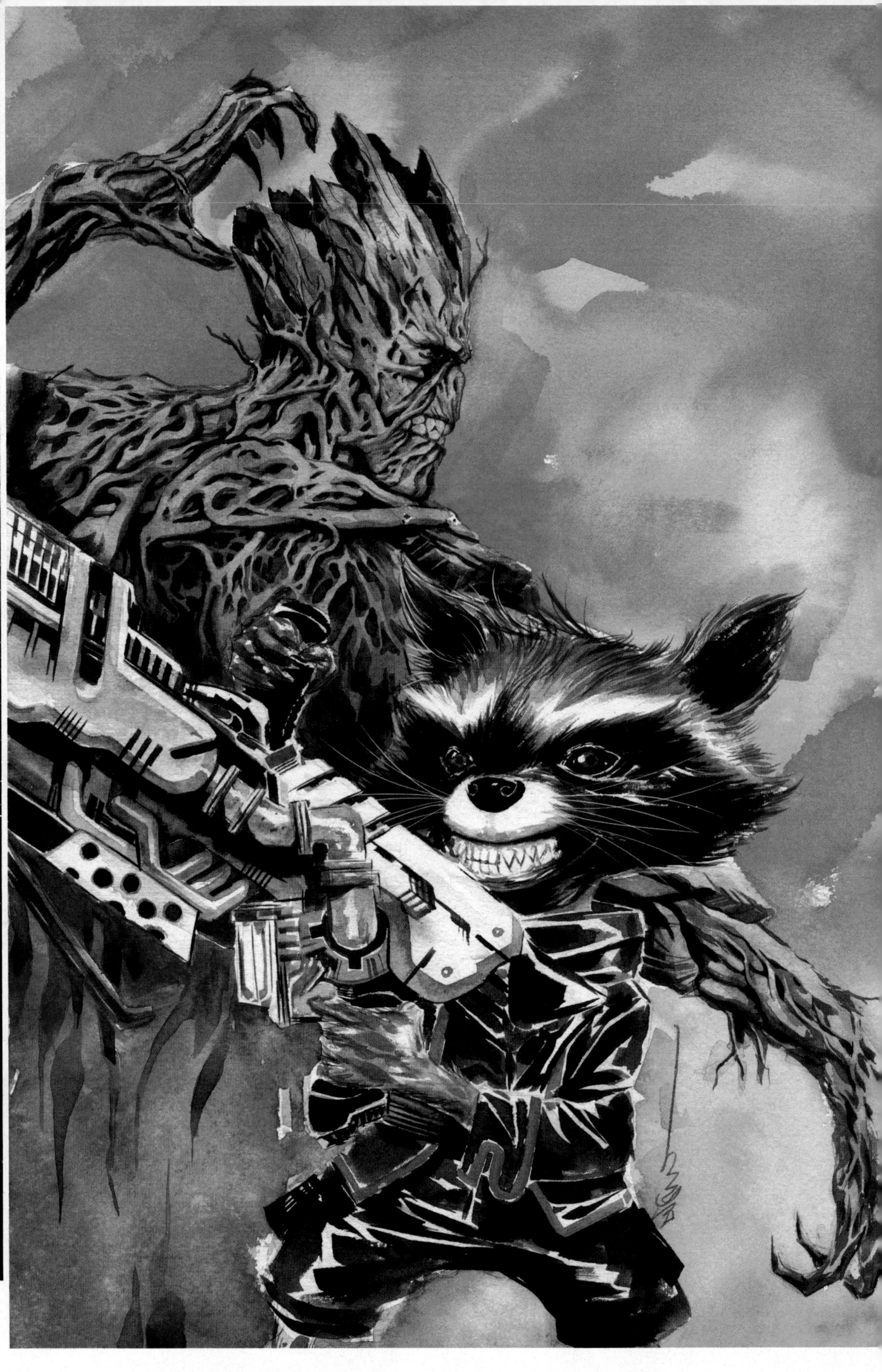

#21 ROCKET RACCOON & GROOT VARIANT BY DUSTIN NGUYEN

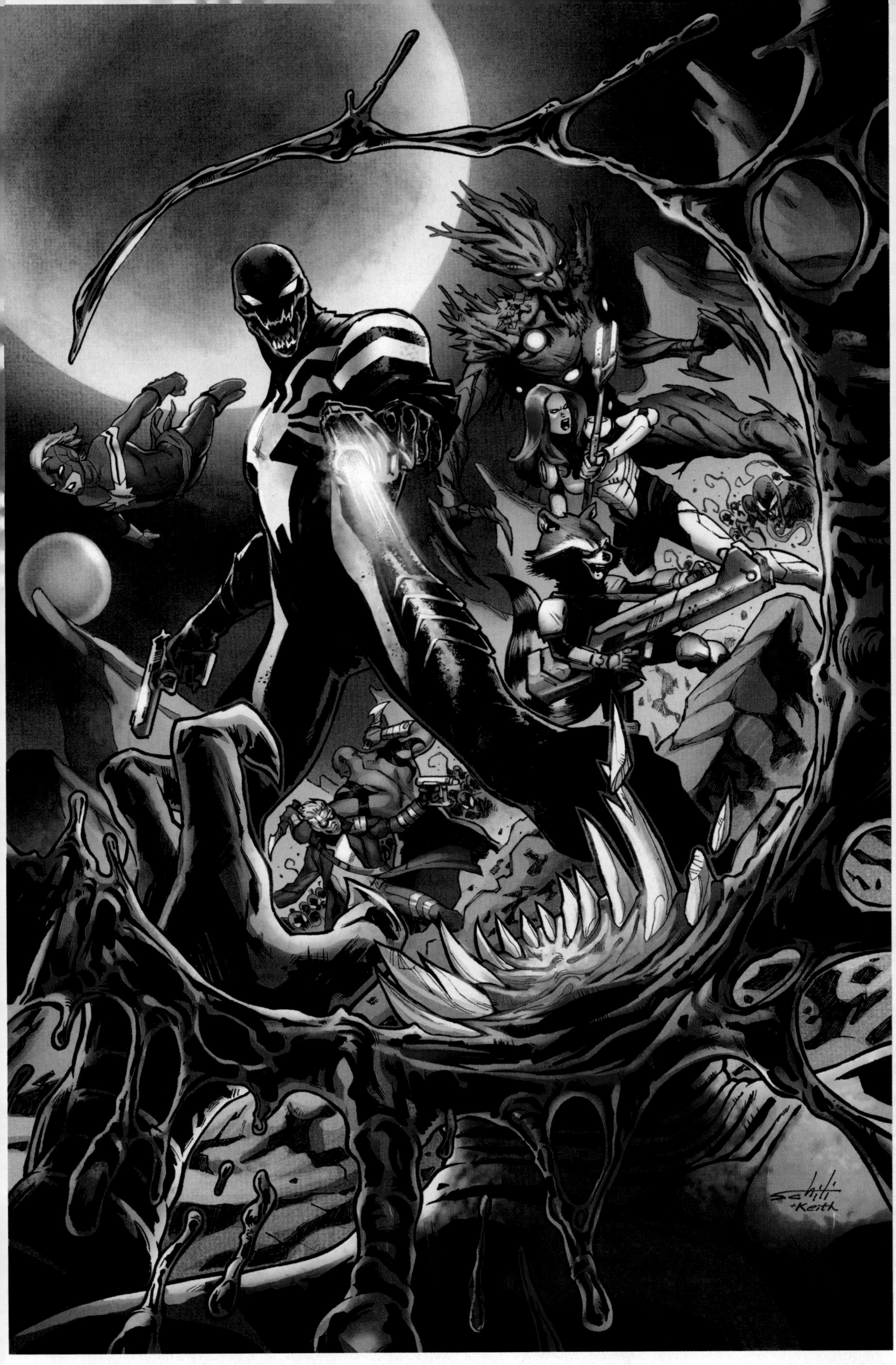

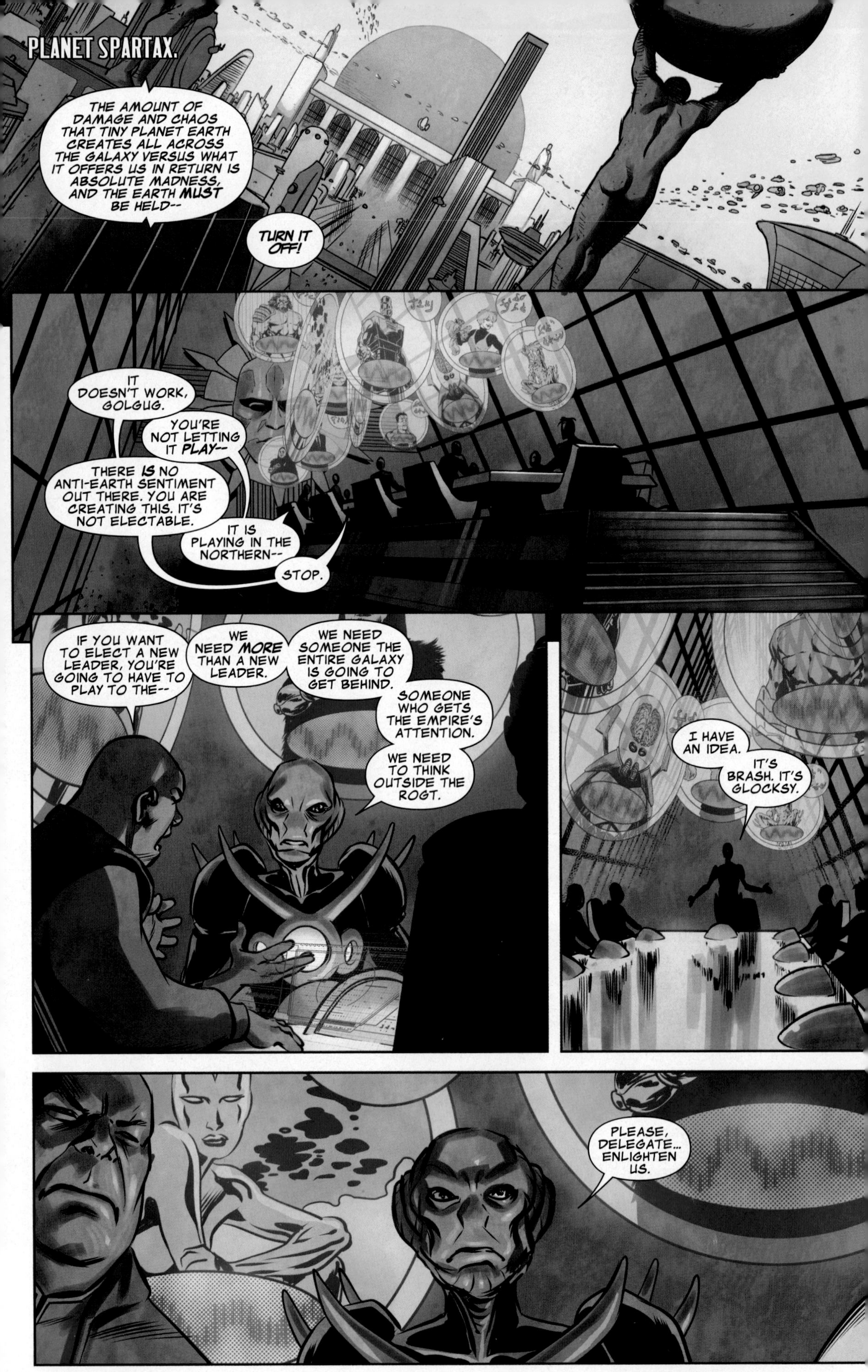
PLANET SPARTAX.
THE AMOUNT OF DAMAGE AND CHAOS THAT TINY PLANET EARTH CREATES ALL ACROSS THE GALAXY VERSUS WHAT IT OFFERS US IN RETURN IS ABSOLUTE MADNESS, AND THE EARTH MUST BE HELD--
TURN IT OFF!
IT DOESN'T WORK, GOLGUG.
YOU'RE NOT LETTING IT PLAY--
THERE IS NO ANTI-EARTH SENTIMENT OUT THERE. YOU ARE CREATING THIS. IT'S NOT ELECTABLE.
IT IS PLAYING IN THE NORTHERN--
STOP.
IF YOU WANT TO ELECT A NEW LEADER, YOU'RE GOING TO HAVE TO PLAY TO THE--
WE NEED MORE THAN A NEW LEADER.
WE NEED SOMEONE THE ENTIRE GALAXY IS GOING TO GET BEHIND.
SOMEONE WHO GETS THE EMPIRE'S ATTENTION.
WE NEED TO THINK OUTSIDE THE ROGT.
I HAVE AN IDEA.
IT'S BRASH. IT'S GLOCKSY.
PLEASE, DELEGATE... ENLIGHTEN US.

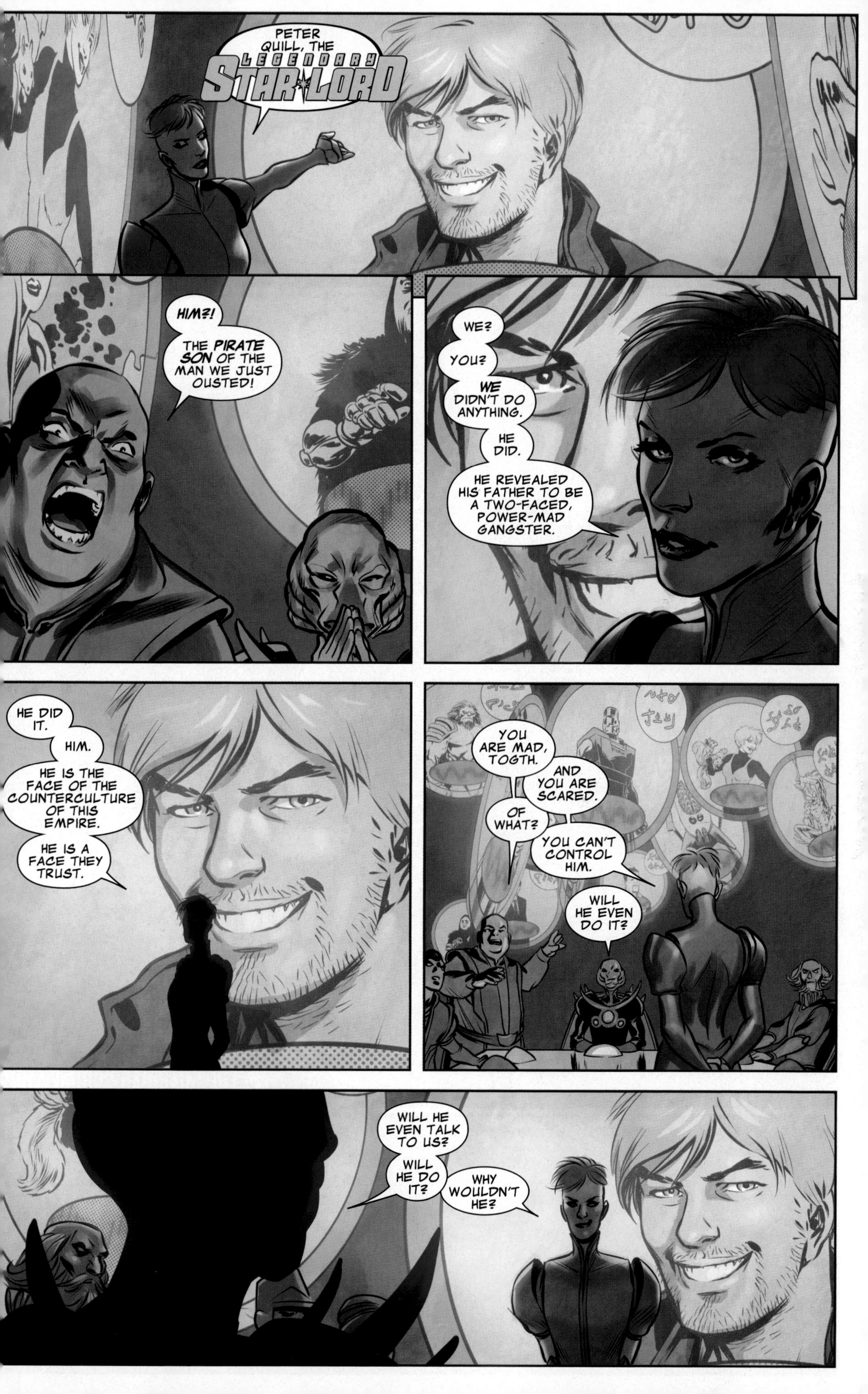
PETER QUILL, THE LEGENDARY STAR-LORD
HIM?! THE PIRATE SON OF THE MAN WE JUST OUSTED!
WE?
YOU?
WE DIDN'T DO ANYTHING.
HE DID.
HE REVEALED HIS FATHER TO BE A TWO-FACED, POWER-MAD GANGSTER.
HE DID IT.
HIM.
HE IS THE FACE OF THE COUNTERCULTURE OF THIS EMPIRE.
HE IS A FACE THEY TRUST.
YOU ARE MAD, TOGTH.
AND YOU ARE SCARED.
OF WHAT?
YOU CAN'T CONTROL HIM.
WILL HE EVEN DO IT?
WILL HE EVEN TALK TO US?
WILL HE DO IT?
WHY WOULDN'T HE?

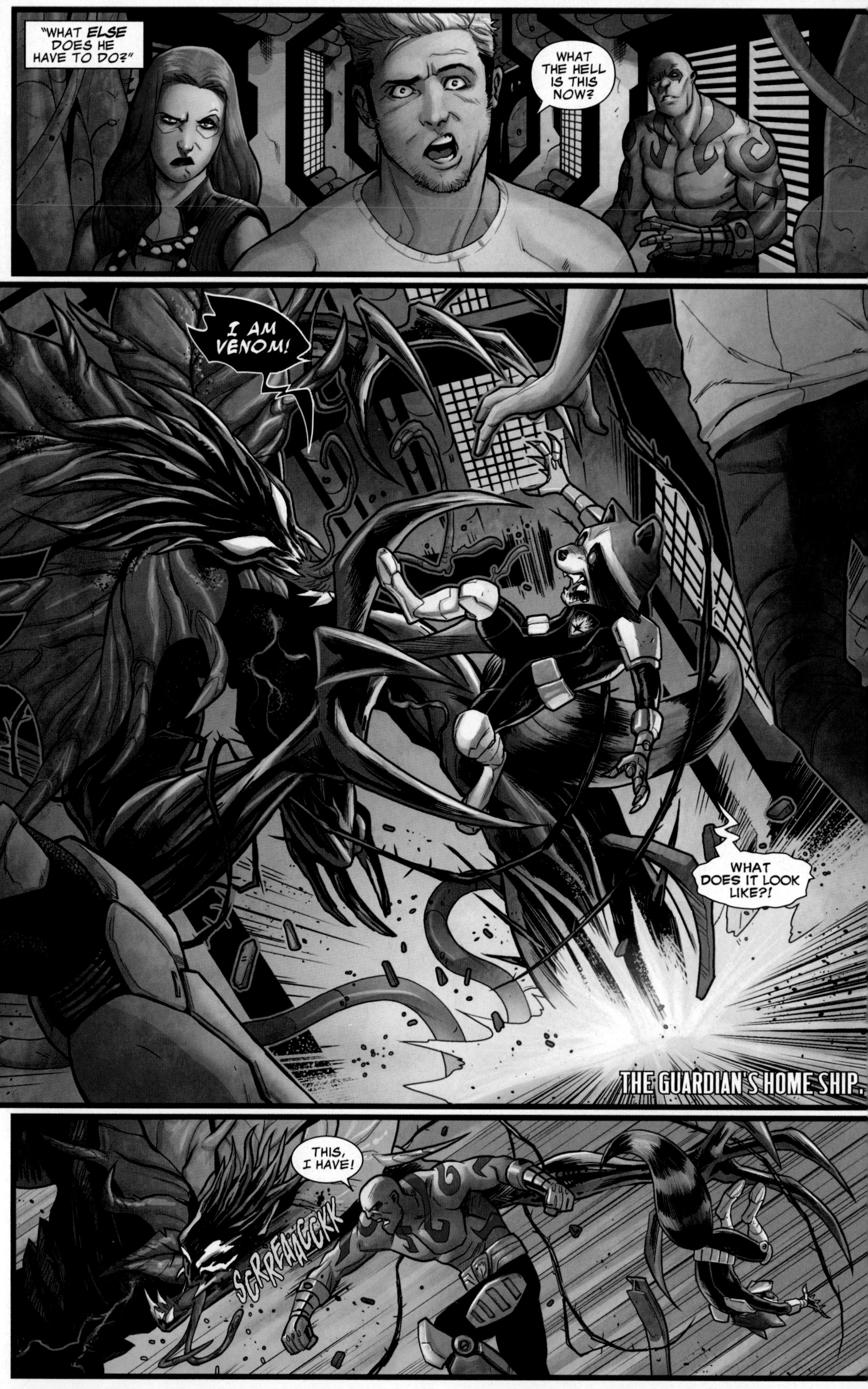
"WHAT ELSE DOES HE HAVE TO DO?"
WHAT THE HELL IS THIS NOW?
I AM VENOM!
WHAT DOES IT LOOK LIKE?!
THE GUARDIAN'S HOME SHIP.
THIS, I HAVE!
SCRREAAGCKK

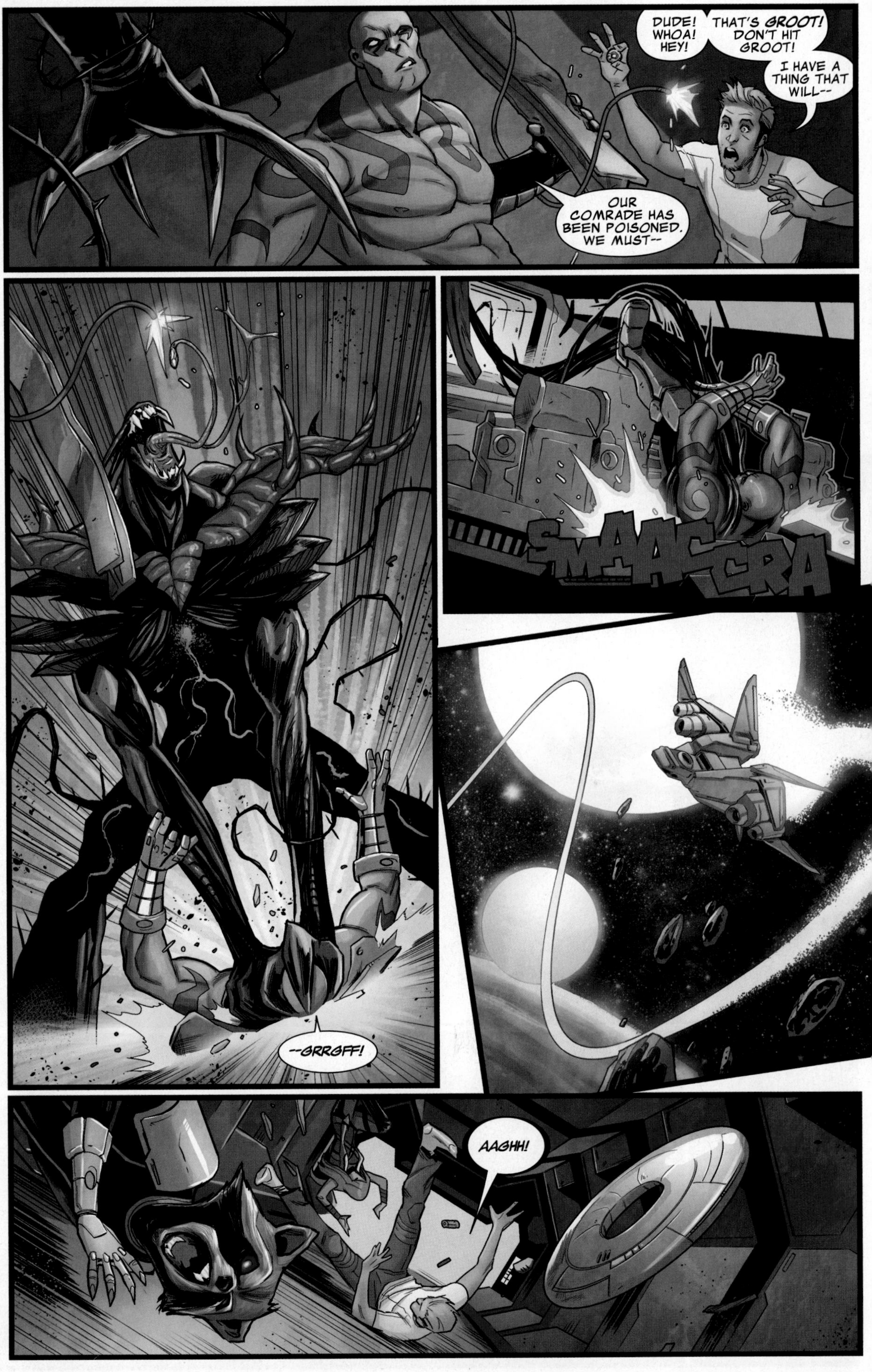
DUDE! WHOA! HEY!
THAT'S GROOT! DON'T HIT GROOT!
I HAVE A THING THAT WILL--
OUR COMRADE HAS BEEN POISONED. WE MUST--
--GRRGFF!
SMAAC
CRA
AAGHH!

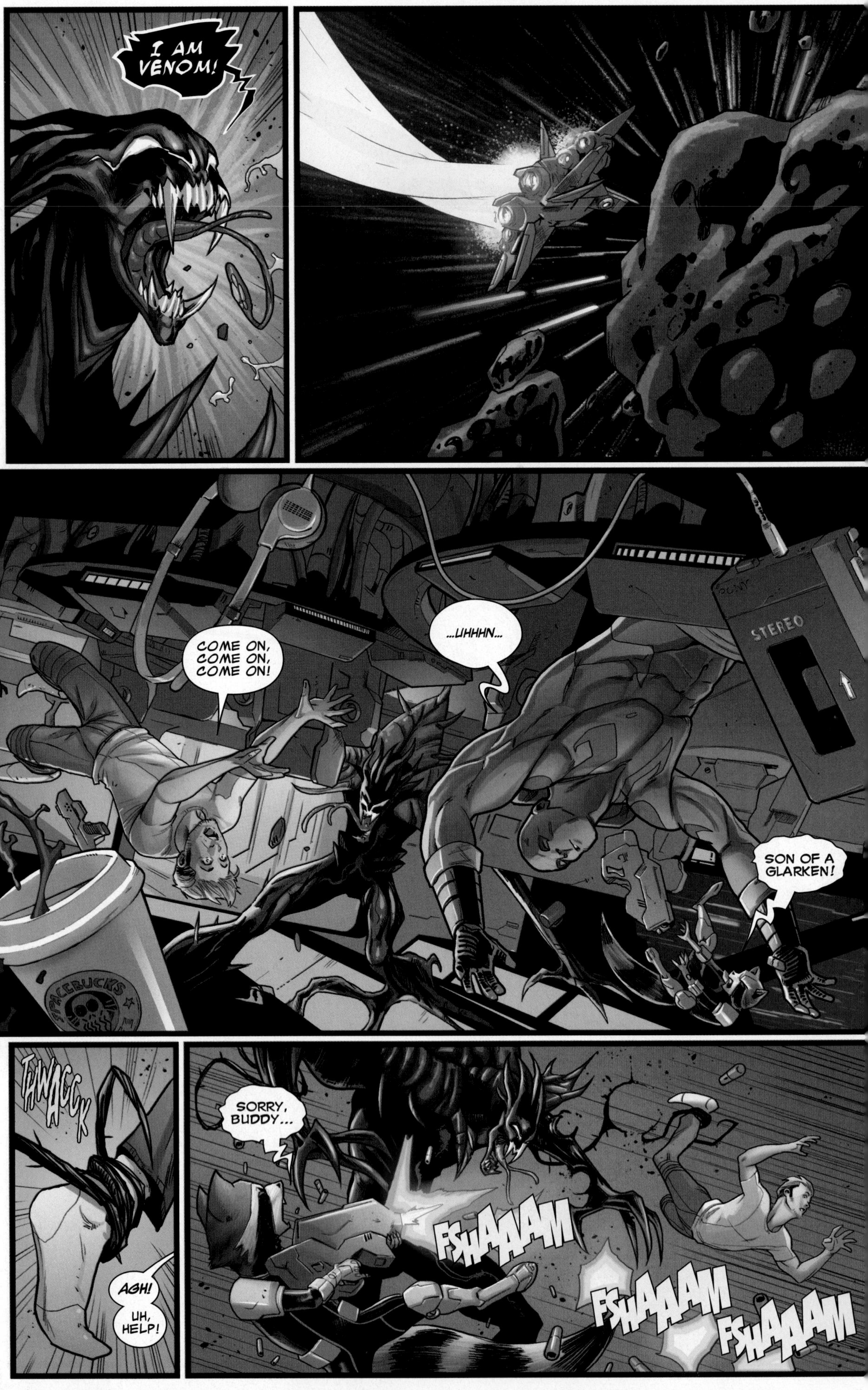

I AM VENOM!
COME ON, COME ON, COME ON!
...UHHHN...
STEREO
SON OF A GLARKEN!
SPACEBUCKS
THWACCK
AGH!
UH, HELP!
SORRY, BUDDY...
FSHAAAM
FSHAAAM
FSHAAAM

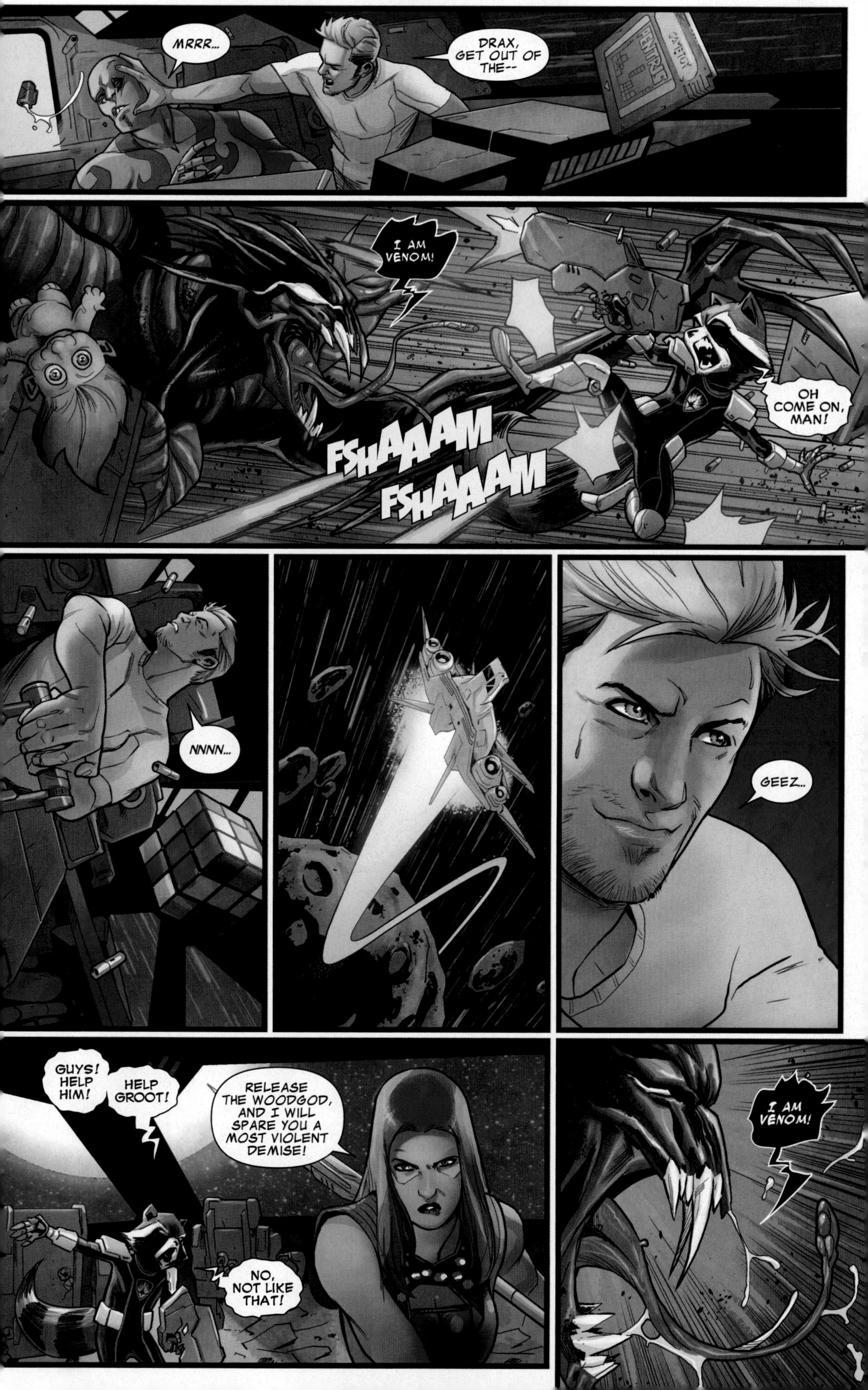
MRRR...
DRAX, GET OUT OF THE--
GAMETOY
I AM VENOM!
OH COME ON, MAN!
FSHAAAM
FSHAAAM
NNNN...
GEEZ...
GUYS! HELP HIM!
HELP GROOT!
RELEASE THE WOODGOD, AND I WILL SPARE YOU A MOST VIOLENT DEMISE!
NO, NOT LIKE THAT!
I AM VENOM!

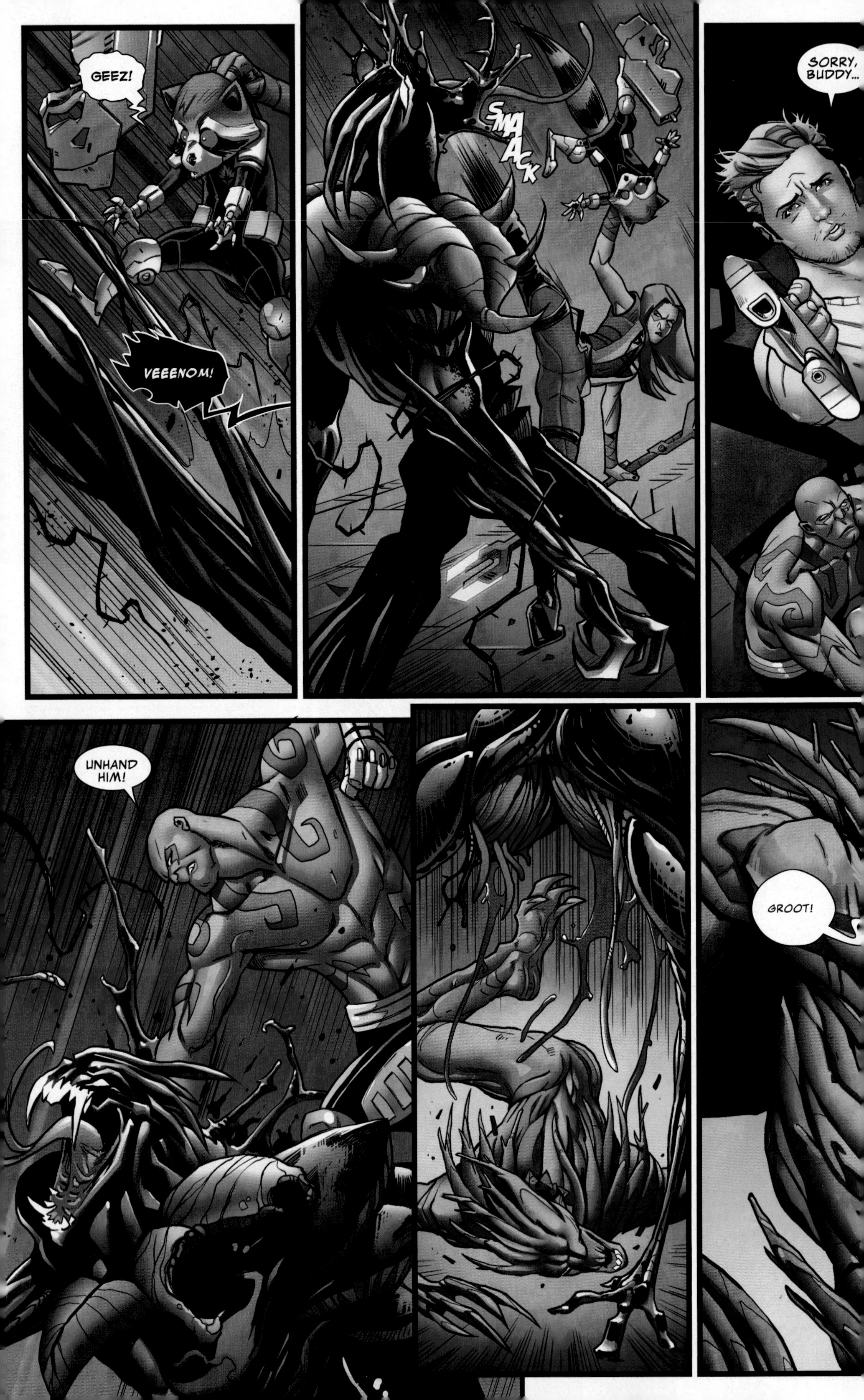
GEEZ!
SMAACK
VEEENOM!
SORRY, BUDDY...
UNHAND HIM!
GROOT!

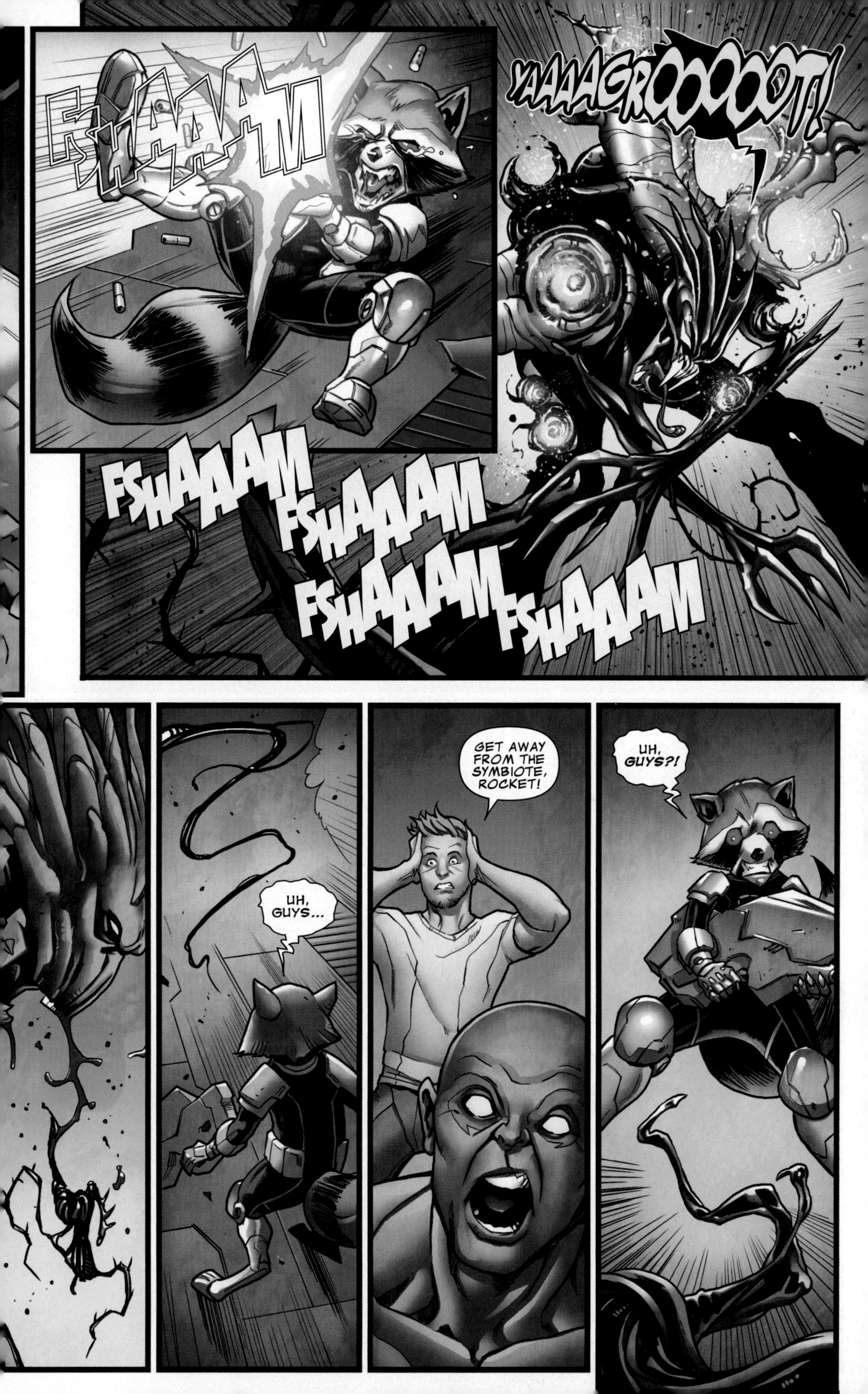
FSHAAAM
YAAAGROOOOOOT!
FSHAAAM
FSHAAAM
FSHAAAM
FSHAAAM
UH, GUYS...
GET AWAY FROM THE SYMBIOTE, ROCKET!
UH, GUYS?!

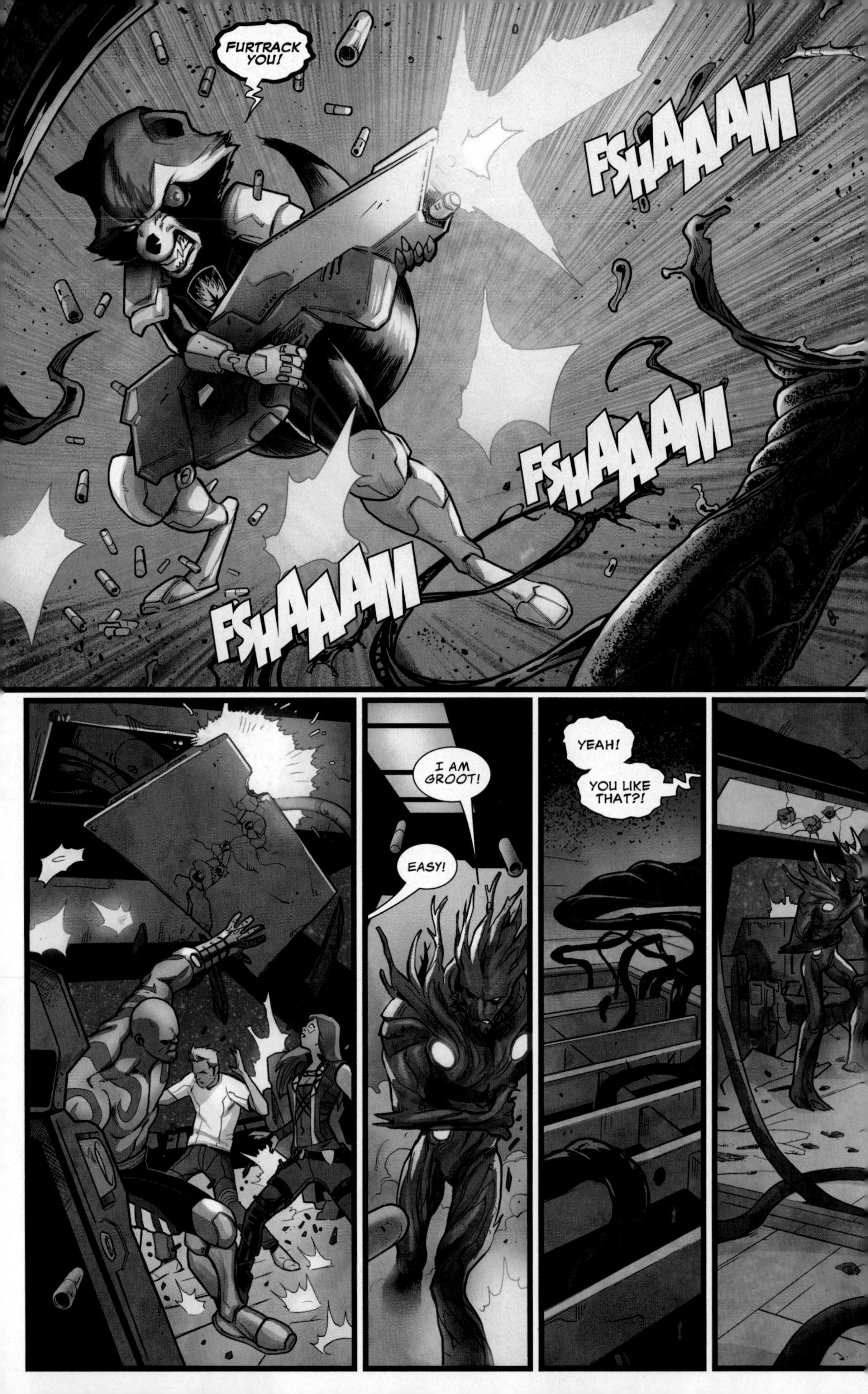
FURTRACK YOU!
FSHAAAAM
FSHAAAAM
FSHAAAAM
I AM GROOT!
EASY!
YEAH!
YOU LIKE THAT?!

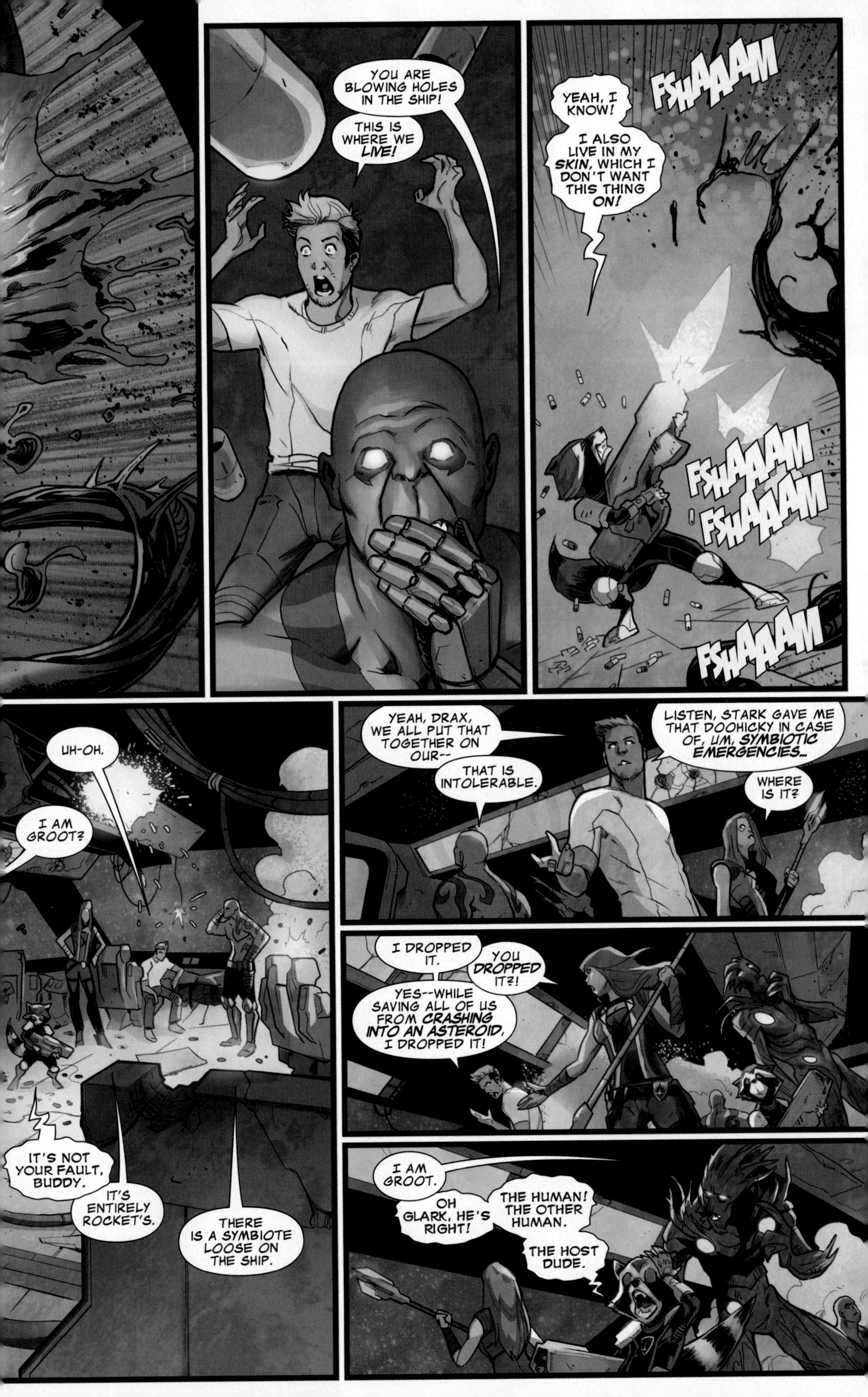
YOU ARE BLOWING HOLES IN THE SHIP!
THIS IS WHERE WE LIVE!
YEAH, I KNOW!
I ALSO LIVE IN MY SKIN, WHICH I DON'T WANT THIS THING ON!
FSHAAAM
FSHAAAM
FSHAAAM
FSHAAAM
UH-OH.
I AM GROOT?
IT'S NOT YOUR FAULT, BUDDY.
IT'S ENTIRELY ROCKET'S.
THERE IS A SYMBIOTE LOOSE ON THE SHIP.
YEAH, DRAX, WE ALL PUT THAT TOGETHER ON OUR--
THAT IS INTOLERABLE.
LISTEN, STARK GAVE ME THAT DOOHICKY IN CASE OF, UM, SYMBIOTIC EMERGENCIES...
WHERE IS IT?
I DROPPED IT.
YOU DROPPED IT?!
YES--WHILE SAVING ALL OF US FROM CRASHING INTO AN ASTEROID, I DROPPED IT!
I AM GROOT.
OH GLARK, HE'S RIGHT!
THE HUMAN! THE OTHER HUMAN.
THE HOST DUDE.

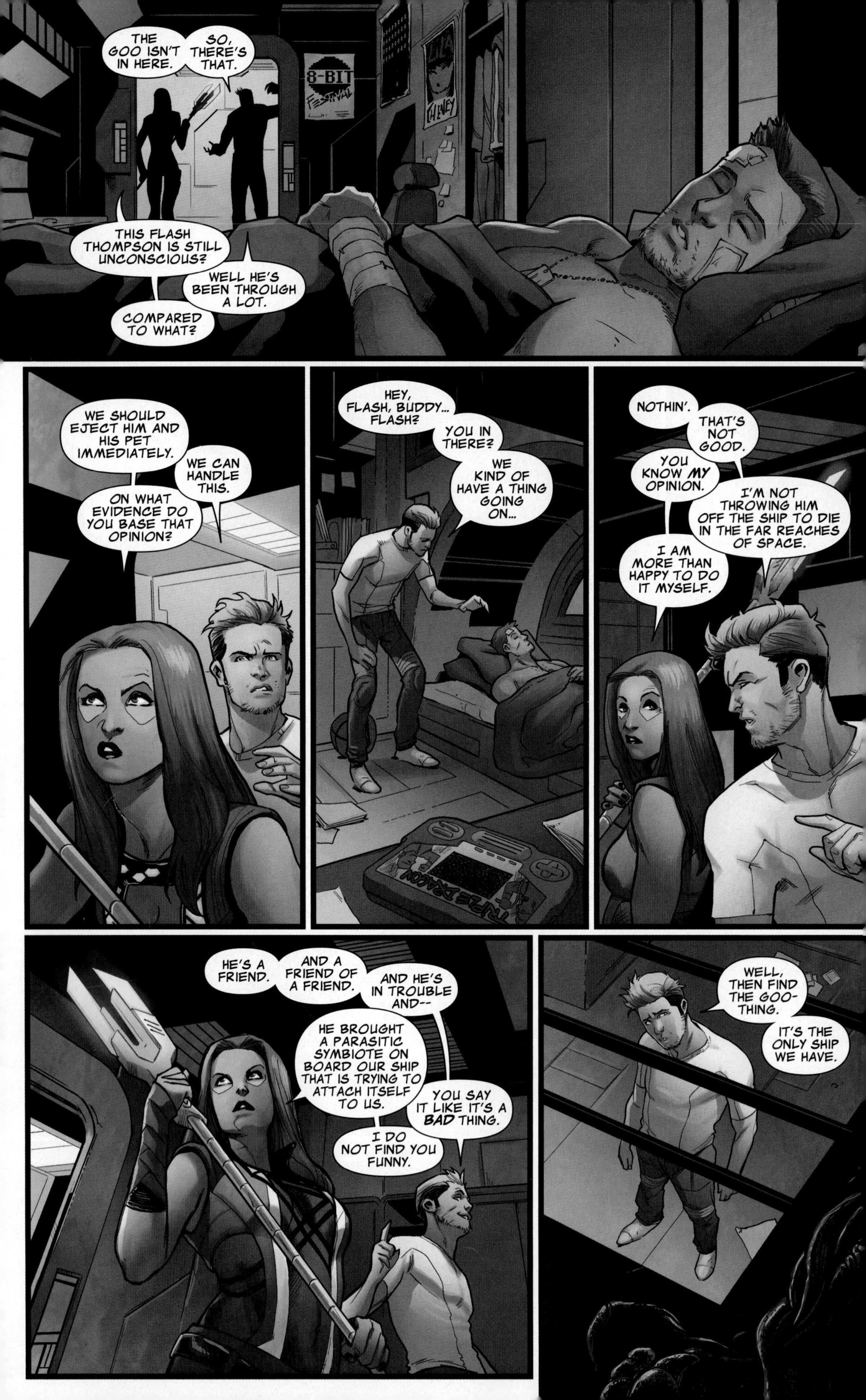

8-BIT FESTIVAL
CHENEY
THE GOO ISN'T IN HERE.
SO, THERE'S THAT.
THIS FLASH THOMPSON IS STILL UNCONSCIOUS?
WELL HE'S BEEN THROUGH A LOT.
COMPARED TO WHAT?
WE SHOULD EJECT HIM AND HIS PET IMMEDIATELY.
WE CAN HANDLE THIS.
ON WHAT EVIDENCE DO YOU BASE THAT OPINION?
HEY, FLASH, BUDDY... FLASH?
YOU IN THERE?
WE KIND OF HAVE A THING GOING ON...
TRIPLE DRAGON
NOTHIN'.
THAT'S NOT GOOD.
YOU KNOW *MY* OPINION.
I'M NOT THROWING HIM OFF THE SHIP TO DIE IN THE FAR REACHES OF SPACE.
I AM MORE THAN HAPPY TO DO IT MYSELF.
HE'S A FRIEND.
AND A FRIEND OF A FRIEND.
AND HE'S IN TROUBLE AND--
HE BROUGHT A PARASITIC SYMBIOTE ON BOARD OUR SHIP THAT IS TRYING TO ATTACH ITSELF TO US.
YOU SAY IT LIKE IT'S A *BAD* THING.
I DO NOT FIND YOU FUNNY.
WELL, THEN FIND THE GOO-THING.
IT'S THE ONLY SHIP WE HAVE.

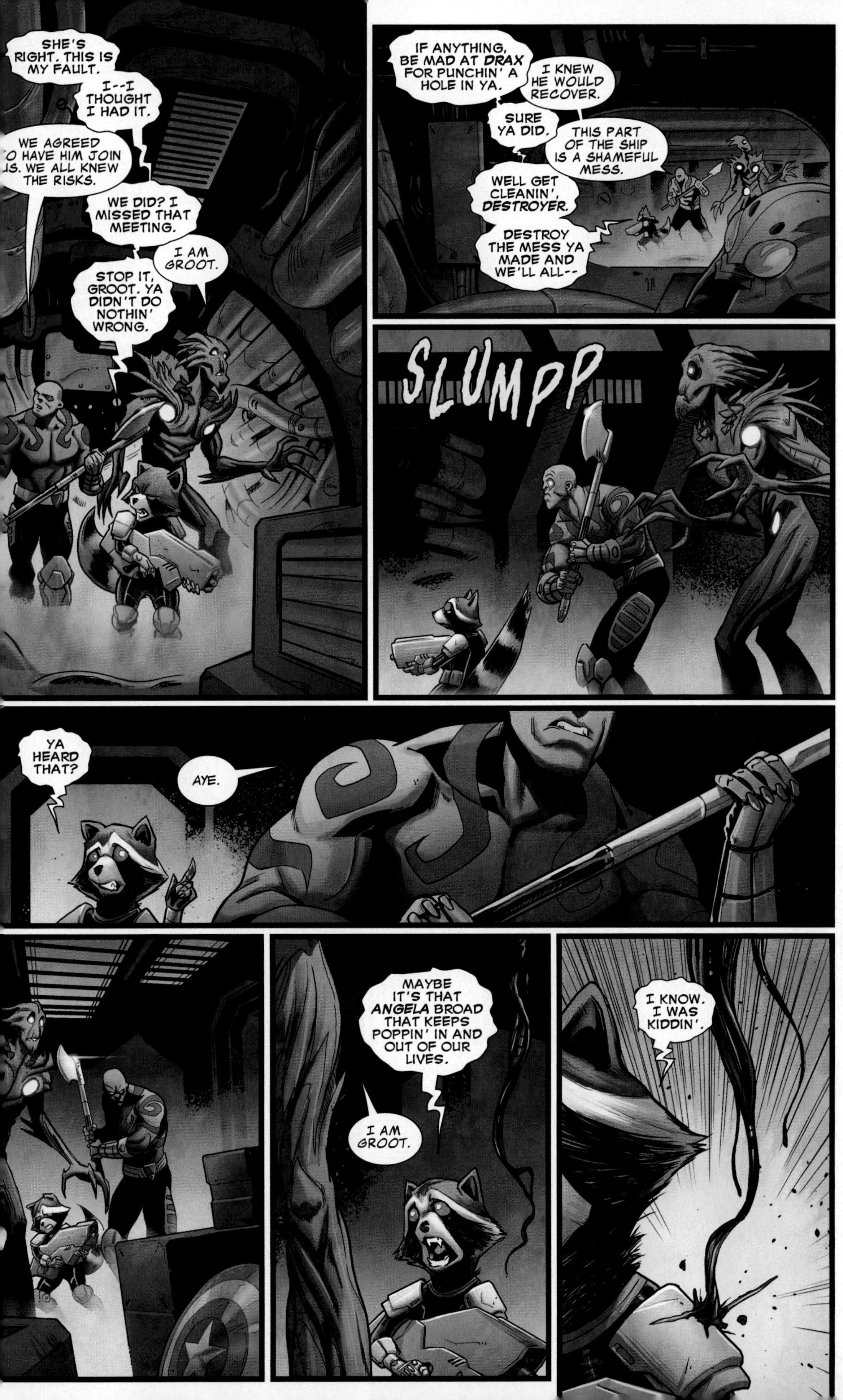
SHE'S RIGHT. THIS IS MY FAULT.
I--I THOUGHT I HAD IT.
WE AGREED TO HAVE HIM JOIN US. WE ALL KNEW THE RISKS.
WE DID? I MISSED THAT MEETING.
I AM GROOT.
STOP IT, GROOT. YA DIDN'T DO NOTHIN' WRONG.
IF ANYTHING, BE MAD AT DRAX FOR PUNCHIN' A HOLE IN YA.
I KNEW HE WOULD RECOVER.
SURE YA DID.
THIS PART OF THE SHIP IS A SHAMEFUL MESS.
WELL GET CLEANIN', DESTROYER.
DESTROY THE MESS YA MADE AND WE'LL ALL--
SLUMPP
YA HEARD THAT?
AYE.
MAYBE IT'S THAT ANGELA BROAD THAT KEEPS POPPIN' IN AND OUT OF OUR LIVES.
I AM GROOT.
I KNOW. I WAS KIDDIN'.

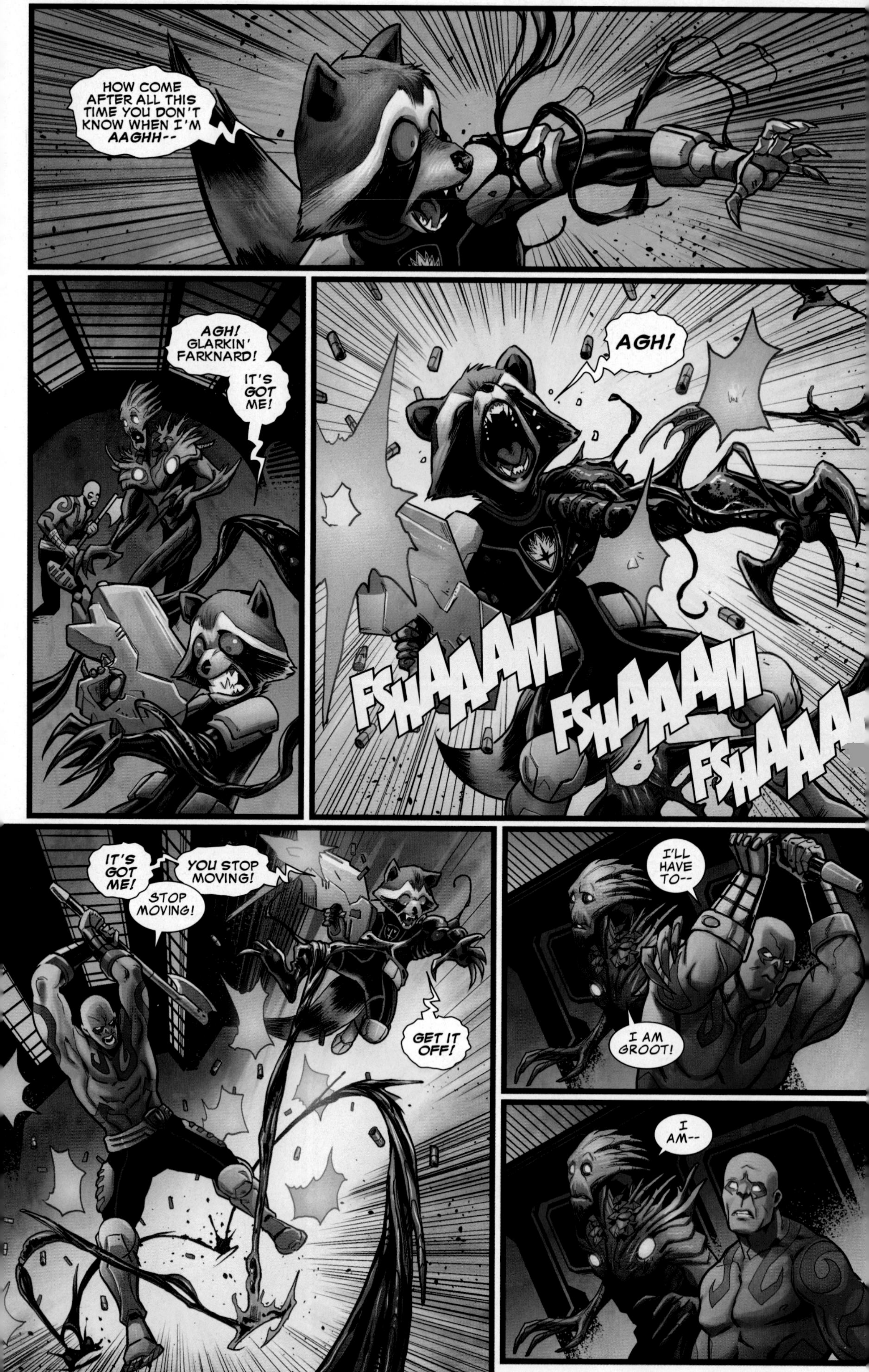
HOW COME AFTER ALL THIS TIME YOU DON'T KNOW WHEN I'M AAGHH--
AGH! GLARKIN' FARKNARD!
IT'S GOT ME!
AGH!
FSHAAAM
FSHAAAM
FSHAAA
IT'S GOT ME!
YOU STOP MOVING!
STOP MOVING!
GET IT OFF!
I'LL HAVE TO--
I AM GROOT!
I AM--

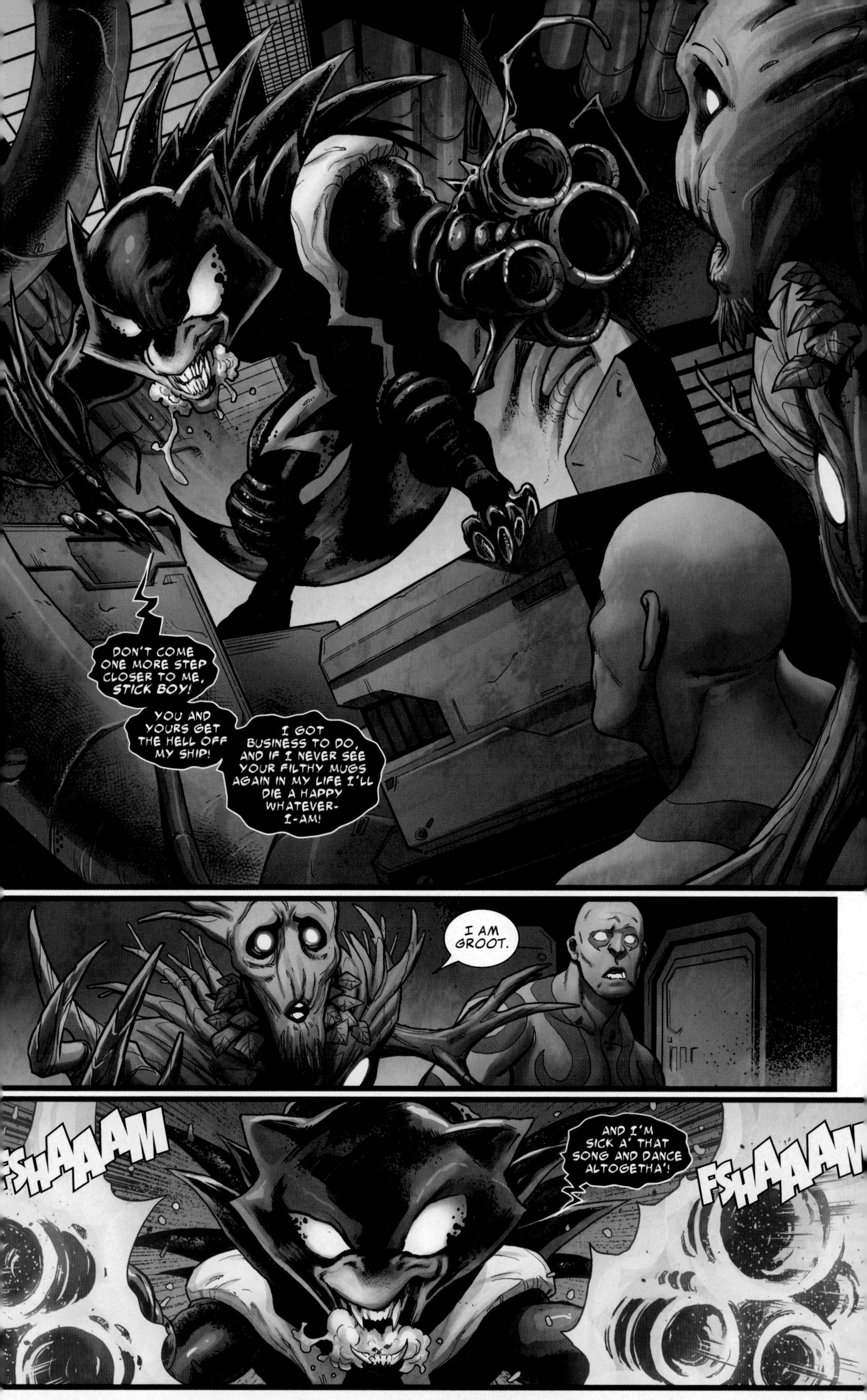
DON'T COME ONE MORE STEP CLOSER TO ME, STICK BOY!
YOU AND YOURS GET THE HELL OFF MY SHIP!
I GOT BUSINESS TO DO, AND IF I NEVER SEE YOUR FILTHY MUGS AGAIN IN MY LIFE I'LL DIE A HAPPY WHATEVER-I-AM!
I AM GROOT.
FSHAAAM
AND I'M SICK A' THAT SONG AND DANCE ALTOGETHA'!
FSHAAAM

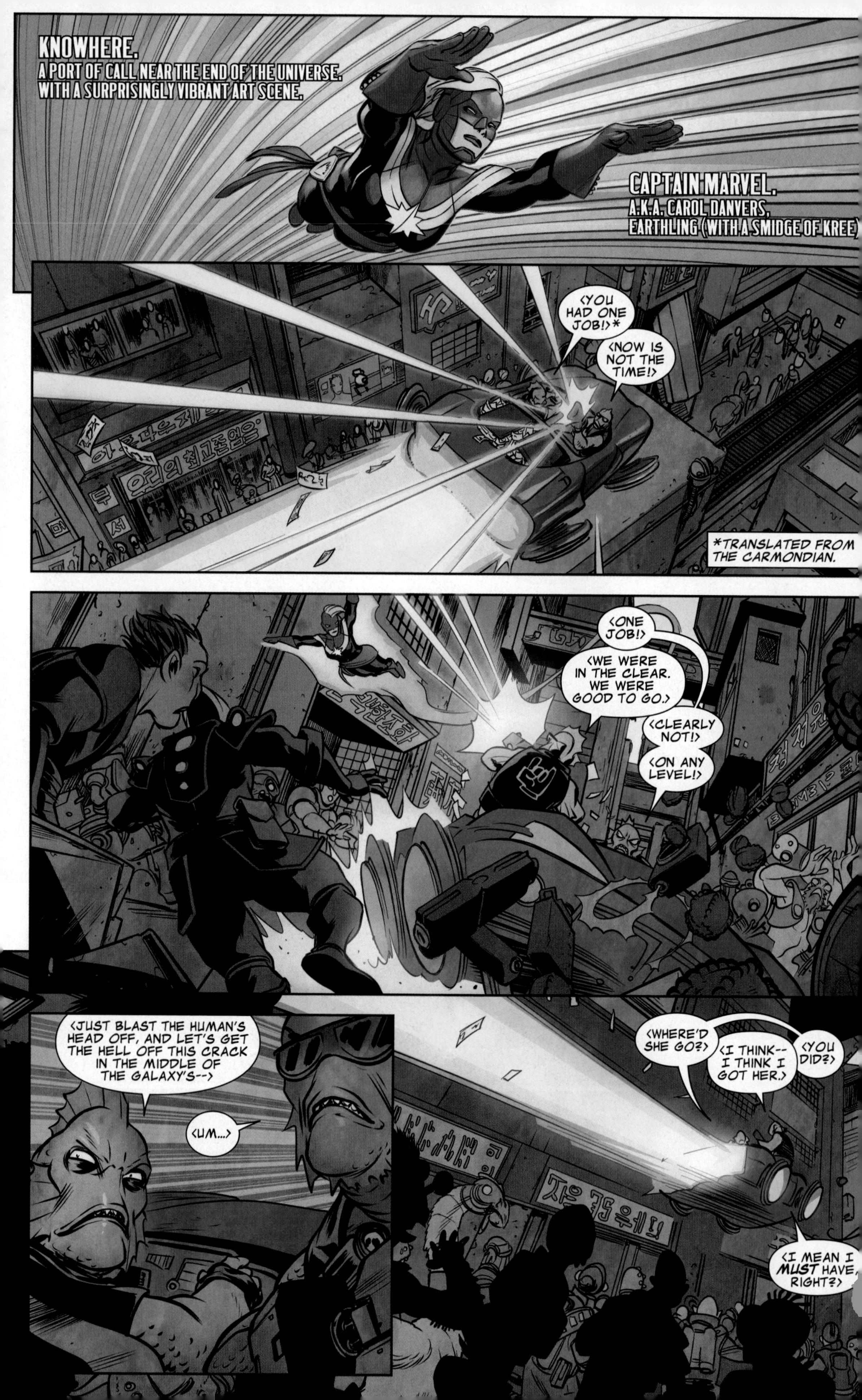
KNOWHERE.
A PORT OF CALL NEAR THE END OF THE UNIVERSE. WITH A SURPRISINGLY VIBRANT ART SCENE.
CAPTAIN MARVEL.
A.K.A. CAROL DANVERS, EARTHLING (WITH A SMIDGE OF KREE)
<YOU HAD ONE JOB!>*
<NOW IS NOT THE TIME!>
*TRANSLATED FROM THE CARMONDIAN.
<ONE JOB!>
<WE WERE IN THE CLEAR. WE WERE GOOD TO GO.>
<CLEARLY NOT!>
<ON ANY LEVEL!>
<JUST BLAST THE HUMAN'S HEAD OFF, AND LET'S GET THE HELL OFF THIS CRACK IN THE MIDDLE OF THE GALAXY'S-->
<UM...>
<WHERE'D SHE GO?>
<I THINK-- I THINK I GOT HER.>
<YOU DID?>
<I MEAN I MUST HAVE, RIGHT?>

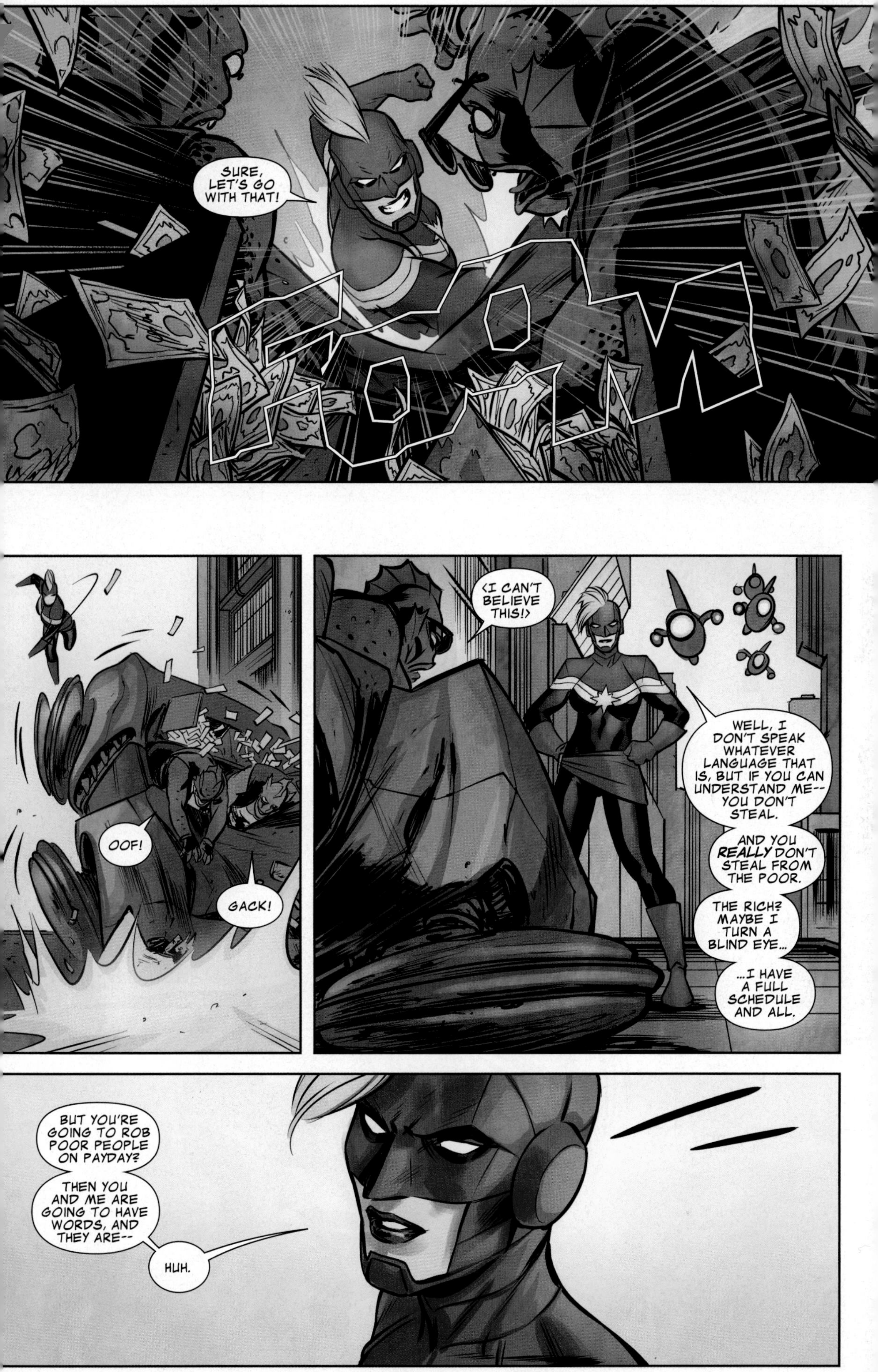
SURE, LET'S GO WITH THAT!
OOF!
GACK!
<I CAN'T BELIEVE THIS!>
WELL, I DON'T SPEAK WHATEVER LANGUAGE THAT IS, BUT IF YOU CAN UNDERSTAND ME-- YOU DON'T STEAL.
AND YOU REALLY DON'T STEAL FROM THE POOR.
THE RICH? MAYBE I TURN A BLIND EYE...
...I HAVE A FULL SCHEDULE AND ALL.
BUT YOU'RE GOING TO ROB POOR PEOPLE ON PAYDAY?
THEN YOU AND ME ARE GOING TO HAVE WORDS, AND THEY ARE--
HUH.

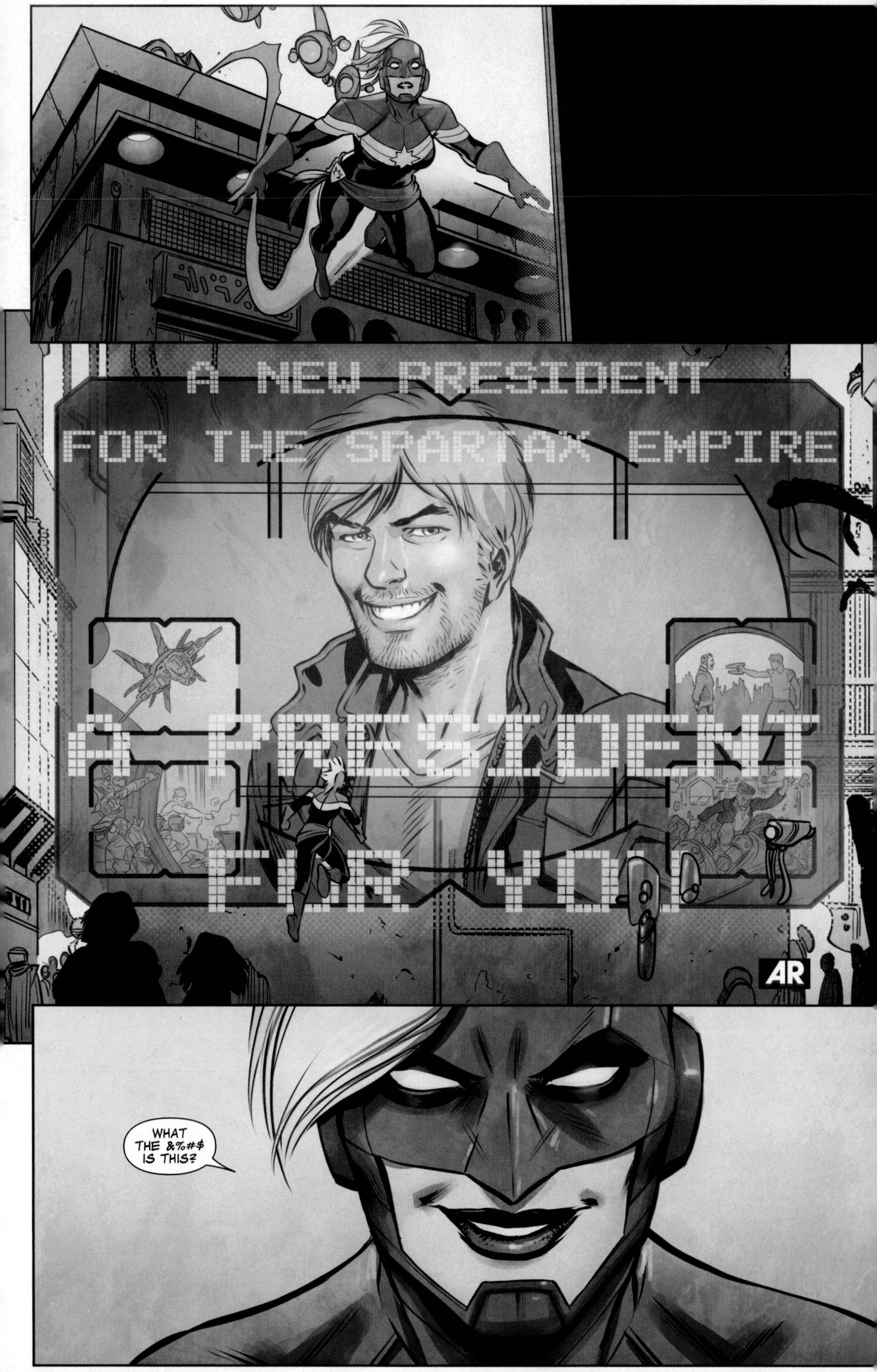
A NEW PRESIDENT
FOR THE SPARTAX EMPIRE
A PRESIDENT
FOR YOU
AR
WHAT THE &%#$ IS THIS?

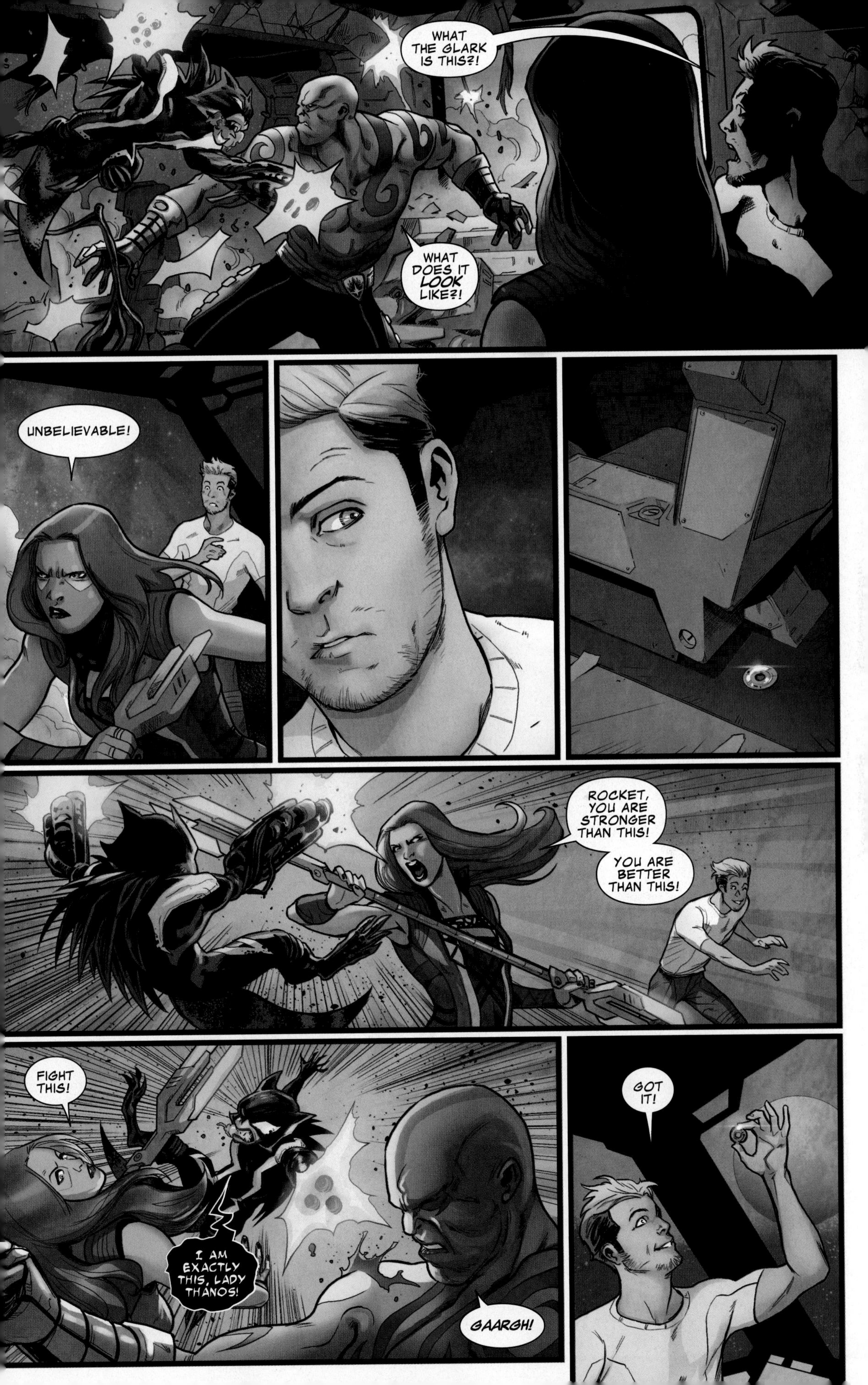
WHAT THE GLARK IS THIS?!
WHAT DOES IT LOOK LIKE?!
UNBELIEVABLE!
ROCKET, YOU ARE STRONGER THAN THIS!
YOU ARE BETTER THAN THIS!
FIGHT THIS!
I AM EXACTLY THIS, LADY THANOS!
GAARGH!
GOT IT!

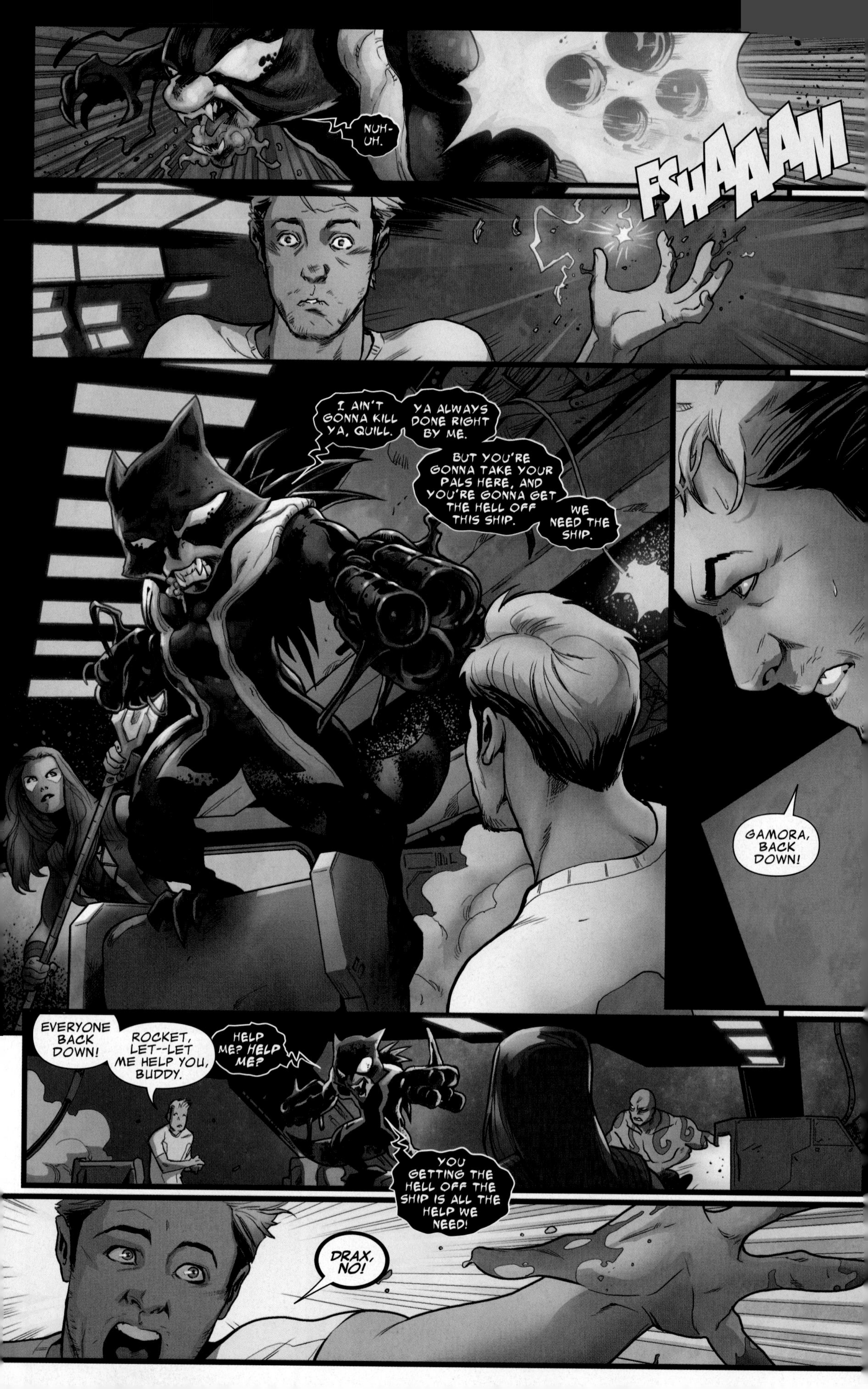
NUH-UH.
FSHAAAAM
I AIN'T GONNA KILL YA, QUILL.
YA ALWAYS DONE RIGHT BY ME.
BUT YOU'RE GONNA TAKE YOUR PALS HERE, AND YOU'RE GONNA GET THE HELL OFF THIS SHIP.
WE NEED THE SHIP.
GAMORA, BACK DOWN!
EVERYONE BACK DOWN!
ROCKET, LET--LET ME HELP YOU, BUDDY.
HELP ME? HELP ME?
YOU GETTING THE HELL OFF THE SHIP IS ALL THE HELP WE NEED!
DRAX, NO!

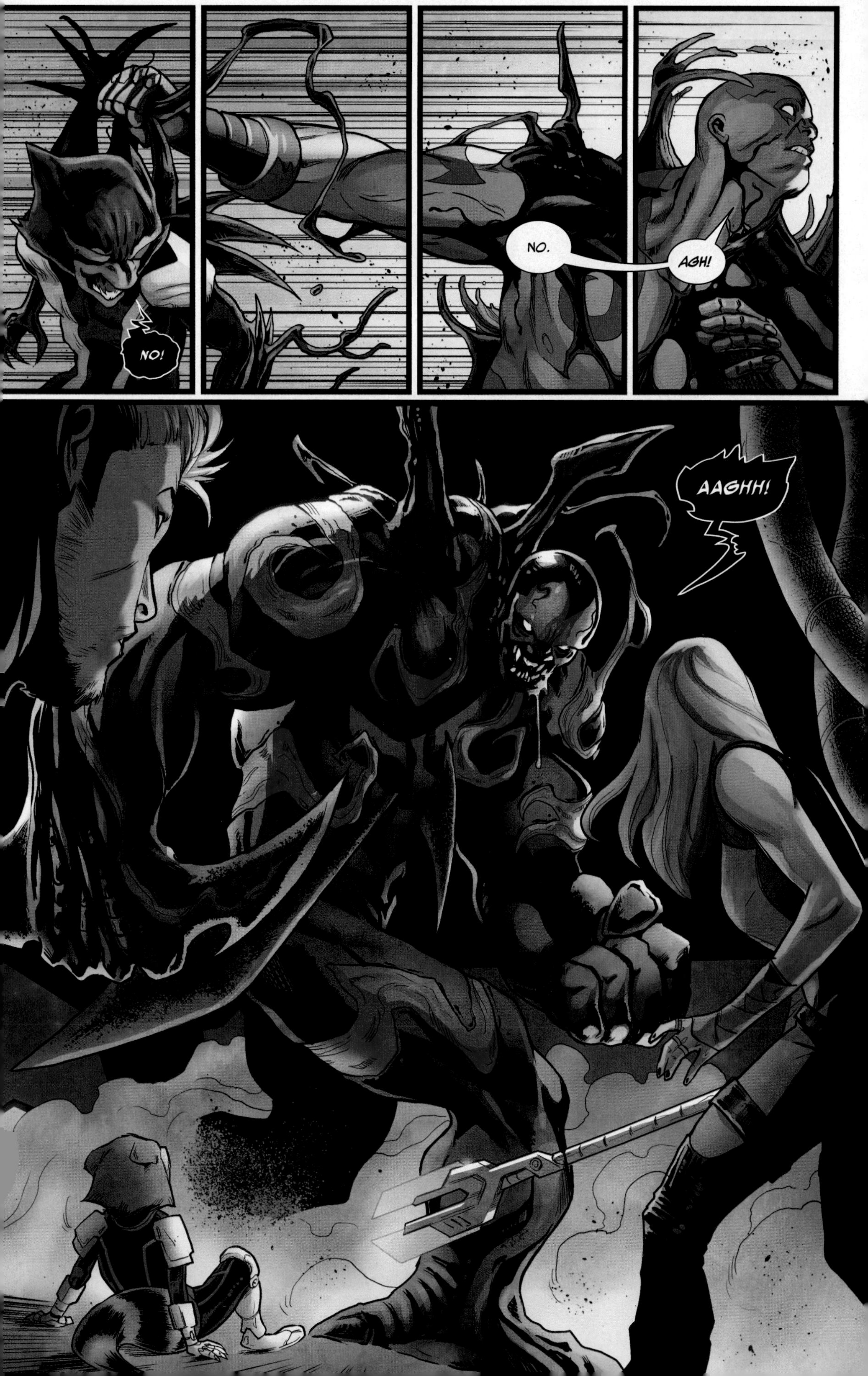
NO!
NO.
AGH!
AAGHH!

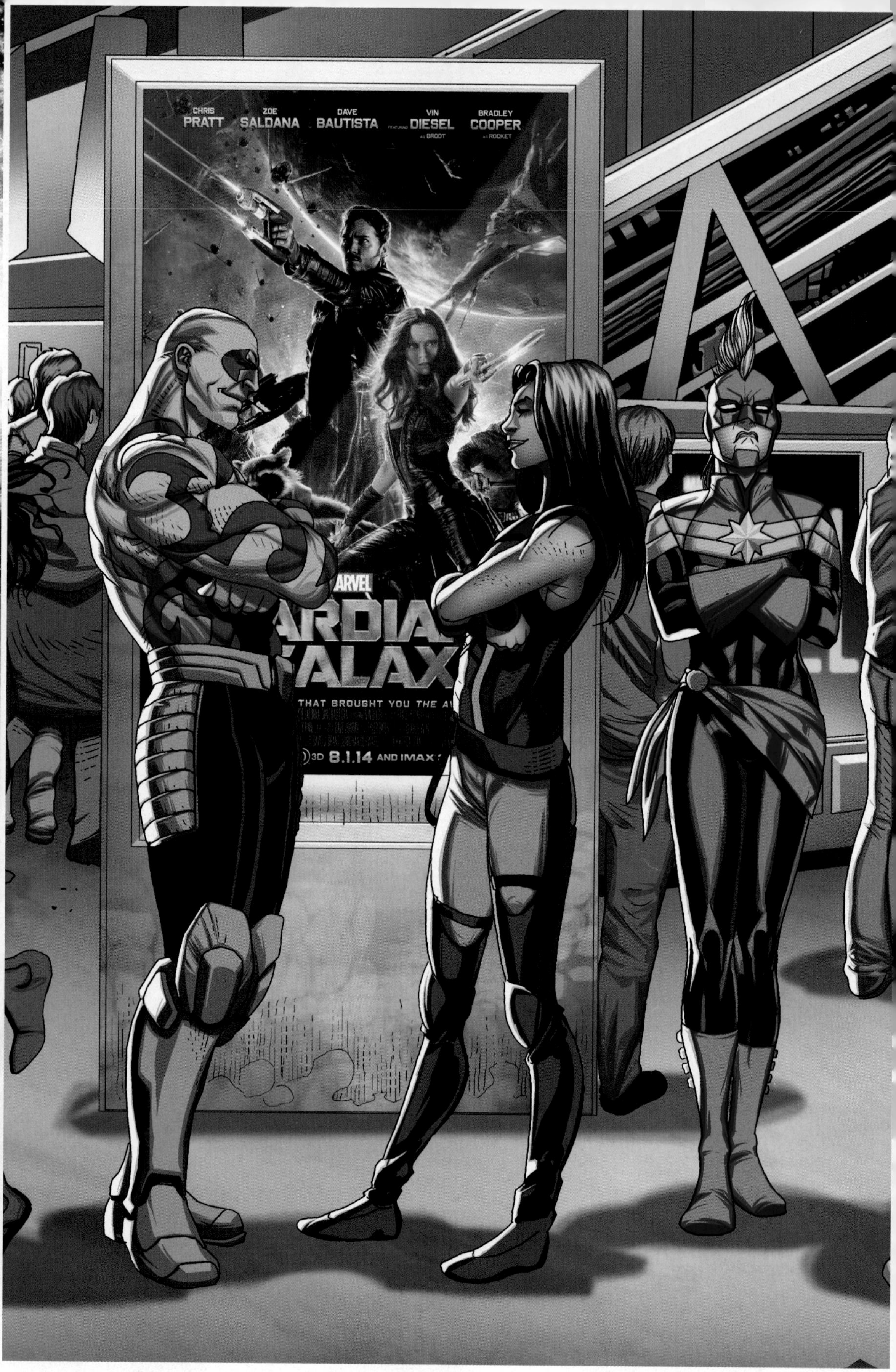
CHRIS
PRATT
ZOE
SALDANA
DAVE
BAUTISTA
VIN
DIESEL
AS GROOT
BRADLEY
COOPER
AS ROCKET
8.1.14 AND IMAX

#23 WELCOME HOME VARIANT BY SALVADOR LARROCA & ISRAEL SILVA

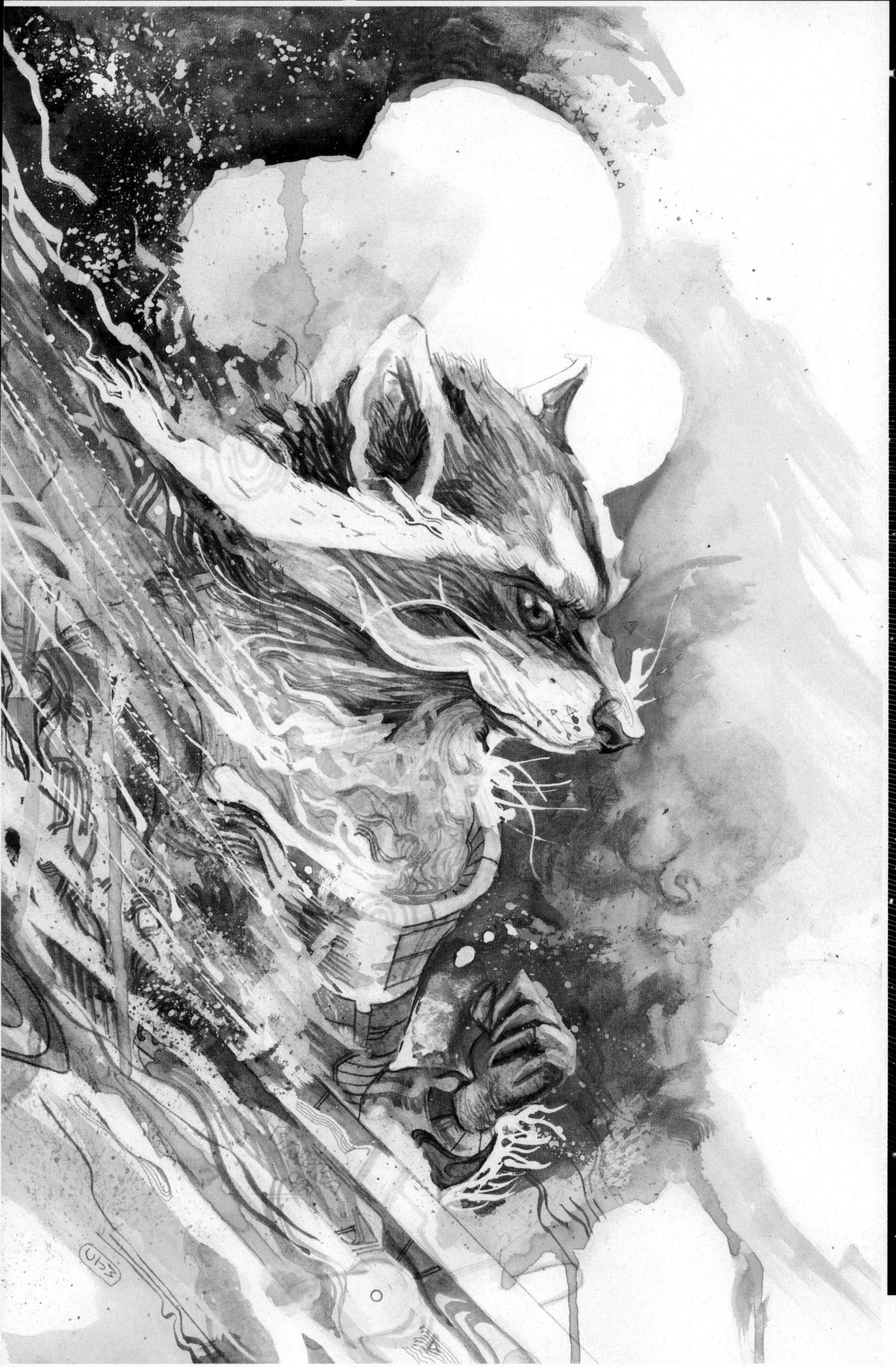

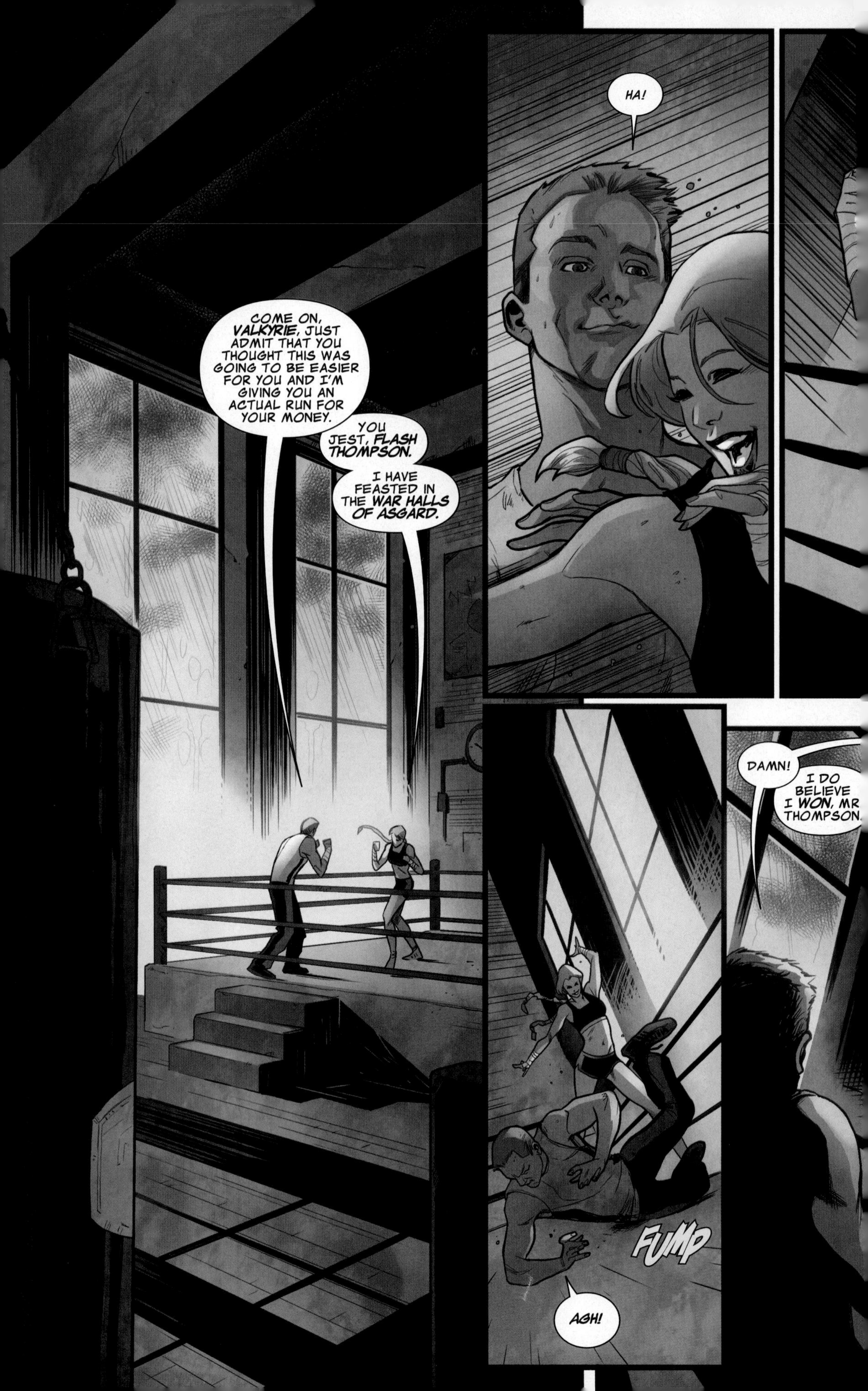
COME ON, VALKYRIE, JUST ADMIT THAT YOU THOUGHT THIS WAS GOING TO BE EASIER FOR YOU AND I'M GIVING YOU AN ACTUAL RUN FOR YOUR MONEY.
YOU JEST, FLASH THOMPSON.
I HAVE FEASTED IN THE WAR HALLS OF ASGARD.
HA!
FUMP
AGH!
DAMN!
I DO BELIEVE I WON, MR THOMPSON.

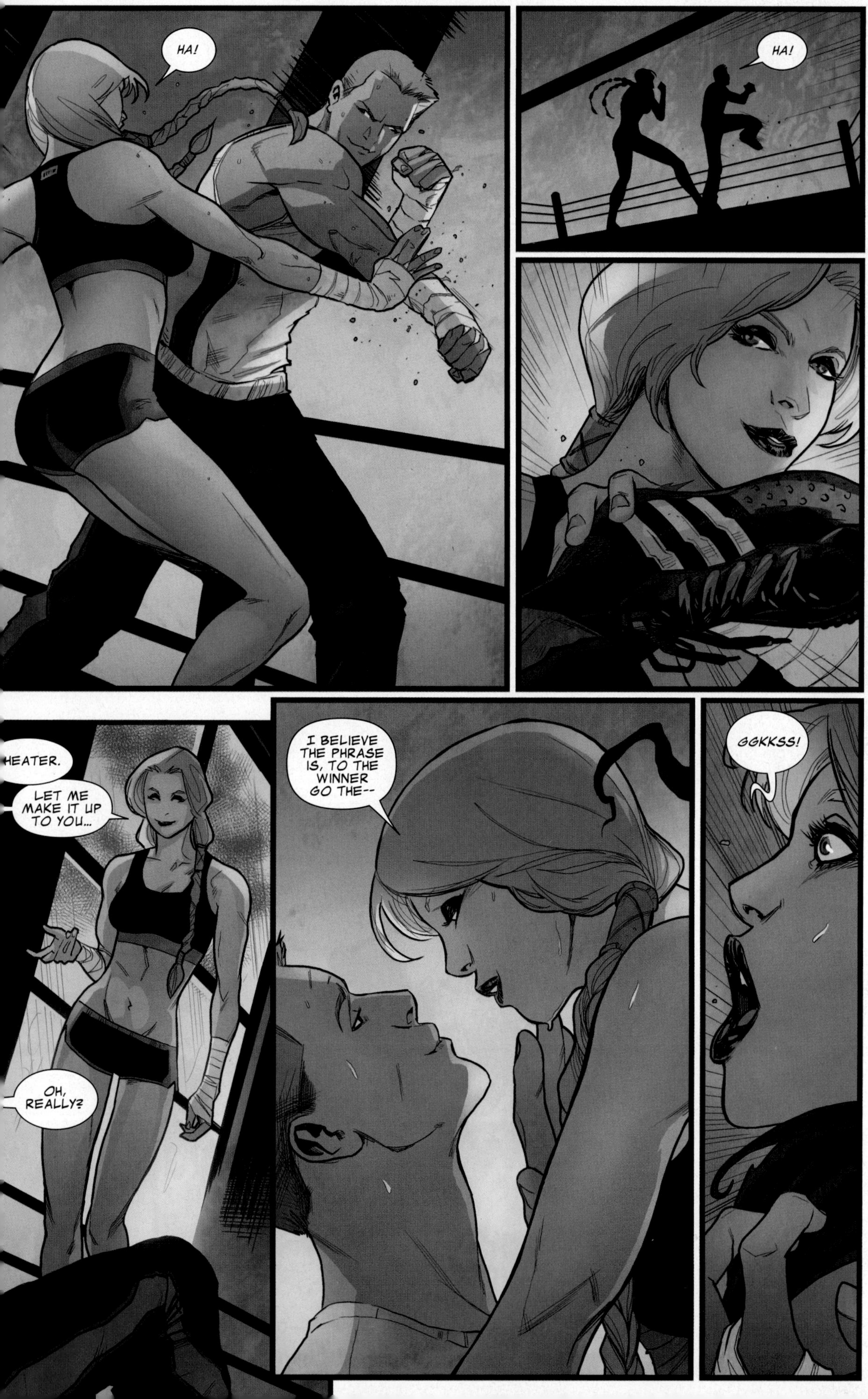
HA!
HA!
HEATER.
LET ME MAKE IT UP TO YOU...
OH, REALLY?
I BELIEVE THE PHRASE IS, TO THE WINNER GO THE--
GGKKSS!

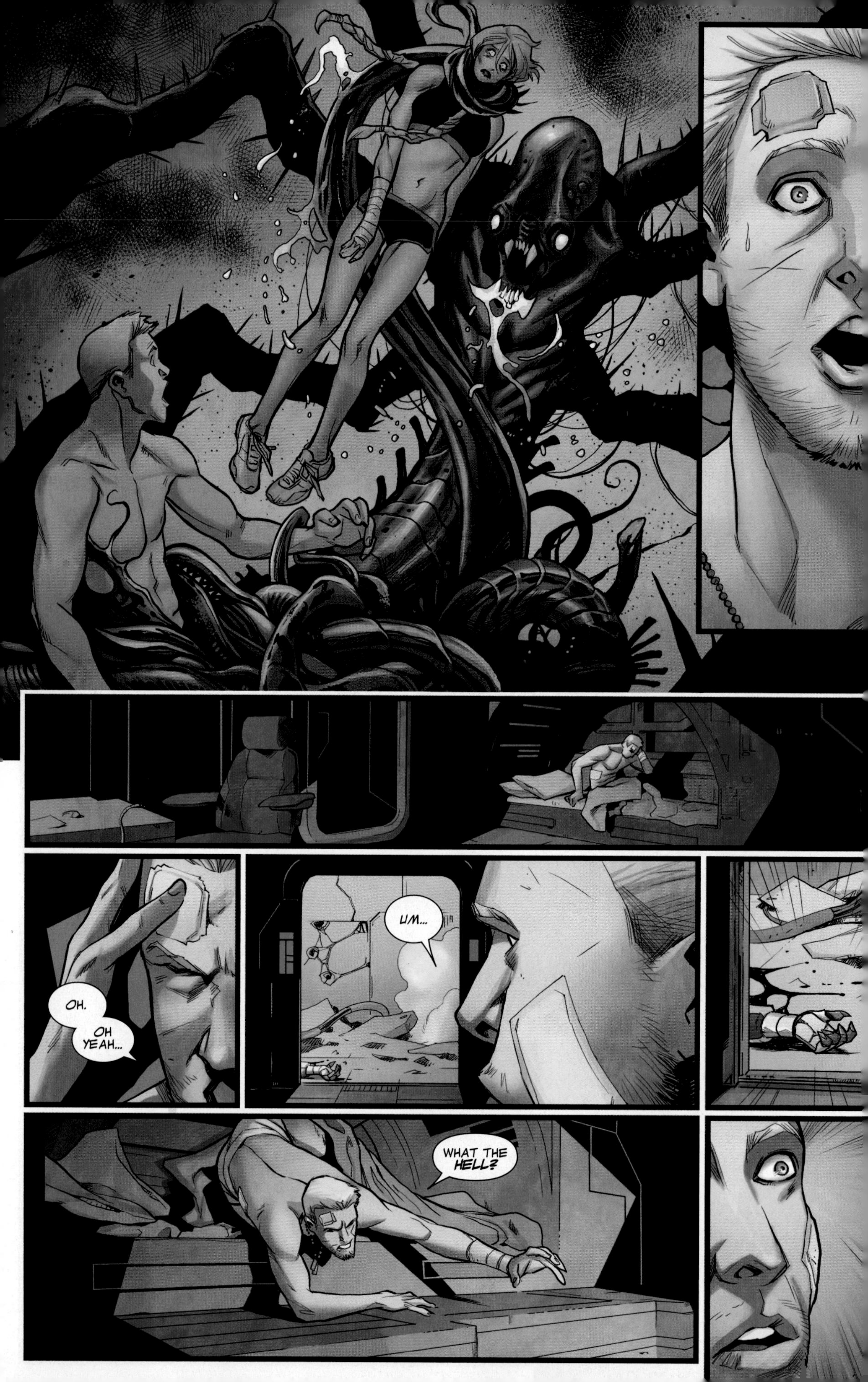
OH.
OH YEAH...
UM...
WHAT THE HELL?

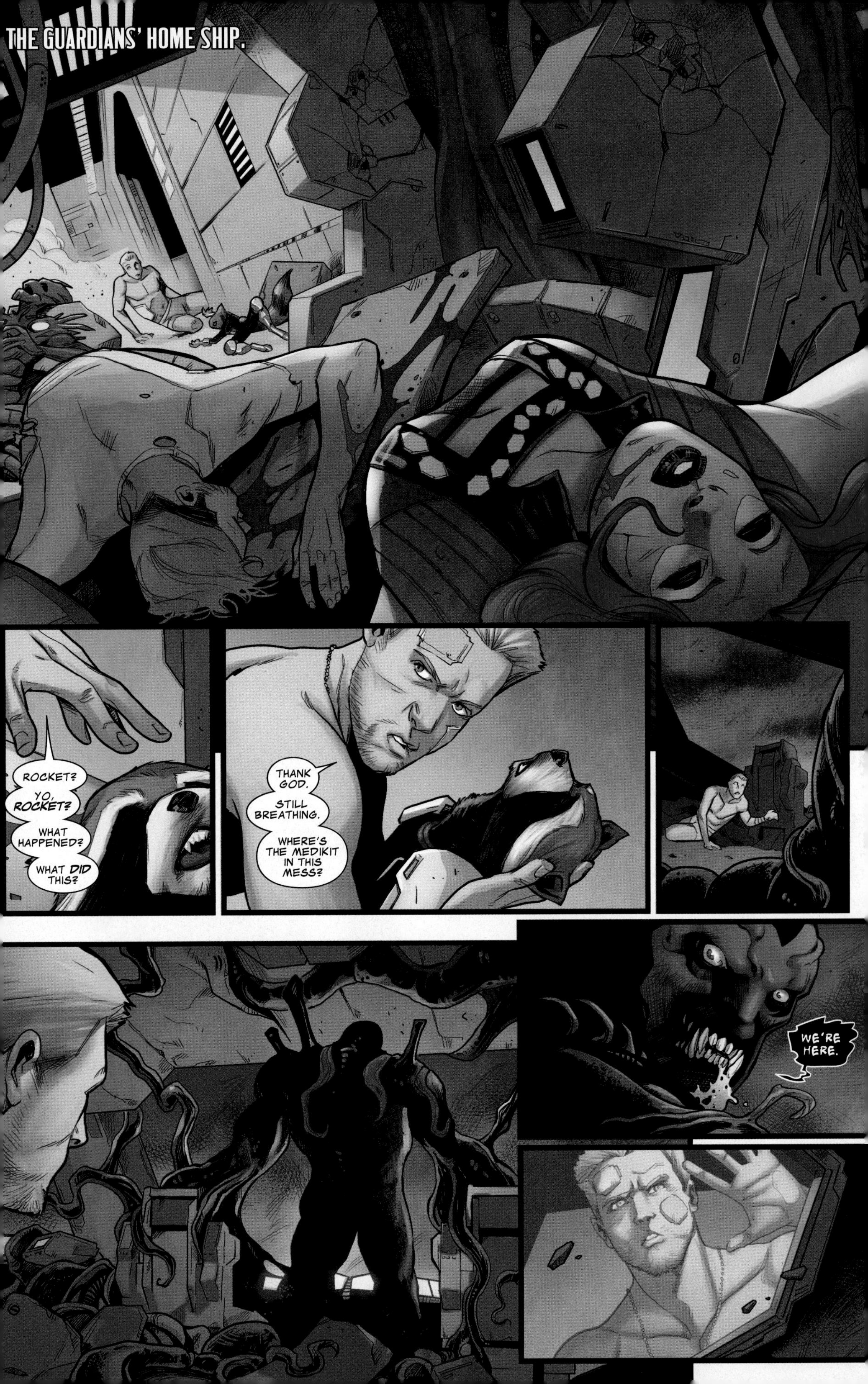
THE GUARDIANS' HOME SHIP.
ROCKET?
YO, ROCKET?
WHAT HAPPENED?
WHAT DID THIS?
THANK GOD.
STILL BREATHING.
WHERE'S THE MEDIKIT IN THIS MESS?
WE'RE HERE.

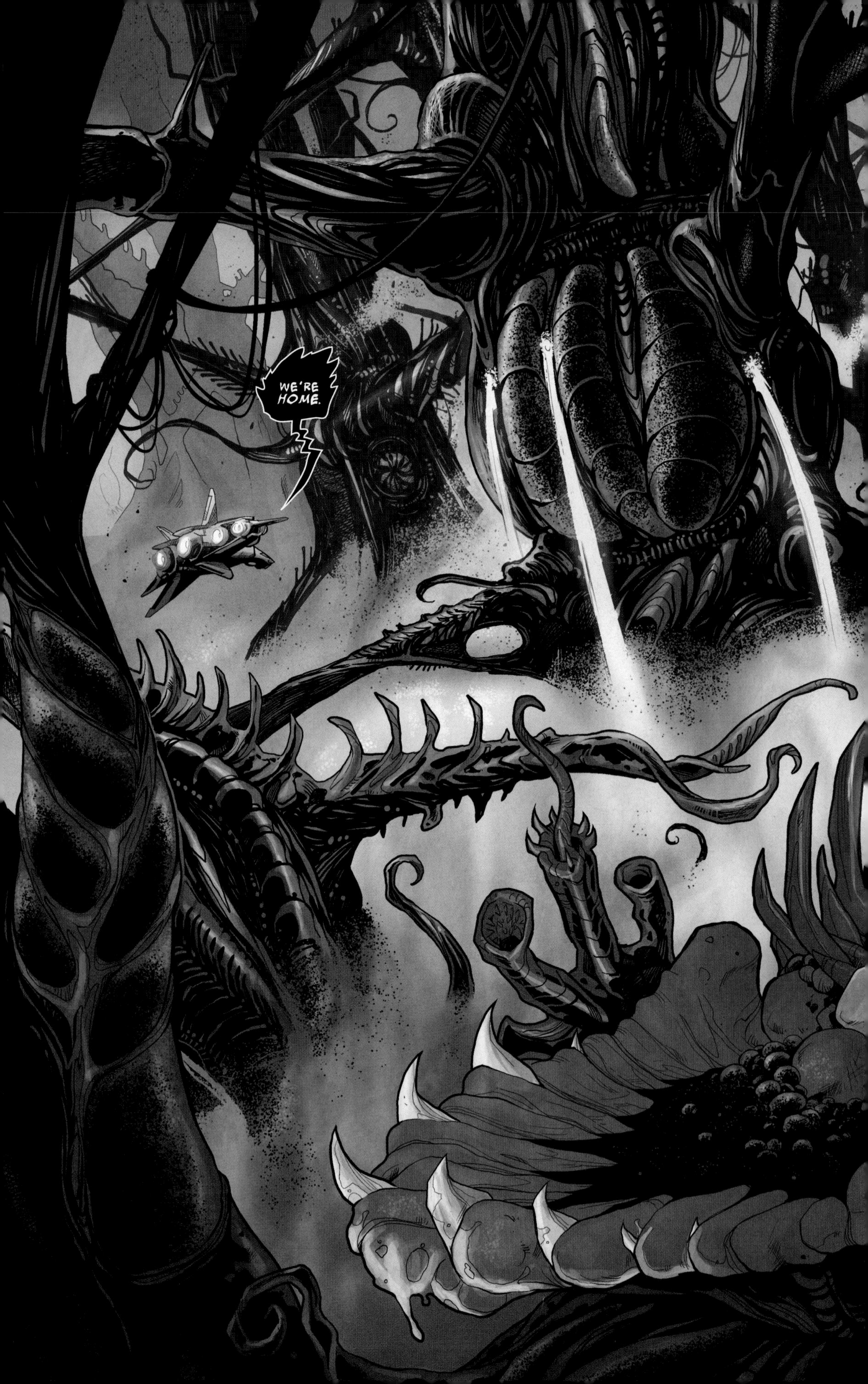
WE'RE HOME.

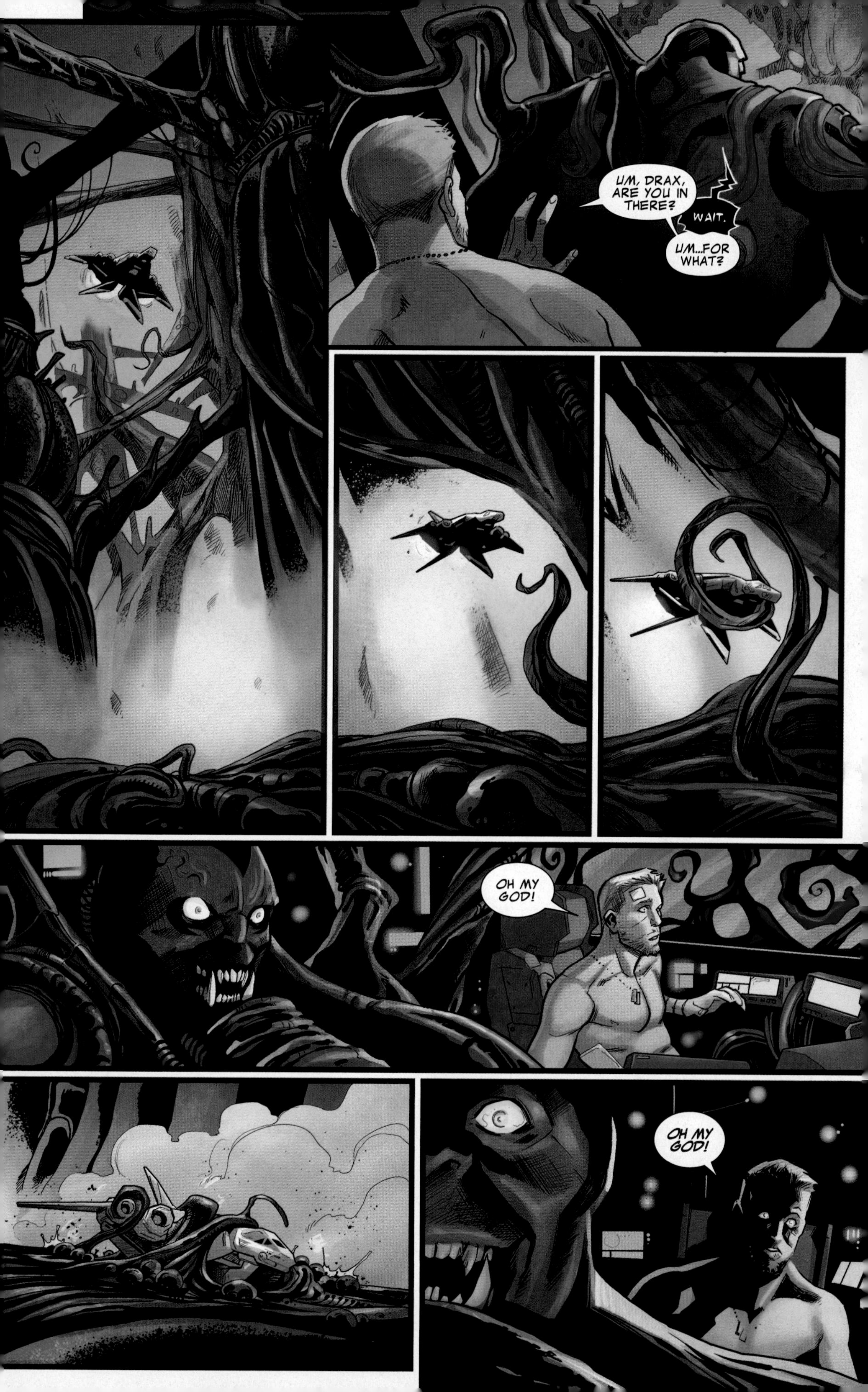
UM, DRAX, ARE YOU IN THERE?
WAIT.
UM...FOR WHAT?
OH MY GOD!
OH MY GOD!

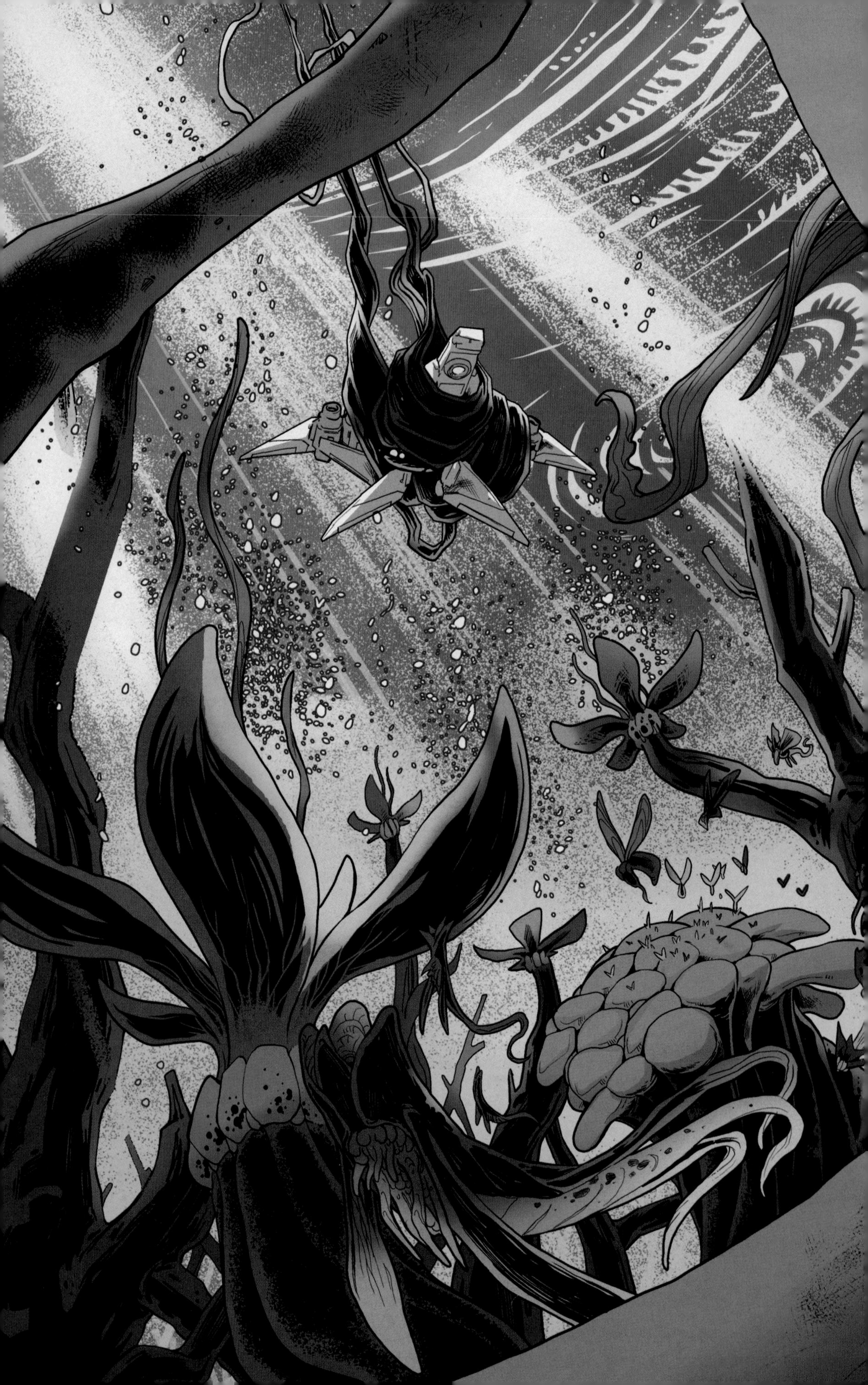

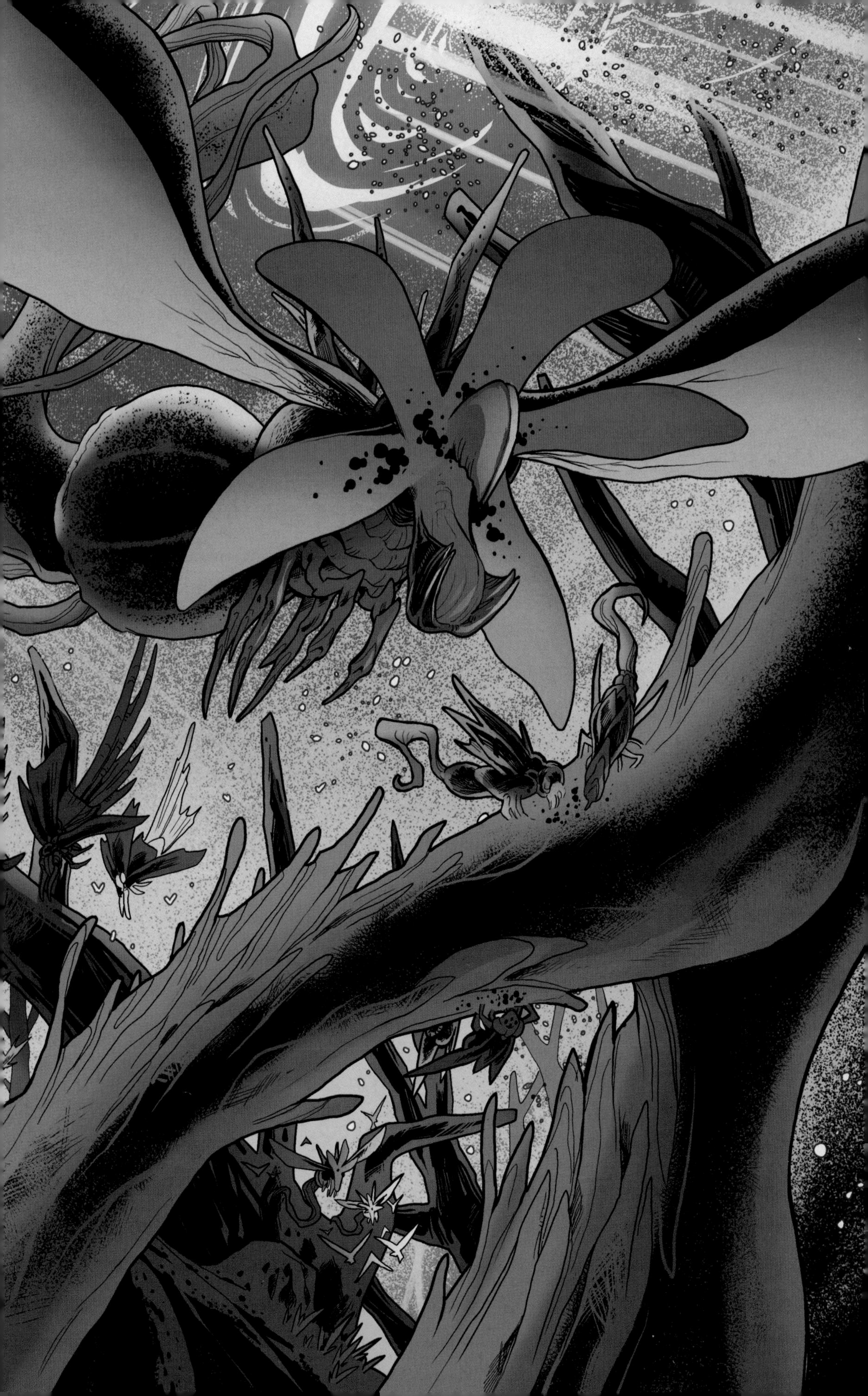

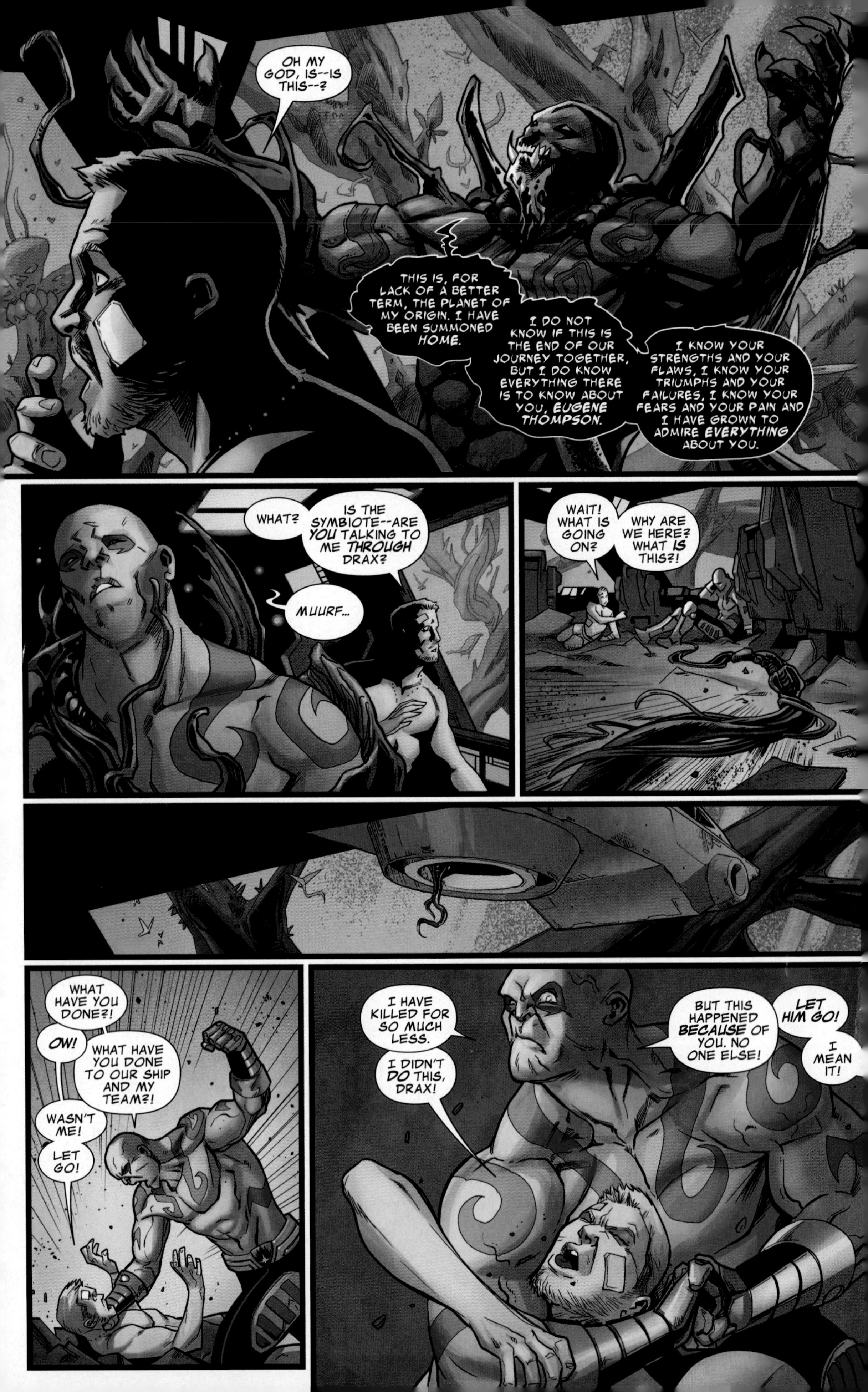
OH MY GOD, IS--IS THIS--?
THIS IS, FOR LACK OF A BETTER TERM, THE PLANET OF MY ORIGIN. I HAVE BEEN SUMMONED HOME.
I DO NOT KNOW IF THIS IS THE END OF OUR JOURNEY TOGETHER, BUT I DO KNOW EVERYTHING THERE IS TO KNOW ABOUT YOU, EUGENE THOMPSON.
I KNOW YOUR STRENGTHS AND YOUR FLAWS, I KNOW YOUR TRIUMPHS AND YOUR FAILURES, I KNOW YOUR FEARS AND YOUR PAIN AND I HAVE GROWN TO ADMIRE EVERYTHING ABOUT YOU.
WHAT?
IS THE SYMBIOTE--ARE YOU TALKING TO ME THROUGH DRAX?
MUURF...
WAIT! WHAT IS GOING ON?
WHY ARE WE HERE? WHAT IS THIS?!
WHAT HAVE YOU DONE?!
OW!
WHAT HAVE YOU DONE TO OUR SHIP AND MY TEAM?!
WASN'T ME!
LET GO!
I HAVE KILLED FOR SO MUCH LESS.
I DIDN'T DO THIS, DRAX!
BUT THIS HAPPENED BECAUSE OF YOU. NO ONE ELSE!
LET HIM GO!
I MEAN IT!

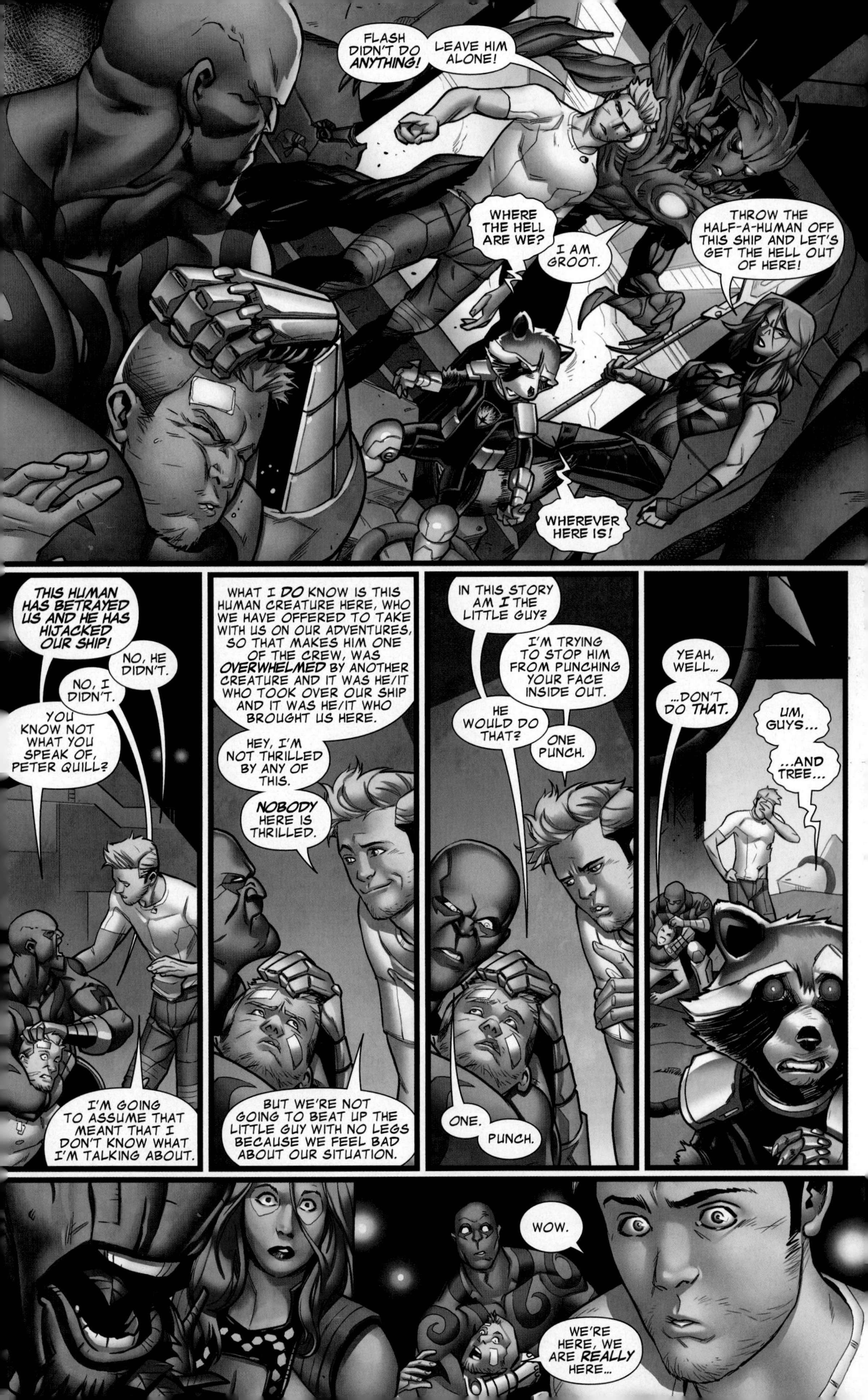
FLASH DIDN'T DO ANYTHING!
LEAVE HIM ALONE!
WHERE THE HELL ARE WE?
I AM GROOT.
THROW THE HALF-A-HUMAN OFF THIS SHIP AND LET'S GET THE HELL OUT OF HERE!
WHEREVER HERE IS!
THIS HUMAN HAS BETRAYED US AND HE HAS HIJACKED OUR SHIP!
NO, HE DIDN'T.
NO, I DIDN'T.
YOU KNOW NOT WHAT YOU SPEAK OF, PETER QUILL?
I'M GOING TO ASSUME THAT MEANT THAT I DON'T KNOW WHAT I'M TALKING ABOUT.
WHAT I DO KNOW IS THIS HUMAN CREATURE HERE, WHO WE HAVE OFFERED TO TAKE WITH US ON OUR ADVENTURES, SO THAT MAKES HIM ONE OF THE CREW, WAS OVERWHELMED BY ANOTHER CREATURE AND IT WAS HE/IT WHO TOOK OVER OUR SHIP AND IT WAS HE/IT WHO BROUGHT US HERE.
HEY, I'M NOT THRILLED BY ANY OF THIS.
NOBODY HERE IS THRILLED.
BUT WE'RE NOT GOING TO BEAT UP THE LITTLE GUY WITH NO LEGS BECAUSE WE FEEL BAD ABOUT OUR SITUATION.
IN THIS STORY AM I THE LITTLE GUY?
I'M TRYING TO STOP HIM FROM PUNCHING YOUR FACE INSIDE OUT.
HE WOULD DO THAT?
ONE PUNCH.
ONE.
PUNCH.
YEAH, WELL...
...DON'T DO THAT.
UM, GUYS...
...AND TREE...
WOW.
WE'RE HERE, WE ARE REALLY HERE...

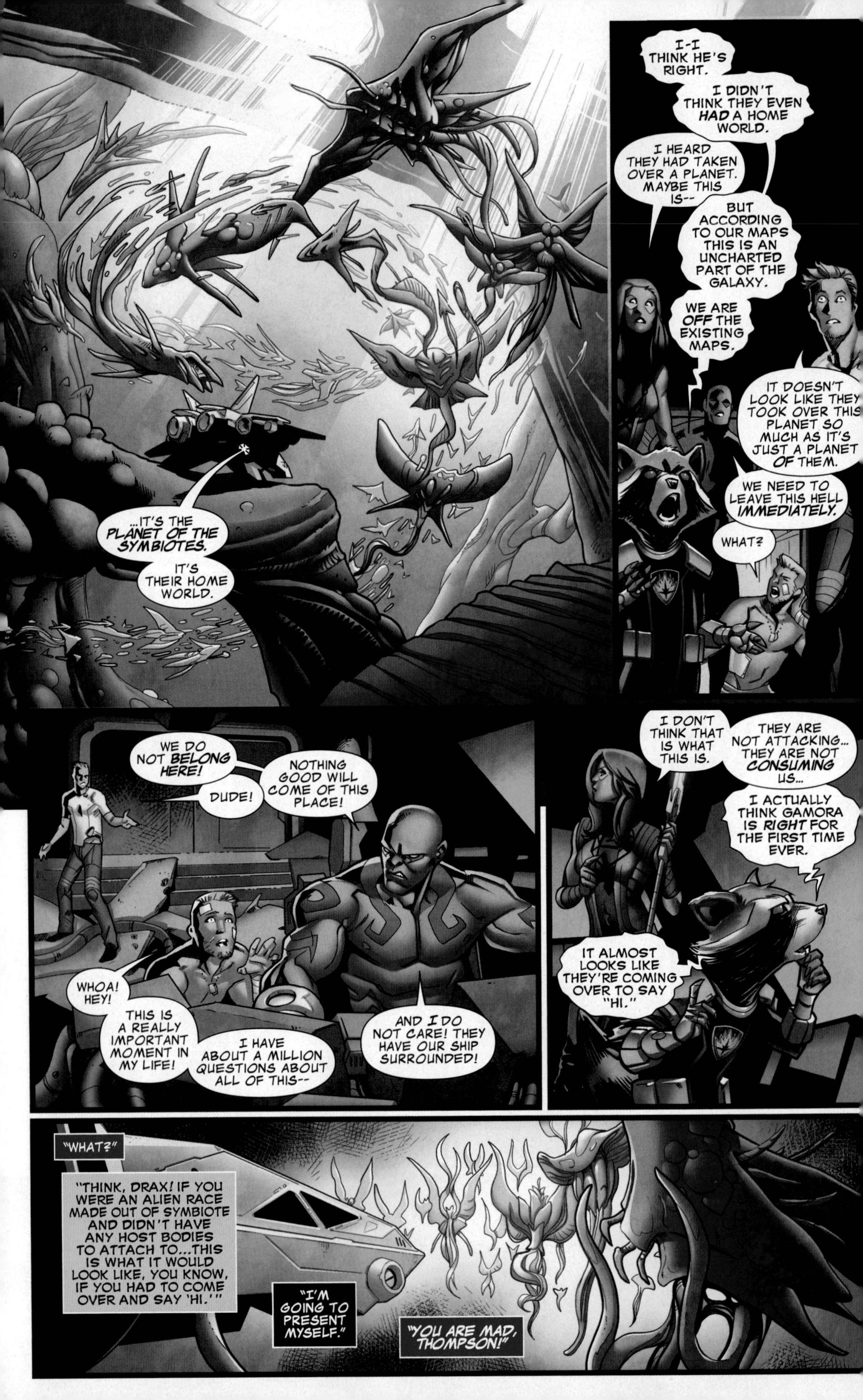
...IT'S THE PLANET OF THE SYMBIOTES.
IT'S THEIR HOME WORLD.
I-I THINK HE'S RIGHT.
I DIDN'T THINK THEY EVEN HAD A HOME WORLD.
I HEARD THEY HAD TAKEN OVER A PLANET. MAYBE THIS IS--
BUT ACCORDING TO OUR MAPS THIS IS AN UNCHARTED PART OF THE GALAXY.
WE ARE OFF THE EXISTING MAPS.
IT DOESN'T LOOK LIKE THEY TOOK OVER THIS PLANET SO MUCH AS IT'S JUST A PLANET OF THEM.
WE NEED TO LEAVE THIS HELL IMMEDIATELY.
WHAT?
WE DO NOT BELONG HERE!
DUDE!
NOTHING GOOD WILL COME OF THIS PLACE!
WHOA! HEY!
THIS IS A REALLY IMPORTANT MOMENT IN MY LIFE!
I HAVE ABOUT A MILLION QUESTIONS ABOUT ALL OF THIS--
AND I DO NOT CARE! THEY HAVE OUR SHIP SURROUNDED!
I DON'T THINK THAT IS WHAT THIS IS.
THEY ARE NOT ATTACKING... THEY ARE NOT CONSUMING US...
I ACTUALLY THINK GAMORA IS RIGHT FOR THE FIRST TIME EVER.
IT ALMOST LOOKS LIKE THEY'RE COMING OVER TO SAY "HI."
"WHAT?"
"THINK, DRAX! IF YOU WERE AN ALIEN RACE MADE OUT OF SYMBIOTE AND DIDN'T HAVE ANY HOST BODIES TO ATTACH TO...THIS IS WHAT IT WOULD LOOK LIKE, YOU KNOW, IF YOU HAD TO COME OVER AND SAY 'HI.'"
"I'M GOING TO PRESENT MYSELF."
"YOU ARE MAD, THOMPSON!"

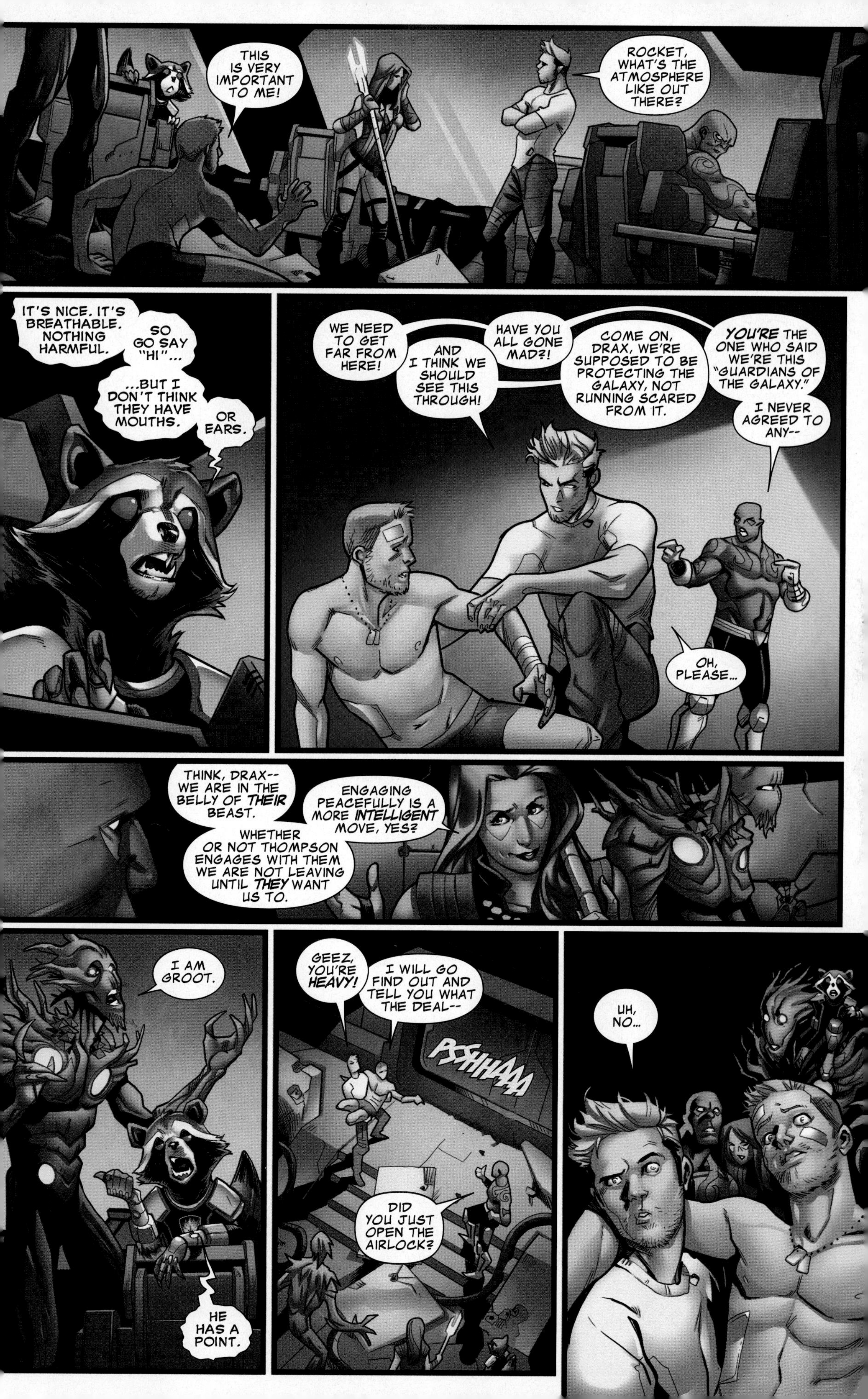
THIS IS VERY IMPORTANT TO ME!
ROCKET, WHAT'S THE ATMOSPHERE LIKE OUT THERE?
IT'S NICE. IT'S BREATHABLE. NOTHING HARMFUL.
SO GO SAY "HI"...
...BUT I DON'T THINK THEY HAVE MOUTHS.
OR EARS.
WE NEED TO GET FAR FROM HERE!
AND I THINK WE SHOULD SEE THIS THROUGH!
HAVE YOU ALL GONE MAD?!
COME ON, DRAX, WE'RE SUPPOSED TO BE PROTECTING THE GALAXY, NOT RUNNING SCARED FROM IT.
YOU'RE THE ONE WHO SAID WE'RE THIS "GUARDIANS OF THE GALAXY."
I NEVER AGREED TO ANY--
OH, PLEASE...
THINK, DRAX-- WE ARE IN THE BELLY OF THEIR BEAST.
ENGAGING PEACEFULLY IS A MORE INTELLIGENT MOVE, YES?
WHETHER OR NOT THOMPSON ENGAGES WITH THEM WE ARE NOT LEAVING UNTIL THEY WANT US TO.
I AM GROOT.
HE HAS A POINT.
GEEZ, YOU'RE HEAVY!
I WILL GO FIND OUT AND TELL YOU WHAT THE DEAL--
PSSHHAAA
DID YOU JUST OPEN THE AIRLOCK?
UH, NO...

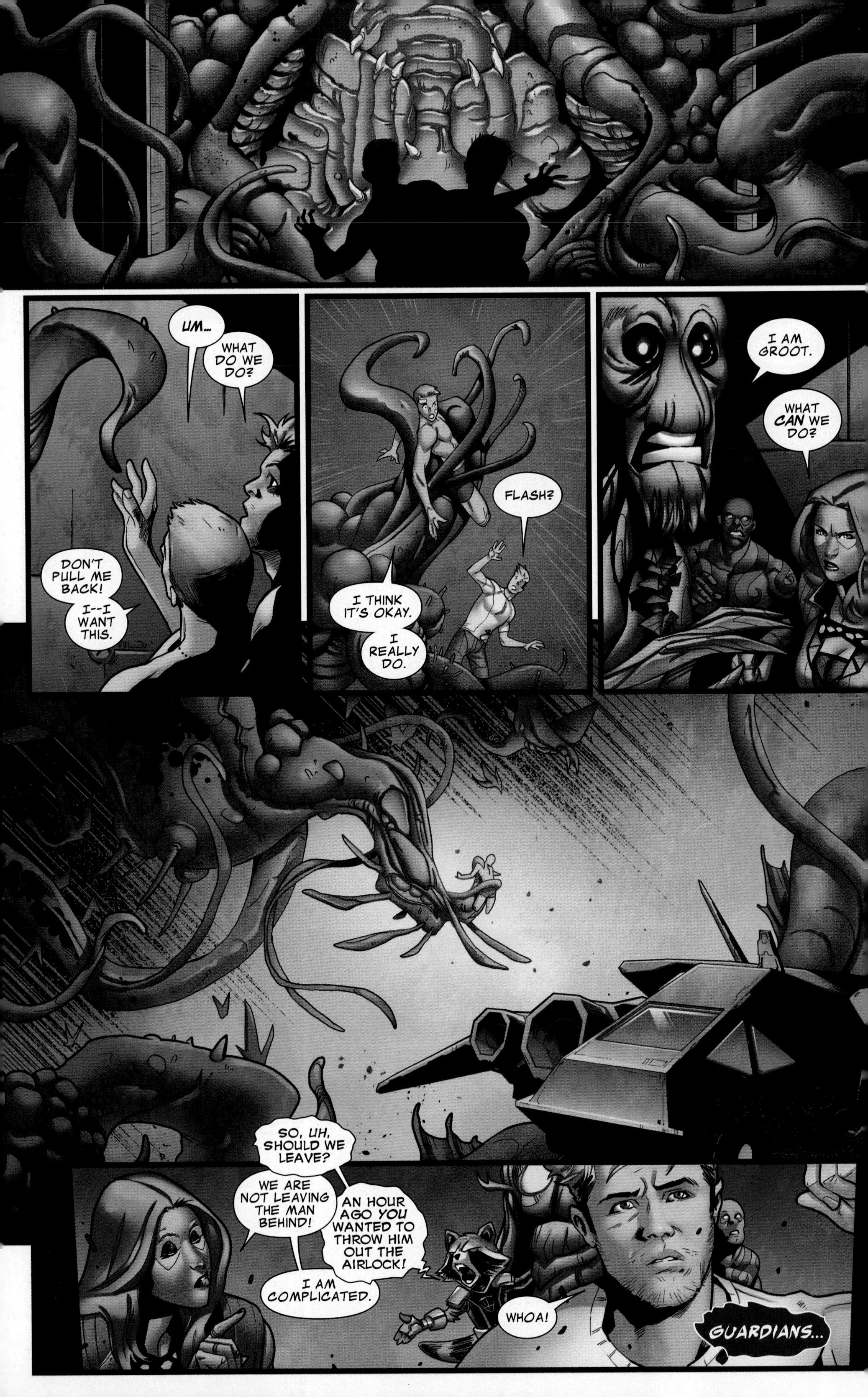
UM...
WHAT DO WE DO?
DON'T PULL ME BACK!
I--I WANT THIS.
FLASH?
I THINK IT'S OKAY.
I REALLY DO.
I AM GROOT.
WHAT CAN WE DO?
SO, UH, SHOULD WE LEAVE?
WE ARE NOT LEAVING THE MAN BEHIND!
AN HOUR AGO YOU WANTED TO THROW HIM OUT THE AIRLOCK!
I AM COMPLICATED.
WHOA!
GUARDIANS...

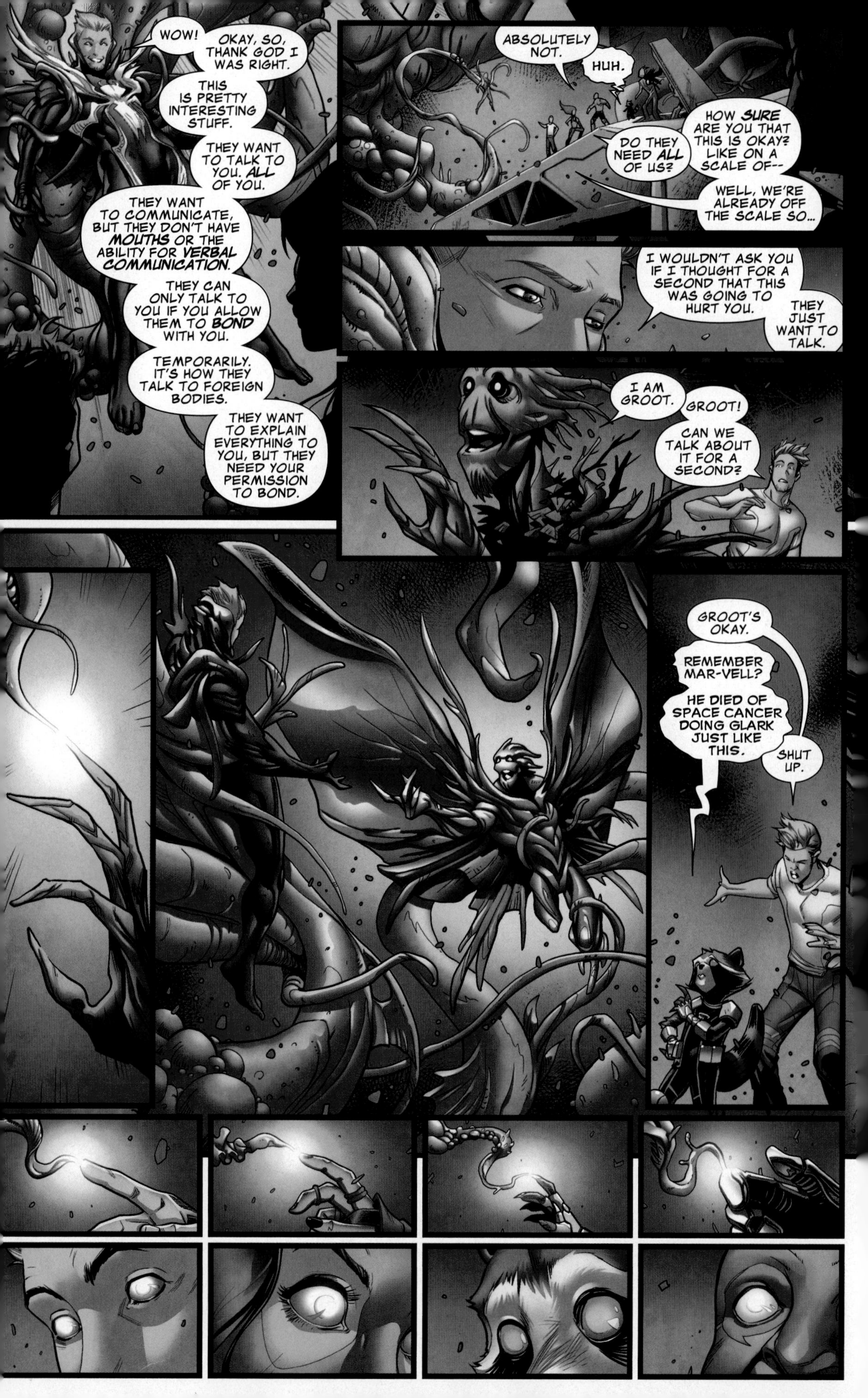
WOW!
OKAY, SO, THANK GOD I WAS RIGHT.
THIS IS PRETTY INTERESTING STUFF.
THEY WANT TO TALK TO YOU. ALL OF YOU.
THEY WANT TO COMMUNICATE, BUT THEY DON'T HAVE MOUTHS OR THE ABILITY FOR VERBAL COMMUNICATION.
THEY CAN ONLY TALK TO YOU IF YOU ALLOW THEM TO BOND WITH YOU.
TEMPORARILY. IT'S HOW THEY TALK TO FOREIGN BODIES.
THEY WANT TO EXPLAIN EVERYTHING TO YOU, BUT THEY NEED YOUR PERMISSION TO BOND.
ABSOLUTELY NOT.
HUH.
DO THEY NEED ALL OF US?
HOW SURE ARE YOU THAT THIS IS OKAY? LIKE ON A SCALE OF--
WELL, WE'RE ALREADY OFF THE SCALE SO...
I WOULDN'T ASK YOU IF I THOUGHT FOR A SECOND THAT THIS WAS GOING TO HURT YOU.
THEY JUST WANT TO TALK.
I AM GROOT.
GROOT!
CAN WE TALK ABOUT IT FOR A SECOND?
GROOT'S OKAY.
REMEMBER MAR-VELL?
HE DIED OF SPACE CANCER DOING GLARK JUST LIKE THIS.
SHUT UP.

THERE ARE MANY STORIES ABOUT
US ACROSS THE GALAXY.

SOME TRUE,
SOME FALSE...

...SOME *CONCOCTED* BY RENEGADE
MEMBERS OF OUR OWN SPECIES.

AND BECAUSE OF
THIS WE ARE KNOWN
BY MANY NAMES...

...WE PREFER TO BE CALLED
THE KLYNTAR.

ALLOW US TO EXPLAIN
OURSELVES USING FAMILIAR
PERSPECTIVES AND THE
VERNACULAR OF YOUR SPECIES...

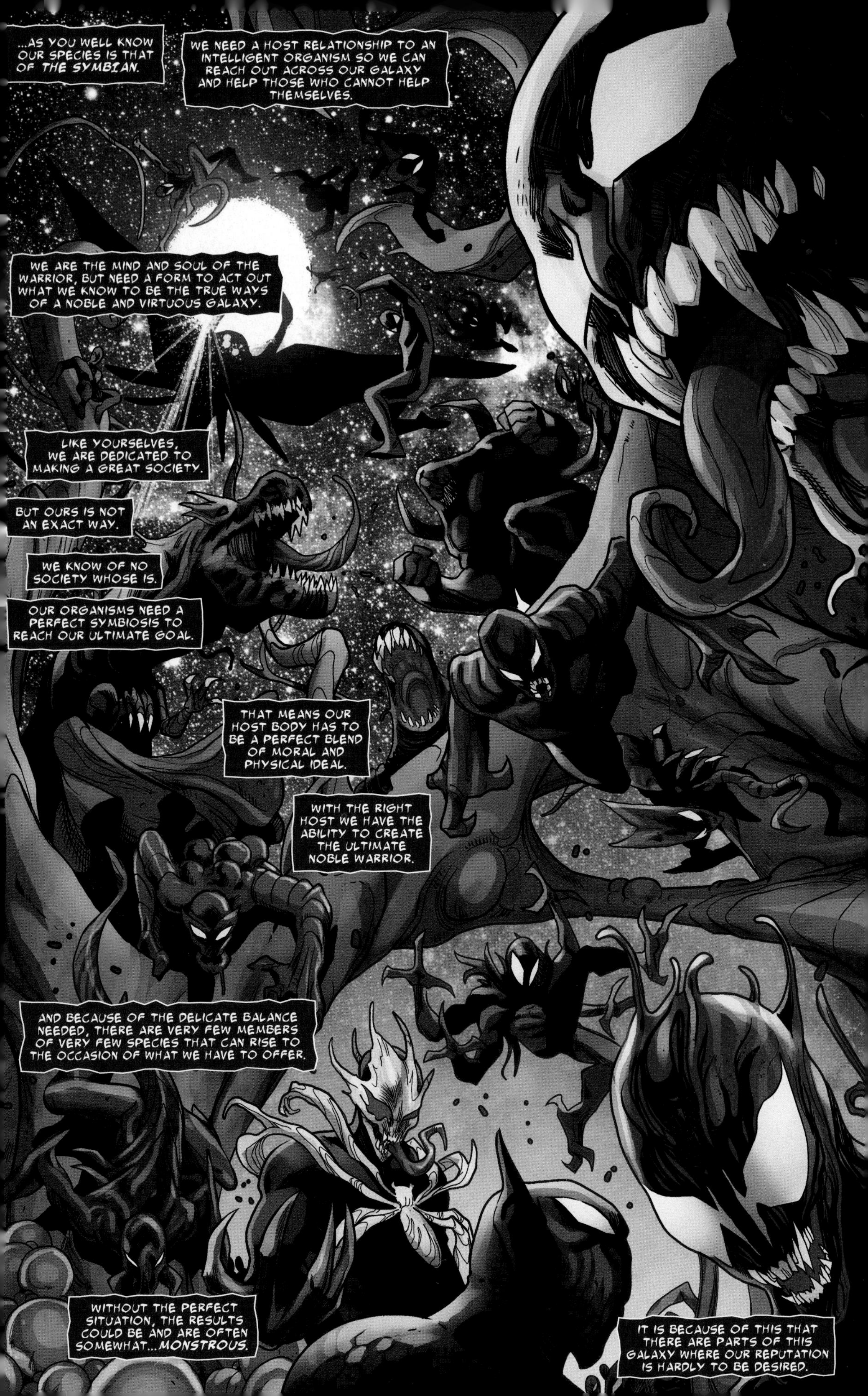
...AS YOU WELL KNOW OUR SPECIES IS THAT OF THE SYMBIAN.
WE NEED A HOST RELATIONSHIP TO AN INTELLIGENT ORGANISM SO WE CAN REACH OUT ACROSS OUR GALAXY AND HELP THOSE WHO CANNOT HELP THEMSELVES.
WE ARE THE MIND AND SOUL OF THE WARRIOR, BUT NEED A FORM TO ACT OUT WHAT WE KNOW TO BE THE TRUE WAYS OF A NOBLE AND VIRTUOUS GALAXY.
LIKE YOURSELVES, WE ARE DEDICATED TO MAKING A GREAT SOCIETY.
BUT OURS IS NOT AN EXACT WAY.
WE KNOW OF NO SOCIETY WHOSE IS.
OUR ORGANISMS NEED A PERFECT SYMBIOSIS TO REACH OUR ULTIMATE GOAL.
THAT MEANS OUR HOST BODY HAS TO BE A PERFECT BLEND OF MORAL AND PHYSICAL IDEAL.
WITH THE RIGHT HOST WE HAVE THE ABILITY TO CREATE THE ULTIMATE NOBLE WARRIOR.
AND BECAUSE OF THE DELICATE BALANCE NEEDED, THERE ARE VERY FEW MEMBERS OF VERY FEW SPECIES THAT CAN RISE TO THE OCCASION OF WHAT WE HAVE TO OFFER.
WITHOUT THE PERFECT SITUATION, THE RESULTS COULD BE AND ARE OFTEN SOMEWHAT...MONSTROUS.
IT IS BECAUSE OF THIS THAT THERE ARE PARTS OF THIS GALAXY WHERE OUR REPUTATION IS HARDLY TO BE DESIRED.

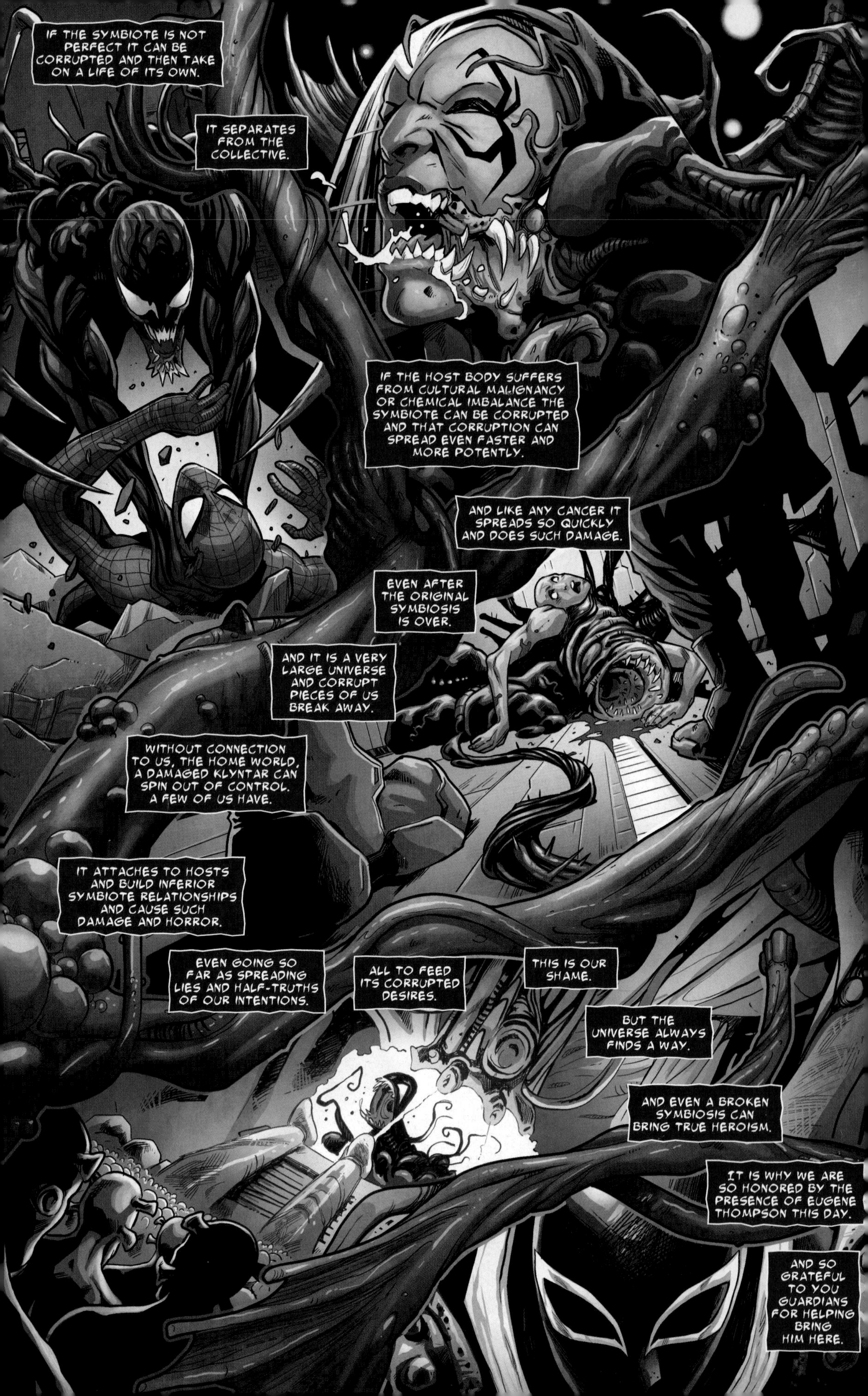
IF THE SYMBIOTE IS NOT PERFECT IT CAN BE CORRUPTED AND THEN TAKE ON A LIFE OF ITS OWN.
IT SEPARATES FROM THE COLLECTIVE.
IF THE HOST BODY SUFFERS FROM CULTURAL MALIGNANCY OR CHEMICAL IMBALANCE THE SYMBIOTE CAN BE CORRUPTED AND THAT CORRUPTION CAN SPREAD EVEN FASTER AND MORE POTENTLY.
AND LIKE ANY CANCER IT SPREADS SO QUICKLY AND DOES SUCH DAMAGE.
EVEN AFTER THE ORIGINAL SYMBIOSIS IS OVER.
AND IT IS A VERY LARGE UNIVERSE AND CORRUPT PIECES OF US BREAK AWAY.
WITHOUT CONNECTION TO US, THE HOME WORLD, A DAMAGED KLYNTAR CAN SPIN OUT OF CONTROL. A FEW OF US HAVE.
IT ATTACHES TO HOSTS AND BUILD INFERIOR SYMBIOTE RELATIONSHIPS AND CAUSE SUCH DAMAGE AND HORROR.
EVEN GOING SO FAR AS SPREADING LIES AND HALF-TRUTHS OF OUR INTENTIONS.
ALL TO FEED ITS CORRUPTED DESIRES.
THIS IS OUR SHAME.
BUT THE UNIVERSE ALWAYS FINDS A WAY.
AND EVEN A BROKEN SYMBIOSIS CAN BRING TRUE HEROISM.
IT IS WHY WE ARE SO HONORED BY THE PRESENCE OF EUGENE THOMPSON THIS DAY.
AND SO GRATEFUL TO YOU GUARDIANS FOR HELPING BRING HIM HERE.

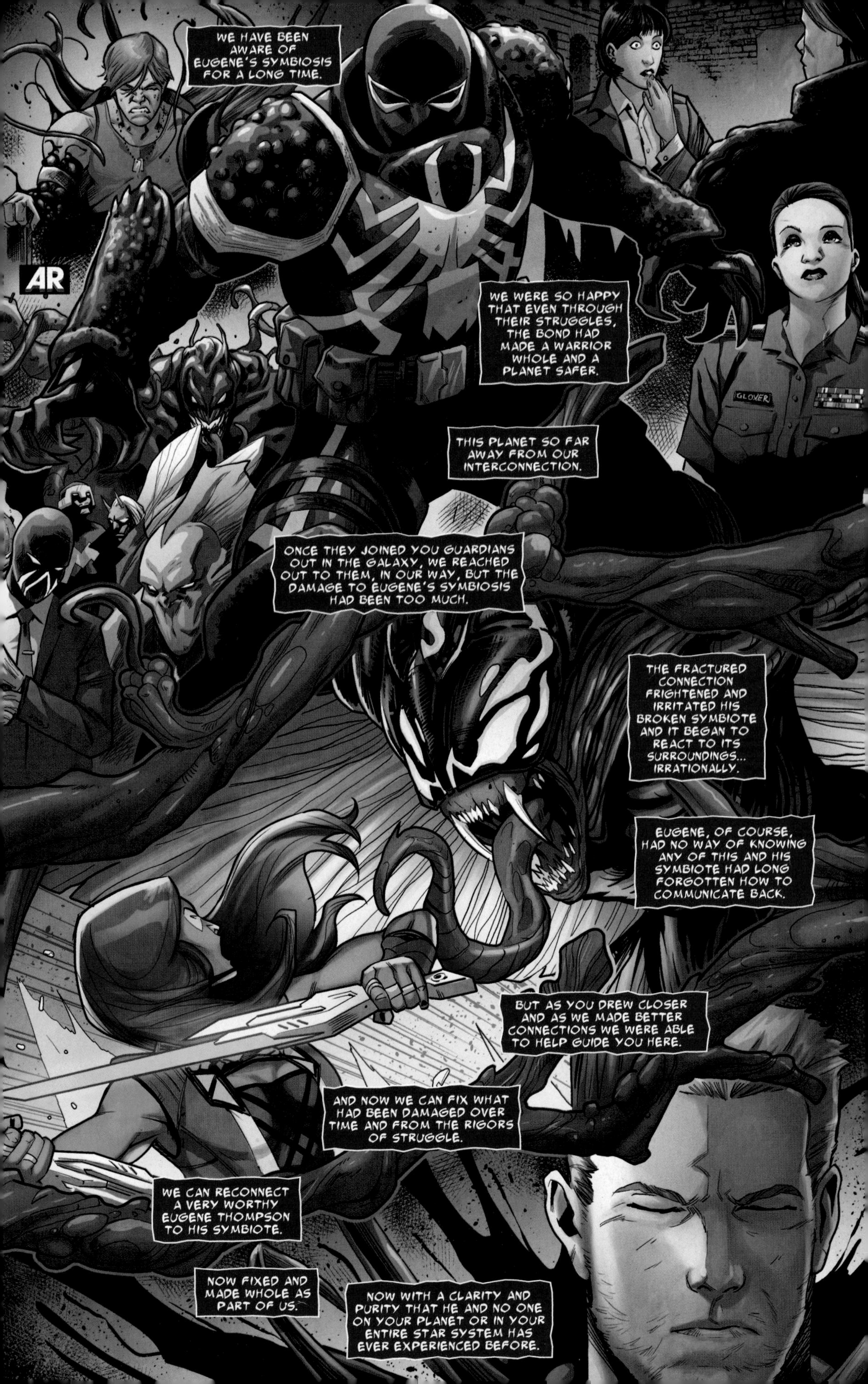
WE HAVE BEEN AWARE OF EUGENE'S SYMBIOSIS FOR A LONG TIME.
AR
WE WERE SO HAPPY THAT EVEN THROUGH THEIR STRUGGLES, THE BOND HAD MADE A WARRIOR WHOLE AND A PLANET SAFER.
GLOVER
THIS PLANET SO FAR AWAY FROM OUR INTERCONNECTION.
ONCE THEY JOINED YOU GUARDIANS OUT IN THE GALAXY, WE REACHED OUT TO THEM, IN OUR WAY, BUT THE DAMAGE TO EUGENE'S SYMBIOSIS HAD BEEN TOO MUCH.
THE FRACTURED CONNECTION FRIGHTENED AND IRRITATED HIS BROKEN SYMBIOTE AND IT BEGAN TO REACT TO ITS SURROUNDINGS... IRRATIONALLY.
EUGENE, OF COURSE, HAD NO WAY OF KNOWING ANY OF THIS AND HIS SYMBIOTE HAD LONG FORGOTTEN HOW TO COMMUNICATE BACK.
BUT AS YOU DREW CLOSER AND AS WE MADE BETTER CONNECTIONS WE WERE ABLE TO HELP GUIDE YOU HERE.
AND NOW WE CAN FIX WHAT HAD BEEN DAMAGED OVER TIME AND FROM THE RIGORS OF STRUGGLE.
WE CAN RECONNECT A VERY WORTHY EUGENE THOMPSON TO HIS SYMBIOTE.
NOW FIXED AND MADE WHOLE AS PART OF US.
NOW WITH A CLARITY AND PURITY THAT HE AND NO ONE ON YOUR PLANET OR IN YOUR ENTIRE STAR SYSTEM HAS EVER EXPERIENCED BEFORE.

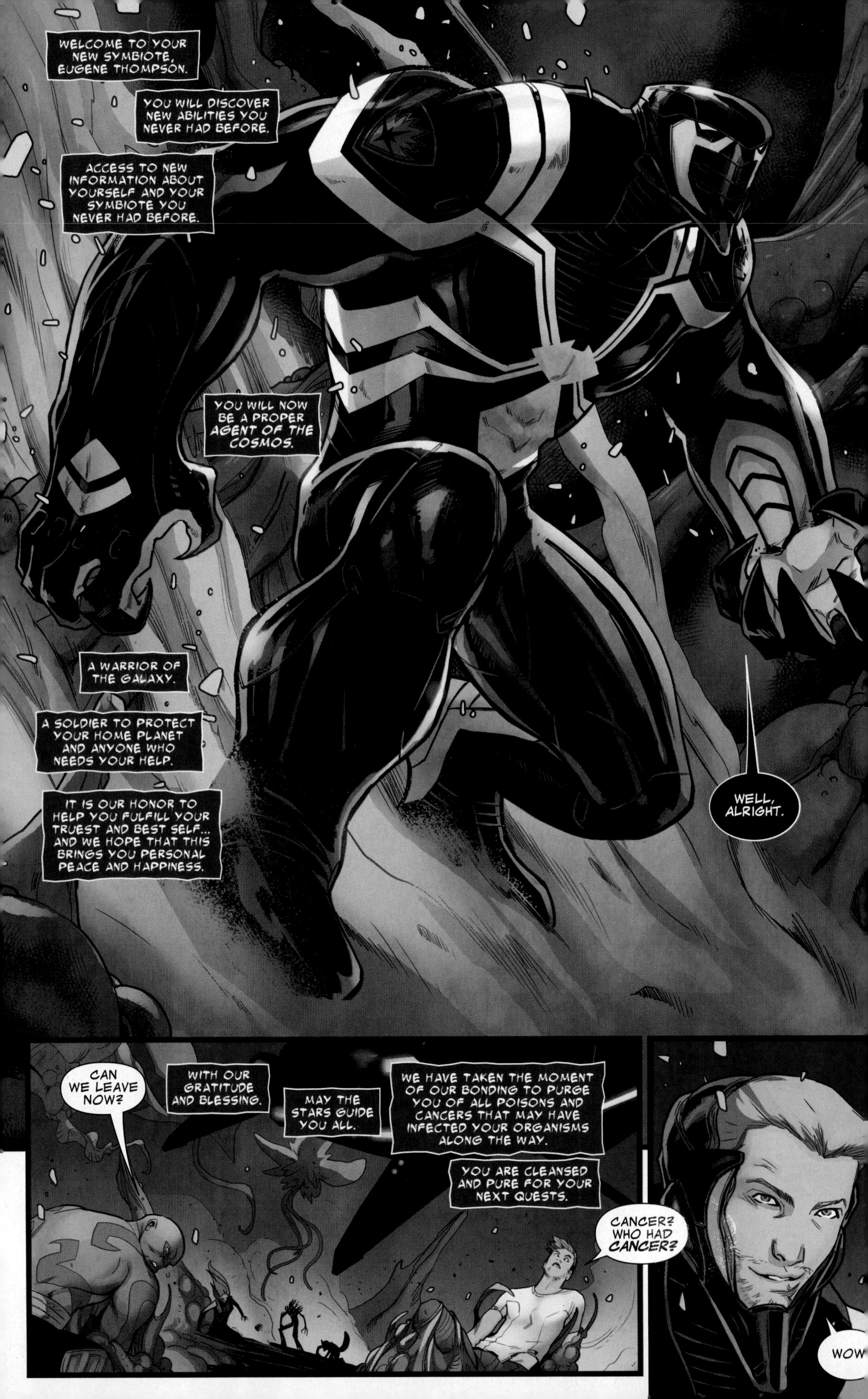
WELCOME TO YOUR NEW SYMBIOTE, EUGENE THOMPSON.
YOU WILL DISCOVER NEW ABILITIES YOU NEVER HAD BEFORE.
ACCESS TO NEW INFORMATION ABOUT YOURSELF AND YOUR SYMBIOTE YOU NEVER HAD BEFORE.
YOU WILL NOW BE A PROPER AGENT OF THE COSMOS.
A WARRIOR OF THE GALAXY.
A SOLDIER TO PROTECT YOUR HOME PLANET AND ANYONE WHO NEEDS YOUR HELP.
IT IS OUR HONOR TO HELP YOU FULFILL YOUR TRUEST AND BEST SELF... AND WE HOPE THAT THIS BRINGS YOU PERSONAL PEACE AND HAPPINESS.
WELL, ALRIGHT.
CAN WE LEAVE NOW?
WITH OUR GRATITUDE AND BLESSING.
MAY THE STARS GUIDE YOU ALL.
WE HAVE TAKEN THE MOMENT OF OUR BONDING TO PURGE YOU OF ALL POISONS AND CANCERS THAT MAY HAVE INFECTED YOUR ORGANISMS ALONG THE WAY.
YOU ARE CLEANSED AND PURE FOR YOUR NEXT QUESTS.
CANCER? WHO HAD CANCER?
WOW

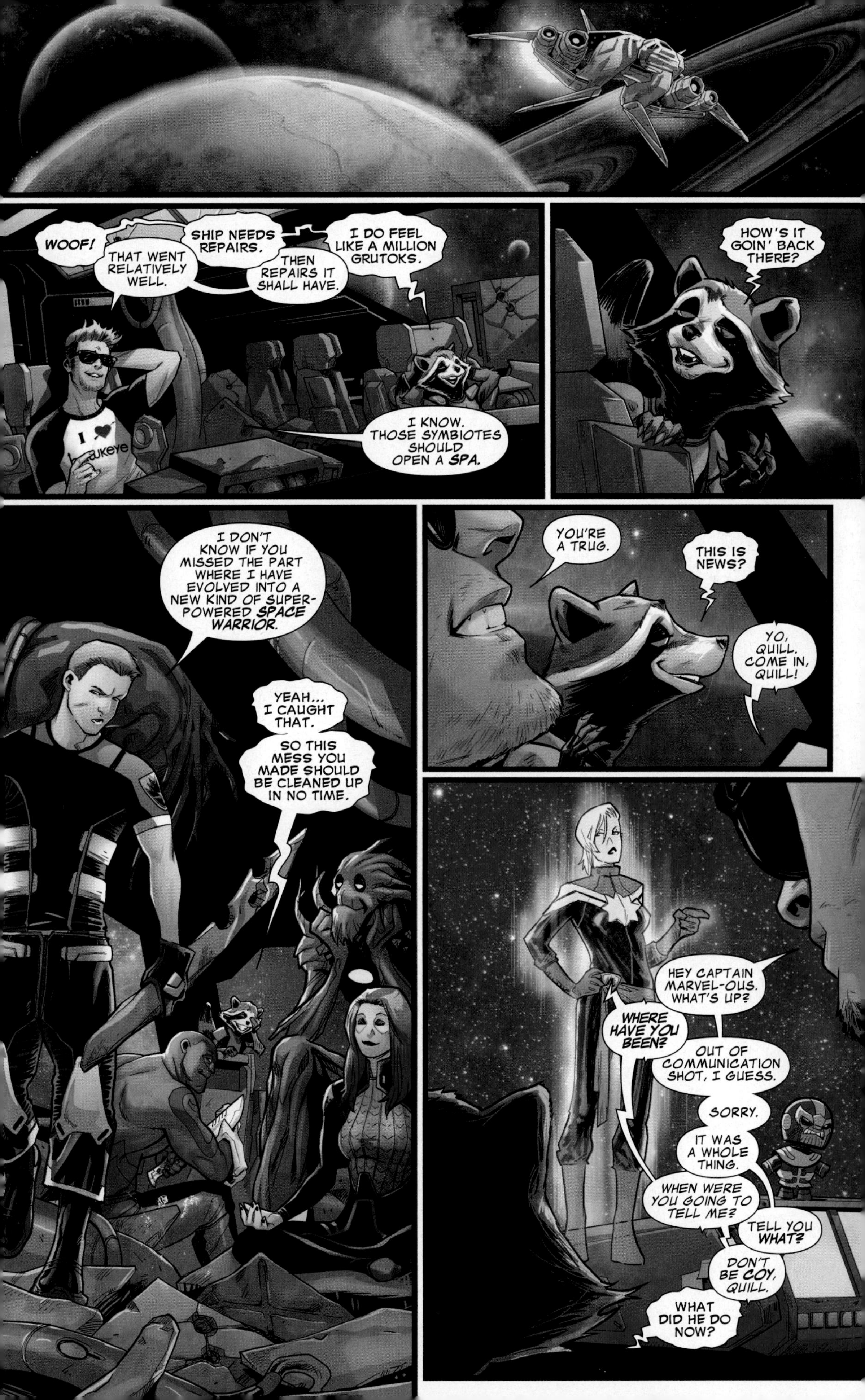
WOOF!
THAT WENT RELATIVELY WELL.
SHIP NEEDS REPAIRS.
THEN REPAIRS IT SHALL HAVE.
I DO FEEL LIKE A MILLION GRUTOKS.
I KNOW. THOSE SYMBIOTES SHOULD OPEN A SPA.
HOW'S IT GOIN' BACK THERE?
I DON'T KNOW IF YOU MISSED THE PART WHERE I HAVE EVOLVED INTO A NEW KIND OF SUPER-POWERED SPACE WARRIOR.
YEAH... I CAUGHT THAT.
SO THIS MESS YOU MADE SHOULD BE CLEANED UP IN NO TIME.
YOU'RE A TRUG.
THIS IS NEWS?
YO, QUILL. COME IN, QUILL!
HEY CAPTAIN MARVEL-OUS. WHAT'S UP?
WHERE HAVE YOU BEEN?
OUT OF COMMUNICATION SHOT, I GUESS.
SORRY.
IT WAS A WHOLE THING.
WHEN WERE YOU GOING TO TELL ME?
TELL YOU WHAT?
DON'T BE COY, QUILL.
WHAT DID HE DO NOW?

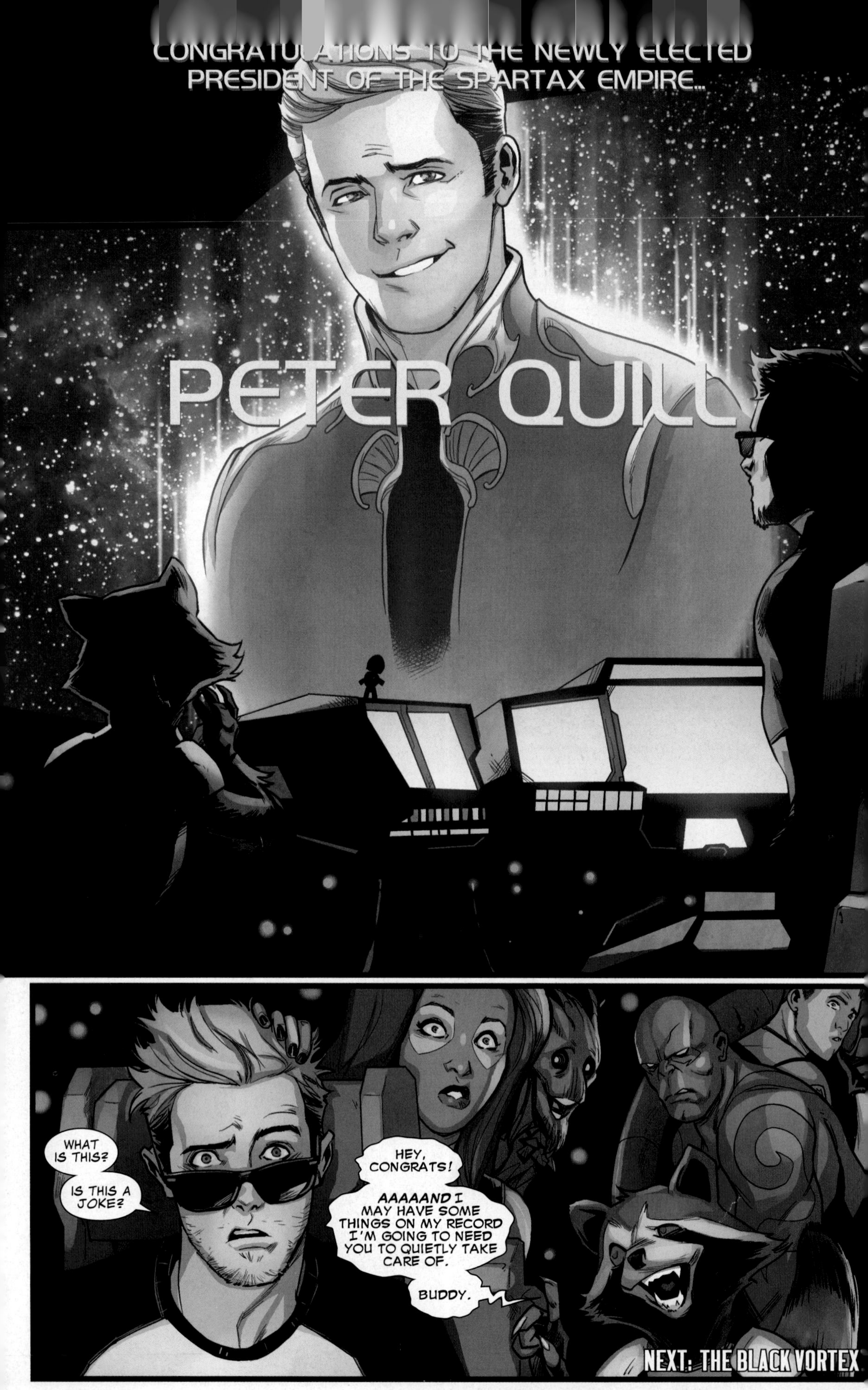
CONGRATULATIONS TO THE NEWLY ELECTED PRESIDENT OF THE SPARTAX EMPIRE...
PETER QUILL
WHAT IS THIS?
IS THIS A JOKE?
HEY, CONGRATS!
AAAAAND I MAY HAVE SOME THINGS ON MY RECORD I'M GOING TO NEED YOU TO QUIETLY TAKE CARE OF.
BUDDY.
NEXT: THE BLACK VORTEX

MARVEL AR AUGMENTED REALITY

MARVEL AUGMENTED REALITY (AR) ENHANCES AND CHANGES THE WAY YOU EXPERIENCE COMICS!

TO ACCESS THE FREE MARVEL AR CONTENT IN THIS BOOK*:

1. Locate the AR logo within the comic.
2. Go to Marvel.com/AR in your web browser.
3. Search by series title to find the corresponding AR.
4. Enjoy Marvel AR!

*All AR content that appears in this book has been archived and will be available only at Marvel.com/AR – no longer in the Marvel AR App. Content subject to change and availa

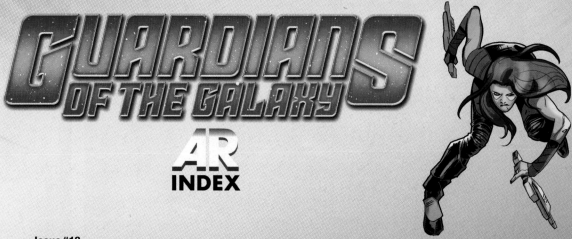

GUARDIANS OF THE GALAXY

AR INDEX

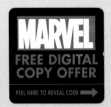